AFRICAN DESCENDANTS
IN COLONIAL AMERICA

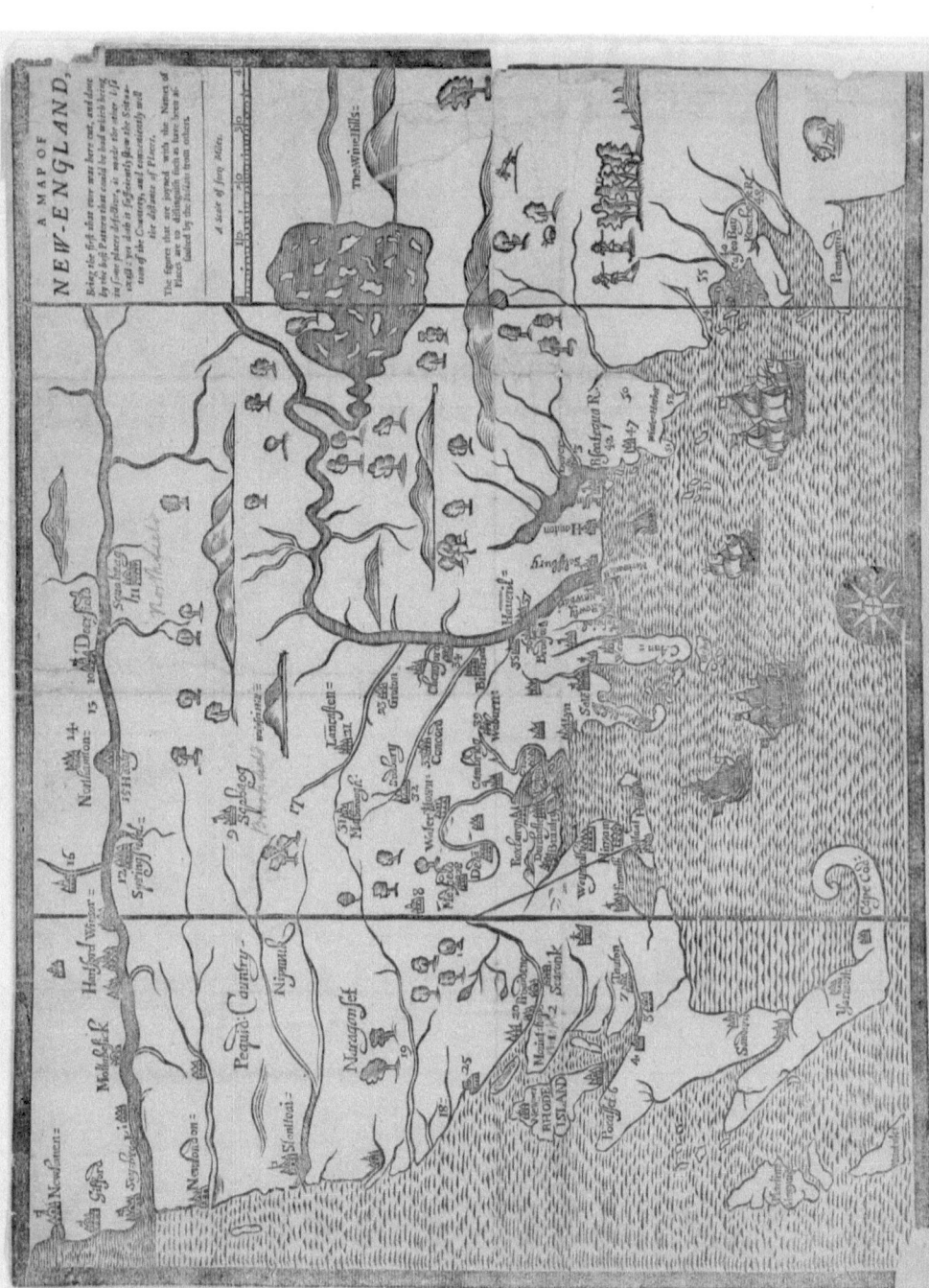

AFRICAN DESCENDANTS IN COLONIAL AMERICA

Impact on the Preservation
of Peace, Security, and Safety
in New England: 1638–1783

Lievin Kambamba Mboma

NASHVILLE, TN

Copyright © 2019 LIEVIN KAMBAMBA MBOMA

All rights reserved including the right to reproduce the book or portions thereof in any form whatsoever. Copyrights Registration Number TXU 2-070-986

Requests for permission should be addressed to Lievin K. Mboma, P.O. Box 23683, Nashville, Tennessee 37202.

ISBN: 978-0-9989716-0-5 (hardcover)/978-0-9989716-1-2 (paperback)/ 978-0-9989716-2-9 (ebook)

LCCN: 2017904205

Frontispiece: A map of New-England: being the first that ever was here cut, and done by the best pattern that could be had, which being in some places defective, it made the other less exact.
Special Colls. Maps 1677b Copy 1, Wine Hills
Map ; 31 x 3 9 cm. Scale ca. 1:900,000.
http://www.masshist.org/database/1739

Cover image: Battle of Bunker's Hill: from the original painting in the possession of the publishers / [graphic] painted by Chappel; engraved by Phillibrown.
Inserted in Washington Irving's Life of Washington (extra-illustrated volume), v. 1, pt. 2, facing p. 481.
Guild Library-Lg.
1 print : engraving, b&w ; image & text 21.3 x 13.8 cm.

Contents

Acknowledgments ix

Preface xiii

Introduction 1

Chapter 1. A Brief History of People of African Descent in Colonial New England 12

Chapter 2. African Americans in the Government of Colonial New England 28

Chapter 3. African Americans as Militiamen and Soldiers in the Colony of New Hampshire 37
African Americans in Law Enforcement in Newmarket, New Hampshire

Chapter 4. African Americans as Militiamen and Soldiers in Colonial Connecticut 60
African Americans as Defenders of Public Safety and Order in Connecticut

Chapter 5. African Americans in the Militia of Colonial Rhode Island 82
Colonial Order for African Americans to Perform Law Enforcement Duties
African American Privateers in Colonial Wars in Rhode Island
African Americans in the Militia during the French and Indian War in Rhode Island

Chapter 6. African Americans as Officers and Militiamen
in Colonial Massachusetts   102
- *Laws of Massachusetts Bay Colony on the Enlistment of Blacks in the Militia*
- *African Americans as Soldiers in the French and Indian War in Colonial Massachusetts*
- *African Americans in the Expedition of 1740 in the West Indies*
- *African Americans as Civilian Officers in Colonial Boston*

Chapter 7. African American Militiamen and Soldiers
in the Revolutionary War: 1770–1783   151
- *Lemuel Haynes*
- *Crispus Attucks*
- *Black Soldiers during the Battles of Lexington, Concord, Cambridge and Bunker Hill Battles*
- *Peter Salem*
- *Salem Poor*
- *Prince and the Secret Mission for the Arrest of Major General Prescott*
- *The Arrest of a British Soldier by Ceasar, a Connecticut African American*
- *African American Seamen and the Beginning of the Navy in America*
- *Laws Governing the Capture of Enemy War Ships and Privateering*
- *The American Navy*
- *Active African Americans in the Continental and State Naval Forces*

Chapter 8. Black Government-by-Proxy
in Colonial New England   192
- *The Black Governors in Connecticut in the Colonial and Earlier Republic Era*
- *Black Governors in Rhode Island during the Colonial and Earlier Republic*

Black King in New Hampshire
Officers of the Black Government
Power of the Black Functionaries
    and Their Jurisprudence
Sociological Aspects of the Blacks' Election Day
Political Aspects of the Blacks' Election Day
The Significance of the Blacks' Election Day
The Parades during the Inauguration
    of Black Governors in Connecticut

Chapter 9. Summary and Conclusion   235

Appendix   239

Selected Bibliography   243

Index of Personal Names   253

Acknowledgments

Leading to the completion of *African Descendants in Colonial America*, I benefited from the enormous assistance of many Tennessee State University (TSU) scholars. Among those who made contributions, Assistant Professor Jewell Parham deserves credit for her contributions as senior editor of this work. As a professor of African American literature, children's literature, and English composition, she brought tremendous support and expanded ideas to this work. Several professors in the Department of History, Geography & Political Science did a yeoman's task of one sort or another to aid in the publication of *African Descendants in Colonial America*. Professor Bobby Lovett, author and former Dean of the School of Arts and Sciences (now the Department of Liberal Arts), reviewed the entire first draft of the manuscript and provided salient suggestions for improvement. Professor Erik Schmeller and Professor Adebayo Oyebade rendered considerable input and guidance. Following their constructive criticism and comments, I was able to collect authoritative data to substantiate the argument presented in this document. I also credit Professor Michael Montgomery for reading the entire manuscript after the completion of the editing process. He is a full professor and currently teaches in the Department of Criminal Justice at TSU and is the Graduate Program Coordinator for the Department. His interests are in correctional leadership, training, and research. TSU Professor Michael Wright also deserves recognition. His guidance and constructive commentary improved the first draft of this manuscript. Ernest Miah, TSU senior librarian, has earned my indebtedness for his superior moral support. His encouragement was the foundation upon which I was able to stand as I began the arduous trek to accomplish my goal, which was to close a wide gap in the historical records that tell of African and African American contributions to the security and public safety of colonial

New Englanders and their properties. Finally, my hearty thanks go to Ms. Barbara VanHooser, reference librarian. She helped with the first draft of *African Descendants in Colonial America* by giving me sage advice when I began researching and gathering data. Furthermore, she gave useful tidbits when I began to write the outline for the book. Mrs. Rhonda Kavan, the TSU Writing Center coordinator and my former English tutor, has shaped my English skills since I began my education at the university. She continues to help me when I need academic assistance. She assisted with the line editing/proofreading process concerning this project. I cannot forget Dr. Daniel Patterson, the reading instructor who walked with me along this journey. My cup runs over with gratitude for the cadre of TSU professors who assisted to fulfill my mission to write this book. Because of these valuable persons, the outcome of this study—*African Descendants in Colonial America*—is a better publication.

I have gained enormous help from the generosity of other professionals from area schools. Dean Reavis Mitchell of Fisk University and Professor James Quirin of Fisk University gave me constructive criticism after they revised the first draft. Professor James Williams, former director of the Gore Center at Middle Tennessee State University, reviewed this manuscript during its infancy and nurtured the research thesis to a more mature status. Moreover, I am very grateful to him for encouraging me to collect data from original sources. Due to his advice, I traveled to Massachusetts, Connecticut, Rhode Island, and New Hampshire to perform research that introduced me to authentic resources. In addition, I acknowledge the contributions of Professor Mark M. Lane, an American history instructor at Nashville State Community College, for his suggestions to improve the manuscript. He spent time reading the document line-by-line and offering constructive commentary. I acknowledge my sincere gratitude for Professor Moses E. Ochunu, Vanderbilt University, who assisted me with composing the description for *African Descendants in Colonial America*. Finally, I appreciate the efforts of Tremaine T. Sails-Dunbar, a student at Vanderbilt University Divinity School. He spent hours proofreading the manuscript, and his observations prompted suggestions that were beneficial to the outcome of *African Descendants in Colonial America*.

In addition to experts of various professions who have assisted me to write this manuscript, I gratefully acknowledge my mentors in the field of history. Dr. Tom Kannon, a Tennessee State archivist, mentored me while I worked on this project. Sometimes he interrupted his own work to analyze data I had collected. Also, I am grateful to Professor Marvin Dulaney. Even though he did not participate directly in this project, he taught me techniques for writing about history when he revised a previous manuscript, *The Employment of African Americans in Law Enforcement, 1803–1865*. He spent much time with me in Texas when I was working on a different project. He went beyond his academic contributions when he transported me from the hotel where I was staying and took me to Arlington University, where I did part of my research. Additionally, he provided an office to accommodate me as I wrote the manuscript. A. Paige Hendrickson of Motlow State Community College edited and proofread five chapters of the manuscript. As a writing tutor, former archivist, and current college librarian, she was able to relate to the project significantly. I also credit Dr. Raymond Sarbach Kinzounza for proofreading and editing the manuscript. Dr. Kinzounza spent much time reviewing the manuscript and fact-checking. I really appreciate his unconditional contributions to my work. As a pastor and a Nashville Public Library branch manager, he employed his expertise with an empathy that is very much needed to fully understand the subject of my manuscript.

I received enormous support from various librarians and archivists in New England. Thanks so much to the Massachusetts Historical Society librarians, especially Dan Hinchen, an assistant reference librarian, and Betsy Boyle, a librarian assistant. In addition to guiding me through data collection, Hinchen made other contributions to this project. He proofread and fact-checked the chapters which discussed African American contributions in Massachusetts and the proxy-government. In addition, Hinchen made plausible recommendations after reviewing the manuscript. Betsy Boyle collected pertinent data on African American men enlisted or impressed into the Massachusetts militia between April 28 and May 2, 1758.

In New Hampshire, Valerie Cunningham, author of *Black Portsmouth: Three Centuries of African-American Heritage*, deserves my sincere appreciation. She read the first draft of the manuscript and made worthwhile recommendations. Bill Copeley of the New Hampshire Historical Society deserves recognition. Nichole Cloutier, a special collections librarian, guided me positively when I was conducting my research at the Portsmouth, Public Library in New Hampshire. Moreover, I received assistance from the following: Reference Librarians at Salem Public Library, Nancy T. Peluso, the access services group head at Connecticut State Library; Joseph Coffill, a reference librarian, Lynn Public Library; Liz Cashman, a reference librarian, Worcester Public Library; Danielle G. Barney, a reference librarian, Framingham Public Library; Mary O'Connell, reference librarian at Bridgewater Public Library; and Ann Thornton, a reference librarian, Marblehead, Massachusetts, contributed enormously by sending me material needed to make completion of the manuscript a strong argument and creditable publication. In Newmarket, New Hampshire, Carrie Gadbois, a library director, and CaJane W. Frechette, assistant librarian, furnished material on the Honorable Wentworth Cheswell. James Lyman from the same library sent documentation on Hopestill and Wentworth Cheswell (father and son, respectively). Finally, data on black governors were provided by Charlotte Rowell, III of Seymour, Connecticut.

Stephanie S. Rodriguez, the southeast branch manager of the Nashville Public Library, deserves kudos for reading the entire manuscript and guiding me in directions that were fruitful. Kristen Howell, a Nashville Public Library associate, deserves credit for assisting with technical services. Similarly, Saber Abdelhalim, Megan Sheridan, and Wesley Berhow, assisted me with formatting the document. As a Nashville Public Library associate, they were always available to provide help whenever I needed his services.

I owe words of appreciation to Charles Sutherland and Keata Brewer of E.T. Lowe Publishing.

In addition to scholars and librarians, the input from friends cannot be overlooked. Hajar Khailani, Greg Ozubu, Ron Wood, and Robert Pullen gave me unconditional support while I conducted the research for this book. I am grateful to Collin Hassen, who read the full manuscript. Moreover, I am grateful to everyone who supported this project from inception to completion.

Finally, I thank my family for the sacrifices they made while I was giving much attention to the manuscript. Thank you, dear family, for demonstrating your love for me by your selfless acts. You embraced my dream and gave me the time and space to make *our* dream a reality.

Preface

As an African and a criminal justice major, I was curious to know the contributions Africans and people of African descent made in colonial New England regarding public safety. Two questions motivated this research: (1) Were Africans and African Americans permitted to contribute to the preservation of peace, security, and safety in colonial New England? (2) Were Africans and African Americans permitted to hold government positions in colonial New England? The search for the answers to these questions increased my desire to investigate further and to understand the contributions of African Americans to the security of the colonies throughout the various wars of the colonial period, as well as during the American Revolution, even though many of them were servants and slaves.

Africans were brought to Colonial New England in 1638, arriving first in the Massachusetts Bay Colony. At that time, Africans who arrived in the colonies were identified in colonial records, baptismal documents, and the wills of their masters as servants. In contrast, early New England historians called the Africans "slaves." In Massachusetts, Connecticut, New Hampshire, and Rhode Island, slavery was not legalized by express laws. There is a consensus among New England historians that the communities detested slavery. In Rhode Island, Roger Williams was the first anti-slavery government official. Following his lead were Hazard Robinson and others. The inhabitants of Massachusetts preferred importing white people over Africans. Similarly, in Connecticut, the importation of African slaves was rejected by the citizens of that colony.

The questions must be asked then: Were these Africans given the same liberties as white servants? What kind of freedom did Africans have? Were they permitted to form social organizations and to select their own leaders?

These questions, and the many others that evolved during my work on this project, could not be answered without conducting practical and objective research. Finding authoritative information required piecing together the scanty records on the contributions made by Africans (free, servants, and slaves) in the matter of public safety during colonial conflicts. Despite the intriguing quest, answers to my questions have been difficult to find because data is scarce. However, I have made the best possible effort to gather and organize available information. Materials collected for this investigation were gathered from various sources. Archival materials I have consulted include books written by local New England historians, colonial government documents, and church records. Furthermore, I perused collections of military data maintained by New England historical societies to identify the names of African military men. The Connecticut, New Haven, Maine, New London, and Massachusetts' historical society collections contain records of military data, including muster rolls of men who served in colonial wars. The muster rolls were the official lists of officers and men in a military unit or a ship military company. Sometimes African American names can be found among enlistees. Similarly, the Society of the Colonial Wars has important documentation that mentions names of black men who served in military conflicts. In New Hampshire, the *Provincial Papers, Documents and Records Collection* lists the names of a few African Americans who served during the colonial wars, and comparable information is recorded in the state public library and archives in Hartford, Connecticut. Similarly, in the Massachusetts Office of the Secretary of State there is abundant documentation about soldiers and sailors of the American Revolution, including records that identify African American service men. Moreover, in the *Acts and Resolves, Public and Private, of the Province of the Massachusetts Bay, data* on African American military men can be found. Many of the materials listed here have been made available online by the libraries and societies that maintain them.

With respect to the local historians, Deloraine Pendre Corey of Malden and Thomas Tracy Bow and George Sheldon of Deerfield, Massachusetts, are among authors who listed the names of African American colonial soldiers in their books. In Rhode Island, Howard Chapin conducted impeccable research on the Rhode Island soldiers and sailors involved in the colonial wars. In Chapin's collections, African Americans were credited for their military deeds. In the same colony, William Babcock Weeden's *Early Rhode Island* (1910) mentions the names of African Americans who served as privateers or soldiers. Arthur Latham Perry, in his book *Origins in Williamstown* (1894), recorded the muster roll of the company of His Majesty's service under the command of Ephraim Williams, Jr., in which, the names of African Americans were also mentioned.

Regarding black government, I consulted various documents. At Hartford State Library, I was given a research report by Katherine J. Harris that she compiled upon the request of the Connecticut State Historical Commission. Recorded in the report are the names of black governors. Additionally, a list of African Americans who served as governors was donated to me by the librarians at Hartford Public Library. Many local historians recorded limited information on the election and the coronation of black governors or kings, respectively. Judiciary officers of the black government were noted histories of New England states. In Connecticut, Rhode Island, and Massachusetts, there are recorded histories that give accounts of the election of black governors. To illustrate, George Simon Roberts (1906) discussed in *Historic Towns of the Connecticut River Valley (1904)* the election and voting methods African Americans followed to select their governor. In the same colony, Henry Reed Stiles, physician and noted historian, mentioned the election of African American governors *The History and Genealogies of Ancient Windsor, Connecticut*. In New Hampshire, Charles Warren Brewster's book, *Rambles about Portsmouth: Sketches of Persons, Localities, and Incidents of Two Centuries* discusses the judiciary system of the African American government, including the election of the African king in that colony at Portsmouth. In Rhode Island, William Johnston, author of *Slavery in Rhode Island* (1894), wrote the most notable information on the election of African American governors in the colony. In the same colony, Wilkins Updike recorded pertinent information on the election process and coronation of the African American governor in Narragansett. Some of the books mentioned above can be found online in Google Books or in libraries.

The names of people and places were collected from historical documents and government records. During the Colonial Era, the terms "nigger," "Negro," and "white slaves" were expressed commonly. While some African Americans had conventional first and last names, slaves often took the names of their masters with the descriptive term "Negro" added. For example, in records from Massachusetts, Rhode Island, Connecticut, and New Hampshire, I found names such as "Peter, Negro." A free African American was sometimes identified as "servant." Legal terms employed by colonial officials to indicate the status of people of color included "Bondsman," "Free Negro," "Negro Servant of…" "Mulatto," "Negro Man of …," and "Nigger." It is unknown whether the terms reflected the same negative connotation as they do currently. These terms were always employed to identify Africans and African Americans when their names were mentioned in legal documents, vital records, and colonial laws.

Finally, the author takes full responsibility for the contents and ideas expressed in this book. The history of any people at any given time is worth recording for posterity. The omission of important data about any group of people results in the incomplete construction of the history of that population. In addition, scholars are incapable of conducting qualitative research on issues concerning groups who have missing data. Hard-to-find and limited records present a challenge for scholars to examine the population and give full disclosure of these groups. This was the reality regarding the examination of the legacy of African descendants in colonial America. The author dealt with nearly insurmountable difficulties in the quest to piece together the impact made by people of African descent in the preservation of peace, security, and safety in New England during the colonial wars.

As literature of the impact of African Americans in the maintenance of peace in colonial New England is scarce, many questions remain unanswered. For a better understanding, I searched for answers to the following questions to see whether Africans and African Americans were permitted to serve in the militia:

- Did laws exist concerning slavery?
- Were there laws to govern who could participate in the militias and military duty?

- Did laws govern the rights and roles of servants?
- Could the master's job determine what part slaves or servants could play regarding militia duties?
- Generally, what was the relationship between servants or slaves and their masters?

African Descendants in Colonial America reveals dates of Africans in New England who might have carried arms in defense of the colony. It is essential to mention these names that are on record since everyone was permitted to carry arms during the earlier years of the settlements. Colonial officials ordered each family to bear arms for the protection of their communities against the enemies of the English. Furthermore, revelations concerning earlier African settlers in New England show that they had the same rights as English servants with respect to the security of the colonies prior to the establishment and enactment of militia laws that said otherwise.

Additionally, I collected information regarding laws established to control people of color. Slavery laws and the relationship between colonists and slaves cannot be separated, as both go hand-in-hand. Established slave laws sometimes dictated how masters treated their subjects. For this reason, it was imperative for me to investigate laws related to the militia and military. Like these militia and military laws, earlier established laws in Massachusetts and Rhode Island on the abolition of slavery were detailed. Laws governing the control of slaves and servants impacted the lives of Negroes as well as the English colonists. There existed a some collaboration between masters and slaves. The mutual relationship between owners and bondsman diminished the skepticism for employing African bondsmen (slaves) in the militia. Because commanders often overlooked the militia law to disregard men of color, military officers frequently took their servants or slaves on expeditions.

African Descendants in Colonial America details the inconsistencies in the New England colony militia laws due to the pressure of many wars. At first in colonial New England, African Americans were excluded from militia and military duties, but with the frequency and magnitude of wars, colonial officials were forced to call upon the black population to help defend the territory and to protect lives and properties. In colonies such as Massachusetts, Connecticut, and New Hampshire, where their General Assemblies enacted laws excluding African bondsmen from militia and military services, generals on the battlefield authorized enlisting African Americans. In addition, the General Assembly did not have control over how local officials in villages, on plantations, and in towns conducted enlistment practices.

Consequently, in areas where local officials held African Americans as servants and slaves, their enlistment in the militia was not a matter of question. Furthermore, in the regions where Native Americans made frequent incursions, local officials expected everyone to help defend the territory. Women, children, and African bondsmen were included. From the work of George Henry Moore, records show that children and women carried weapons to protect their plantations and villages.[1]

This research also explores the role African Americans played during the Revolutionary War. The contributions of high-profile African American soldiers or militias are well explained. The impact made by African Americans such as Crispus Attucks, Peter Salem, and Salem Poor have been examined attentively. Moreover, the roles men of color played on battlegrounds and in collaboration with their white counterparts have been addressed.

Finally, during my research, I became immersed in the political and military maneuvering employed by government officials before the total inclusion of African Americans in the Continental Army. The roles played by military officials such as General Washington to enlist Africans and their descendants greatly enriched the premise upon which *African Descendants in Colonial America* is based.

---

1. George Henry Moore, *Notes on the History of Slavery in Massachusetts*, New York, Appleton& Co, 1866, p. 243.

Introduction

Historians have investigated the contributions of people of color in the military during the Revolutionary War; nonetheless, some of these same researchers and others have paid less attention to the roles played by Africans and African Americans during the Colonial Era. Comparatively, little writing has addressed what men of color did in the defense of the colonies, in the preservation of public safety, and in wars such as King Philip's War, King George's War, Queen Anne's War, and the French and Indian War. For nearly four centuries, since the arrival of Africans in colonial New England, little is known about the contributions they made in colonial territories. This same scarcity of record-keeping was realized by Joseph Thomas Wilson and Dudley Taylor Cornish, thus leading them to publish *The Black Phalanx: African American Soldiers in The War of Independence, The War of 1812, and The Civil War 1861–1865*. During their research, Wilson and Cornish discovered the dearth of history about African American soldiers and the role they played in colonial America. It is noteworthy that the authors of *The Black Phalanx* did not mention the names of African slaves or servants who sacrificed their lives for liberty in defense of the New England colonies.

As the topic of black contributions to the protection of the colonies and the preservation of public safety has remained unexplored for centuries, it is necessary to reconstruct the duties of African Americans to acknowledge their input to the welfare of the territory during colonial wars. It is fair to note that the topic is vital because it is part of American history and needs to be treated as such. Moreover, it is significant to examine this topic because the processes utilized for the enrollment of African Americans during colonial wars were the same processes observed years later during the Revolutionary War and the Civil War.

Students and scholars specializing in American history, and more specifically, American military history, can scrutinize how the colonists and government officials in early America and during the antebellum period were inconsistent in the way they involved African Americans in security protocols.

During King Philip's War (1675–1678), King William's War (1689–1697), Queen Anne's War (1702–1713), King George's War (1744–1748), the Revolutionary War (1775–1783), and the Civil War (1861–1865), African Americans were excluded from the military by law. But under the pressure of the military conflicts, local commanders and generals disregarded the language of the law that prevented the inclusion of men of color from participating in military maneuvers. Rather, when situations to protect the colonies became crucial, local commanders and generals employed blacks for defense, protection, and the preservation of peace and safety. Moreover, when the conflicts worsened during wars, government officials disregarded the laws excluding African Americans from serving in the militia or military. Officials were forced to revoke the laws that prohibited African Americans from being an integral part of the military. The inconsistent policies of military folkways regarding the enlistment of African Americans were passed from generation to generation until the Civil War. The anomalies that war created for consigning blacks to perform military duties legally and illegally were so imperative that I was driven to explore how and why blacks began to play integral roles in the military strategies of colonial America.

When I attempted to gather data, librarians and archivists at the Massachusetts Historical Society and the Malden, Salem, and Lynn Public libraries believed research concerning Africans and African Americans' active role to protect early New England colonies had not been conducted. To the librarians, my approach to the subject was their introduction to the idea. Piecing together the data on African American soldiers during the Colonial Era proved to be an ardent challenge. But by consulting various historical documents, I slowly began to gather the names of African American soldiers who made outstanding contributions to the welfare of colonial America. Before beginning my quest, I was duly advised that collecting data on the contributions made by Africans and African Americans during the colonial wars would be very difficult because military men were sometimes not identified by race on the muster rolls. Fortunately, slave soldiers were occasionally listed on the muster roll. Several librarians and archivists informed me that colonial military records were not recorded in the local public libraries. According to them, such information was recorded in state archives. Moreover, the names of African American soldiers were difficult to access due to the recording method employed at the time.

As in Massachusetts, I was advised the same at the Rhode Island Black Heritage Society: Colonial military records were not a part of the Rhode Island Black Heritage Society library holdings. However, in Newport, the caretaker of the Newport Historical Society library possessed the books of a librarian named Howard Chapin. Chapin, as the author of *Rhode Island Men in Colonial Wars,* listed the names of colonial soldiers; however, the names were not listed by race. Therefore, information was not accessible to identify African American soldiers and militias who fought during the colonial wars in Rhode Island because they were not listed by race on the Rhode Island colonial muster rolls.

At the Public Library in Portsmouth, New Hampshire, data on African American colonial soldiers were not recorded at the time of my research. Then I was given access to the archives. After investigating many documents, I discovered little was written about men of color, whether African slaves, servants, or free men. After calling upon other local libraries in New England, I found that these institutions did not have colonial records, specifically records of African Americans who served during the colonial wars. I was especially surprised that the African American Museum in Boston had the same dearth of information. In other New England towns, librarians offered the same negative response to my request. It appears that in times past, military data regarding Africans and their descendants warrant record-keeping, during that era, compounding matters, Africans themselves record the impact they made upon public safety. Contrary to the libraries noted above, in Hartford, Connecticut, at the public library archives, I found a few names of African Americans who served in colonial wars.

In summary, in the Northern colonies, the contributions made by black people regarding their efforts toward internal security during the colonial wars have been largely overlooked. Until now, few researchers have been devoted to investigating and understanding the subject in question.

Scholars have discussed the involvement of African bondsmen and their contributions to the internal security of colonial New England. Prominent among such scholars include Lorenzo Johnston Greene (1942), Benjamin Quarles (1988), Laura Eliza Wilkes (1919), and William Piersen (1988). Greene's *The Negro in Colonial New England, 1620–1776* covers a plethora of topics that show how men of color were woven inextricably into New England society. His book covers 156 years of slaves being transported to colonial America and discusses how the presence of slaves influenced early American economy, politics, religion, and military prowess. In his book *Black Mosaic: Essays in Afro-American History and Historiography*, Benjamin Quarles listed a few names of African Americans who served during the colonial wars in New England. Likewise, Laura Eliza Wilkes extended the focus of African and African American contributions to colonial safety in *Missing Pages in American History: Revealing the Services of Negroes, in the Early Wars in the United States of America*. She recorded names of African American colonial soldiers in New England. Additionally, Wilkes addressed laws enforced by colonial officials for the exclusion and inclusion of African Americans in the military. William Piersen discussed law enforcement duties of black governors. In addition to the works of the authors previously mentioned, muster rolls recorded in various documents of the historical societies in New England identified names of African Americans who served in colonial wars from various regions. In the collections of Connecticut, Rhode Island, and Massachusetts, the muster rolls of colonial wars have the recorded names of African Americans who were in service. Moreover, the *Society of Colonial Wars* gathered significant information about military men who served. Among these were African Americans.

In colonial documents, sometimes the names of African American soldiers were recorded. In New Hampshire, in the colonial papers and the *Report of the Adjutant-General*, the names of African American soldiers were listed. Also, militia laws were documented in the records of the Connecticut and Rhode Island colonies. In Massachusetts, in the *Laws of the Province and Colony of Massachusetts Bay*, militia and military laws were recorded. In these documents, laws that excluded

African Americans from performing military and other law enforcement duties such as guarding, watching, and warding are mentioned. To be more precise, the historical societies maintain archives of documents that have information which was recorded by local authors in 1800s. The Maine Historical Society indicates the enlistment of African Americans in the Company of Major Benjamin Church in 1689.[1] In the *Report of the New Hampshire Adjutant-General of 1866*, the names of black men who fought for the protection of the colonies are recorded. Howard M. Chapin, a former archivist in the Rhode Island Historical Society, gathered information on the Rhode Island men who served during the colonial wars. In his book, *Lists of Rhode Island Men in the French and Indian War*, the names of African Americans are noted.

In New England, some authors ignored discussing militia and military duties performed by African Americans. Samuel Gardner Drake and George Henry Moore, earlier New England historians writing during the second half of the nineteenth century, overlooked the responsibilities and contributions of black militiamen during the colonial wars. Drake, who examined the Indian wars in *The Book of the Indians of North America*, did not list African Americans who participated in the defense of the colony. And although Moore thoroughly described the conditions of African and African American slavery, he did not mention the sacrifices made by African Americans to protect colonial lives and properties. It is noteworthy that Moore recorded many laws which excluded or included people of African descent in militia training, but he did not credit the contributions black men made during the various colonial wars. Thomas Hutchinson, the royal governor of Massachusetts (1769–1771) and author of *History of New England* in 1765, talks about the Indian wars briefly. He omitted much regarding the military contributions of the English, as well as those of African Americans. Benjamin Church, a patriot soldier and writer in New England, failed to discuss the impact made by African slaves in the colonial wars. However, he

---

1. Major Benjamin Church of Massachusetts employed Negroes for his expedition against the Indians for the protection of the town and the fort. The information regarding the enlistment of African Americans during this expedition was recorded in *The Collection of the Maine Historical Society*, 1896, p. 5. See also Drake, *History of Philip's War, Commonly Called the Great Indian War, of 1675 and 1676*, 1827, pp. 156, 157,177.

revealed the contribution made by a black man who served the town of Taunton, New Plymouth Colony. Church did not mention in *History of Philip's War, Commonly Called the Great Indian War, 1827* the enlistment of African Americans who fought. Yet, Church marched with African militiamen for the defense of the territory of Maine.

In books written by local historians in many New England towns, names of black people who protected lives and property and defended the territory against the French and Indians occasionally were mentioned. William Barry, author of *History of Framingham* (1847), discussed the enlistment of African Americans who served during colonial wars. In his *History at the Battle of Lexington* (1825), Elias Phinney listed African Americans who fought in the war at Lexington, Massachusetts—the battle that launched the American Revolution. Emory Washburn discussed in *Historical Sketches of the Town of Leicester, Massachusetts* the services of Peter Salem to the colony. George Washington Williams, an African American author and soldier, indicated that African Americans guarded the young colonies in America. He noted that African bondsmen played important roles in protecting the population against Indian attacks. Thomas Tracy Bow, the author of *History of the Town of Hingham, Massachusetts*, revealed the names of African Americans who served during the French and Indian wars. George Sheldon's article, "Negro Slavery in Old Deerfield,"[2] recorded the names of African bondsmen who fought in the French and Indian wars.

Authors Lorenzo Johnston Greene, William Piersen, Jeremy Belknap a New Hampshire historian, and George Henry Moore a historian and librarian placed more emphasis on slavery and the social lives of African bondsmen. Piersen and Greene described the relationships between Africans and their masters and wrote about the election and coronations of African American governors in Connecticut and Rhode Island. Contrary to Greene and Piersen, I have focused my research on the role played by Africans and African Americans in the defense and security of the New England colonies and on laws that governed the lives of people of African descent. While Greene and Piersen considered

---

2. George Sheldon "Negro Slavery in Old Deerfield." *The New England Magazine*, 1893, p. 50.

the lives of people of color in all the colonies as a unit, in this research, I discuss separately the contributions of people of African descent in the militia of each New England colony. Moreover, my research reveals the impact made by African bondsmen in such colonial conflicts as King Philip's War. In the work of Greene (1942), military services performed by African slaves and free Africans in colonial wars in New England were recorded. He listed the names of African Americans who served in colonial wars as soldiers and sailors. Even though Greene listed a few names of African slave soldiers, the historian did not focus on the slaves' contributions to the war.

In addition to colonial wars, I cover militia and military services of African Americans during the Revolutionary War. I explored the change of policy by the state and Continental officials with respect to the enlistment of African Americans to the Continental militia and army. Similarly, I discuss the election and function of black governors. Attention is given to the black government-by-proxy in Connecticut, New Hampshire, and Rhode Island. In this research, I selected high-profile African Americans who made exceptional contributions during the American Revolutionary War. Similarly, African Americans who served during the Cambridge and Lexington alarms at the beginning of the war are discussed.

However, it is difficult to fully piece together the military movement of people of African descent due to insufficient data. In a like manner, many questions regarding the contributions of African Americans in politics in colonial New England were not discussed by the authors whom I have mentioned in this book. At the time of this writing, my research revealed no evidence suggesting that African Americans were politically active in the colonies during the Colonial Era. Even though African Americans were excluded from engagement in political activities in the colonial government, in the black government they performed political duties.

During the Colonial Era, military contributions made by African Americans were often disregarded. As an illustration, *The Boston News Letter Journal* of June 10, 1706, noted that Boston citizens did not want imported Africans in colonial New England. One of the reasons Bostonians rejected the importation of persons of African descent in the colony was that they did not carry weapons as did the whites in defense of the colony against enemies.³ Such language shows military duties performed by African Americans during the period in question was not known by some people in the colony. In 1887, Robert Rantoul, the author of *Negro Slavery in Massachusetts* that was published by the Essex Institute, noted that African Americans were "never" enlisted in the militia.⁴ Contrary to his account, data shows African Americans indeed were enrolled as soldiers and privateers during the colonial wars even though they were excluded by law. From the writing of these authors, I stipulate that the policy of the enrollment of African Americans in the militia or military differed from town to town and village to village. In towns where the French and Indians attacked the English intensely, African Americans were more than likely called upon to serve in the ranks of the English. For example, in Deerfield, where the French viciously attacked the town, African Americans were enlisted.⁵ It is important to investigate the impact made by Africans and their descendants in militia and military services for the internal security against the enemies and for the preservation of public safety. As the contributions made by people of color during colonial wars have been researched and made known, a gaping hole that existed for far too long in American history has been filled.

I had to persevere to find historical data that recorded the sacrifices made by black people in colonial wars, the many battles that occurred before the Revolutionary War. It is noteworthy that information regarding the contributions of Africans and their descendants was not recorded systematically or chronologically by the scholars and researchers whose work I read. During the Revolutionary War, the inhabitants of many provinces were against arming black people.

---

3. George H. Moore, *Notes on the Slavery History in Massachusetts*, D. Appleton & Co., 1866, p. 107.

4. See Robert Rantoul, "Negro Slavery in Massachusetts" Printed for the Historical Collections of the Essex Institute, July 1, 1887.

5. George Sheldon, *Negro Slavery in Old Deerfield*, [Boston, Mass.: S.n],1893, See also, George Sheldon, *A History of Deerfield, Massachusetts: The Times when the People by Whom it was Settled, Unsettled and Resettled*, vol.2., Press of E.A. Hall & Company, Deerfield , (Mass), 1896. Also see, Lilian Brandt, "Slavery in Massachusetts," vol.21 (1900), p. 92.

For that reason, the impact of African Americans in colonial New England is worth revealing. The early years during the expansion of American territories were critical for colonial officials. Any contributions made for safety and peace in the colonies must be applauded because these were not easy missions to accomplish. Public safety was a priority for the colonists. The protection of the settlers and their belongings was of critical importance during the early years when the foundation of the colonies was being set. As the protection of the settlers was paramount, every resident in the colonies was armed for the defense of land and properties. Charles Brooks and William Henry Whitmore wrote that on September 7, 1643, the General Court of Massachusetts ordered that "arms must be kept in every family."[6] In addition, they noted on May 14, 1645, the General Court ordered that children from ten to sixteen years old were to be instructed on how to use a weapon. The arming of children was not illegal during the Colonial Era. During the early years of American settlement, towns were under-populated. Therefore, women, children, and the elderly were armed for their personal and communal security. Because of the pressure from the frequency of attacks from Native Americans and the few men in the colony, it was acceptable during this time to arm children and women to protect themselves when the men were away.

Upon discovering the tenuous safety of women, children, and the elderly, I wondered about the role of Africans when enemy attacks occurred in the colonies. At this juncture of the research, several questions plagued my thoughts. Were African Americans permitted to protect lives and properties? Did they assume watch duties like other colonial subjects? Did African Americans join the colonists in the fight against enemies? Did men of color fight side-by-side with their white counterparts? Were black men paid for their military service during the Colonial Era? Were they paid a bounty during the American Revolution? The responses to these questions will confirm whether African Americans contributed to the maintenance of peace and security before and after the enactment of the exclusionary militia laws and during the fight

---

6. Quoted in Charles Brooks and William Henry Whitmore, *The History of the Town of Medford, Middlesex County*, 1855, p. 184.

for American independence. According to historical data, English titles such as constable, justice of the peace, sheriff, deputy sheriff, coroner, marshal, deputy marshal, tithing men, lord of the manor, alderman, and mayor were Anglo-Saxon titles introduced in colonial New England by the settlers. As in England, officials in America assigned law enforcement work to agents to maintain law and order in the colonies. Before the introduction of these titles in the colonies, the militia performed law enforcement duties. Did people of African descent hold such titles as justice of the peace, coroner, marshal, sheriff, tithing men, or constable during the Colonial Era?

After discovering the plethora of law enforcement agents in colonial America, a few questions remained in my thoughts: Were African Americans included in the militia of the colony? If so, was the inclusion permanent or temporary? Were men of color enrolled in the militias of all the colonies in New England? Did the colonists overlook the exclusionary militia laws during the wars with enemies by enlisting people of African descent? Did African Americans contribute military might in the French and Indian Wars? Again, answers to these questions will confirm whether African Americans were permitted to preserve peace, security, and safety during the Colonial Era. African Americans were permitted to join the militia; therefore, African descendants enforced law and order jointly with their white counterparts during war times.

During the French and Indian Wars, African Americans were enlisted in the militias of the New England colonies. It was the custom of the time for men to enlist voluntarily in the militia, and others were enlisted by order of the colonial government at the request of the King of England. In New Hampshire during the French and Indian Wars, communal maintenance of law and order was common. Neighborhood watch was maintained consistently. Each man in the neighborhood took his turn at watch by day and night. In addition, guard duties were performed by private citizens.[7]

In addition to militia, army, and privateer services, African Americans served as sentinels in the colonies of their masters. People of

---

7. *Report of the Adjutant General of the State of New Hampshire, for the year ending June 1, 1866,* vol. ii, p. 51.

African descent performed sentinel duties by protecting the properties of their masters—houses, plantations, and mansions. As my research progressed, questions continued to arise in my mind concerning African and African American involvement in the safety of colonial America. For example, during the American Revolution, were black men enlisted in the army? Did they fight side-by-side with the Americans? Did they participate in the Battles of Lexington, Concord, and Cambridge? Did they protect, guard, and perform law enforcement duties? The selective data which I collected from early and modern American historians provided me with information I needed so that I could reconstruct the deeds of African and African American soldiers during the Colonial Era. As the information I have gleaned from my research becomes accessible and available to scholars and students majoring in history and other social science fields, more investigation may be conducted on associated topics. My research is a starting point to revisit records concerning the contributions made by non-whites to public safety in colonial America. Furthermore, my research confirms that African Americans and loyal Native Americans were, at least, temporarily included in the ranks of colonial military men. Usually these parallel groups were excluded from military duties, but under the stress of war, their inclusion became necessary. Possibly resulting from this research, scholars may decide to investigate the contributions of faithful Native Americans to public safety in colonial America. Further examination needs to be conducted to study the continuation of colonial military folkways observed in the early American Republic and during the Civil War.

Chapter 1

A Brief History of People of African Descent in Colonial New England

History reveals that African Americans were imported to colonial Massachusetts on February 26, 1638; by Captain William Peirce or Pierce. After a seven-month voyage from Providence Island colony in the West Indies, Pierce brought with him Africans, cotton, and tobacco to Massachusetts.[1] According to George Washington Williams (1882) and Joseph Felt (1849), Captain Peirce exchanged Indian prisoners from the Pequod War for Africans. Even though these historians noted Africans were introduced into colonial Massachusetts, it was John Josselyn, a Scottish visitor to the Massachusetts Bay Colony, who recorded the existence of Africans in the house of Samuel Maverick. Maverick became the first slaveholder in New England at his small mansion that was fortified and armed with artillery to defend his territory. Josselyn lodged at Maverick's home on Noddle's Island when visiting the island in 1638. Maverick was the king's agent at Noddle's Island. In *Two Voyages to New England* (1865), Josselyn mentioned three African Americans whom he identified as "servants" owned by Maverick. His account has remained authoritative with respect to the importation of Africans to colonial Massachusetts, in particular, and to New England, in general.

---

1. Samuel Roads, Jr., *The History and Traditions of Marblehead*, Press of N. Allen Lindsey & Co., Marblehead, 1897, p. 12. Roads notes that "the year 1636 was an important epoch in the history of the little community at Marblehead. During that year a ship of one hundred and twenty tons burden, the third ever built in the colony, was constructed on the shore, probably on the harbor of the plantation. This vessel was known as the Desire, and for more than two years was employed in the fishing business. A few years later she was sent to the West Indies on commercial voyage, and returning brought a cargo of (salt, cotton, tabocco, and negroes.) These are supposed to have been the first slaves brought into the colony."

Regarding the social status of Africans, George Washington Williams believed that from 1638 to 1641, Africans lived with colonists in a patriarchal relationship. Two years after Africans were imported into colonial Massachusetts (1641), the Body of Liberties was enacted. It was a legal document composed of 100 Articles and this governing body of laws was largely framed up by Nathaniel Ward. John Winthrop (1826) wrote that Ward was a pastor of the church of Ipswich and a minister in England before his migration to Massachusetts Bay.[2] Additionally, he was a law literate and a common law attorney. Possibly, due to his credentials, he was entrusted with the elaboration of the Massachusetts Body of Liberties.

One article of this body of law covered the topic of slavery. The article reads:

> "It is ordered by this court and the authority thereof: that there shall never be any bond slavery, villenage or captivity amongst us, unless it be lawful captives taken in just wars, as willingly sell themselves or are sold to us, and such shall have the liberties, and Christian usage which the law of God established in Israel concerning such persons doth morally require; provided this exempts none from servitude, who shall be judged thereto by authority."[3]

This was the first law that legalized slavery in colonial New England. Even though the laws prohibited slavery among the colonists, slavery for strangers or people of different ethnic backgrounds was legalized. Likely, the slavery of people convicted by the court was justified. Similar view was also articulated by Wilson Waters. In 1917, he noted that in 1641, when the Body of Liberties was adopted, slavery became legal in Massachusetts.[4]

---

2. John Winthrop, *The History of New England from 1630 to 1649, vol.2*. Phelphs and Farnham, 1826, pp. 37, 55.

3. See *The Charters and General Laws of the Colony and Province of Massachusetts Bay*. Published by order of the General Court of Massachusetts. T.B. Wait and Company, 1814, p. 52. See also William Chauncey Fowler, *Local Law in Massachusetts and Connecticut*. Joel Munsell, 1872, p. 147.

4. Wilson Waters, *History of Chelmsford, Massachusetts*. Town, 1917, p. 570.

CHAPTER 1

In 1645, Captain James Smith and his shipmate, Thomas Keyser, brought to the Massachusetts colony two Africans whom they kidnapped in Guinea. The Africans were sold to a man named Williams of Piscataqua (now Portsmouth, New Hampshire). The act was detested by colonial authorities in Boston. As consequence, Keyser and Smith were sanctioned by the magistrates in Boston. Thereafter, the court ordered the return of stolen Africans to their native country.[5] Piscataqua [Portsmouth or Straw Berry Bank] was under the jurisdiction of the Massachusetts colony. In fact, from 1641 to 1679 the New Hampshire colony was part of Massachusetts Bay. The Africans remained in Piscataqua for a short time; then they were returned to Guinea by order of the court (see Appendix 1). In the same year, John Winthrop (1853) noted that one of the colonial ships traveled to the Canary Islands in early November and returned with sugar, wine, salt, and tobacco after visiting Barbados in exchange for Africans. The Africans were carried from the Isle of Maio, Cape Verte, in the Atlantic Ocean about 400 miles from the West African coast.[6] This is another indication that slavery was legal in colonial Massachusetts.

Although Africans were imported in 1638, historians do not know when they were introduced to the Connecticut colony. William Chauncey Fowler (1901) wrote in 1644, "one Hagar" was a slave in New Haven colony. It is unknown whether Hagar was an African or Indian slave. In Hartford, Connecticut, Gysbert Opdyck, an operator of the Dutch commissary at the fort, had an African with him. Louis Berbice, an African from Dutch Guiana, was possibly a servant to Opdyck. William Chauncey Fowler recorded that Berbice was killed by his master. In the language of Fowler, Governor Trumbull believed that Berbice was the first African introduced into Connecticut.[7] As in the colony of Con-

---

5. George Bancroft, *History of the United States, from the Discovery of American Continent, vol.1*. Routhledge, 1861, 1861, p. 132.

6. Charles Deane, *The Connection of Massachusetts with Slavery and the Slave-trade*. Charles Hamilton, 1886, p. 18. Charles Deane notes that in 1644 as a colonial ship went to the Canaries with pipes – staves, and brought home an assorted cargo which she brought in at Barbados in exchange for Africans which she armed carried from the Isle of Maio; one of the Cape Verde Island.

7. William Chauncey Fowler, *The Historical Status of the Negro in Connecticut*: A *paper read before the New Haven Colony Historical Society*. Walker, Evans & Cogwell Company, 1901, p. 4.

necticut, in Rhode Island, there is no record as to when African slaves were introduced into the colony. But in 1652, Roger Williams and his associate enacted a law prohibiting the enslavement of Africans and Indians.[8] This act covered Providence Plantations and Warwick. The Newport colony was not united to the Providence Plantations at the time. Even though the act prohibited slavery in the colony, the institution prevailed throughout many years.

With respect to slaves' social conditions, New England historians wrote African slaves and servants were often treated well by their masters and were considered a part of the family. In Connecticut, William Chauncey Fowler (1901) recorded that slavery was a family institution. Young Africans imported to the colony were always customized to the Europeans' culture such as eating, drinking, sleeping, working, and religious instruction. In the same colony, George Larking Clark (1913) posited that African slaves were cared for well. Connecticut writers Frances Manwaring Caulkins (1874) and Thomas Bailey Aldrich (1894) recorded that blacks in Connecticut were well-treated and had some liberties. In Rhode Island, New Hampshire, and Massachusetts, African slaves and white servants received the same treatment. William Johnston, the author of *Slavery in Rhode Island*, elucidated that slaves were in the same positions as white apprentices and servants. The way slaves were treated depended on the wills of their own masters. Possibly, a master with a mild temperament treated his slaves humanely. On the other hand, an unkind master mistreated his slaves. In general, the inhabitants of New England established a civil relationship with African slaves and servants. From the queries made by Judge St. George Tucker to Jeremy Belknap, to a number of people in Rhode Island and Massachusetts, I discovered that the treatment of Africans was generally quite the same in the New England colonies. To illustrate, in the Belknap Papers (1877), I found that Reverend John Eliot; Samuel Dexter, a Boston merchant; Judge James Winthrop, a graduate of Harvard College and Chief justice of the

---

8. William Harrison Taylor, *Legislative History and Souvenir of Rhode Island 1899 and 1900*. E. L. Freeman & Sons, State Printers, 1900, p. 174. Also see. William McMichael, *Slavery and Its Remedy*. J.S. Davison, 1856, p. 120.

Court of Probate, (all whites) had the same views—Africans lived on good terms with white people.

A similar example indicating kindness to an African slave was the action done by Rowland Hazard who lived in Narragansett, Rhode Island. In 1893, Caroline Hazard recorded in *Thomas Hazard, son of Robt, Called College Tom,* the generosity of Rowland Robinson to African slaves. Robinson and some friends were involved in the slave trade by sending vessels from Franklin Ferry to the coast of Africa. But on one occasion, he felt sorrow when he witnessed the conditions of slaves brought from Africa at the port. Some slaves were feeble and could not stand alone. From that time on, he had a different view of slavery. Instead of selling his share of Africans into slavery, he kept them for his own domestic services. The same account was written by William Johnston (1894) and Thomas Robinson Hazard, author of *Recollections of the Olden Times* (1879). In dealing with people of African descent, Caroline Hazard wrote that Robinson, a slave trader, wept when he saw the physical conditions of slaves after they disembarked the ship upon its arrival in Rhode Island.[9] He witnessed how one of the slaves was incapable of walking without assistance. Robinson's share from the trade was twenty-eight slaves, but he felt unable to sell them. Instead, he employed all of them for his own service and treated them with some humanity. Among Robinson's slaves was one called Abigail. Her son had been left behind in Africa. Upon learning that the mother had been separated from her child, Robinson paid for her to return to Guinea by slave ship to get her son and bring him back to Narragansett. The son, called Prince Robinson, became a body servant of Rowland Robinson and was treated as part of the family. He acted as bodyguard for the entire family, trusted even to keep watch over the daughters of his master.[10] In the same colony, Thomas Hazard advocated the abolition of the slave trade and the abolition of slavery throughout the British domains. Caroline Hazard (1893) wrote that Thomas Hazard was awakened to the evil of slavery. Johnston notes that Hazard refused to take slaves his

---

9. See Thomas Robinson Hazard and Willis Pope Hazard, *Recollection of Olden Times.* J. P. Sanborne, 1879, p. 22; Carolina Hazard, *Thomas Hazard, Son of Robert Call'd College Tom.* Houghton, Mifflin and Company, 1894, p. 45.

10. Ibid., p. 22.

father gave to him. Instead, he preferred performing his farming duties without the assistance of slaves. While Thomas refused to hold slaves, his father, Robert Hazard, was offended by Thomas' approach. The senior Hazard feared that many people would support the abolition of slavery. As a result, he threatened to disinherit his son.

Like in Rhode Island, in 1676, an African slave named Hagar saved her master's children from an Indian attack. According to Benjamin L. Mirick and John Greenleaf Whittier (1832), Hagar courageously protected her master's children who were about six and eight years old. At the first alarm of enemy attack, she quickly carried the youngsters into the cellar where the Indians would not find them. She covered the children with two tubs before going into hiding for herself. When the Indians entered the house, they took every precious good. As the enemies passed regularly around the tubs, they did not discover the children. Another woman in the household by the name of Whittaker, possibly English, went into hiding, too. Angola, an African in Boston, saved Governor Richard Bellingham when he was in danger of drowning in the river. When Angola saw the governor's distress, he retrieved a boat without delay and rescued him. The incident occurred in the river located between Boston and Winisimet. For Bellingham's show of appreciation, John Winthrop (1825) noted the governor gave Angola a gift: a fifty-square-foot plot of land on the highway leading to Roxbury, the piece of land was given to him forever. The property was to be passed from generation to generation among his descendants.[11] These illustrations show that some Africans in early colonial America valued the lives of their masters as highly as the latter valued their own lives.

William Chauncey Fowler (1901) noted that slaves and their masters were attached strongly. During colonial wars, slaves defended the land of their masters. Many slaves enlisted as soldiers in the names of their masters, and others went to war as servants. Like Fowler, in 1836, Governor Isaac Hill of New Hampshire spoke about the cordial relationship between master and slave. In fact, during his address to both Houses of the Legislature, Hill stressed the mutual relationship between slaves and

---

11. John Winthrop, History of New England from 1630 to 1649. Little, Brown, 1853, p. 174.

their masters. In the Colony, Connecticut General Newbury in Windsor established a good relationship with Mark, his African slave. After freeing Mark, the general with his wife traveled from Windsor to Litchfield to visit him. Jabez Haskell Hayden (1900) commented that General Newbury was interested in the life of his former slave. When Newbury visited Mark, he stayed overnight at Mark's house.[12]

In Rhode Island, Thomas Williams Bicknell (1898) further confirms that a strong affection existed between African house and farm servants and their masters. According to him, relationships were common and became permanent. In his language, Bicknell said the relationship established between master and slave was reciprocal. In Massachusetts, Sarah Loring Bailey (1880) talked about Cato, the slave of Reverend Samuel Phillips, who remained for some years at the house of his master, even after being liberated from bondage in 1780. Staying at his master's house indicated that Reverend Master Phillips and his servants had a relationship that was on good terms. If he had been abused by his master or his family, Cato would not have stayed under his master's roof. Cato appreciated his master's good faith toward his servant. The former slave wrote a letter expressing his gratitude to Reverend Phillips:

> I desire therefore to return my hearty & unfeigned thanks for your care over me, your kindness to me, also for your timely checks, your faithful reproofs, necessary corrections, your wise counsel, seasonable advice, for your endeavors being yet (or when) young & my mind tender to frame it such a manner as to lay a foundation for my present & future happiness and also by the blessing of heaven.[13]

The letter was signed by Cato on May 24, 1789.[14]

Like mutual relation, in colonial New England, African Americans were taught language and religion. In Rhode Island, James MacSparran,

---

12. Jabez Hayden, Historical Sketches. Arranged and published by the Windsor Locks Journal, 1900, p. 79.

13. See Sarah Loring Bailey, *Historical Sketches of Andover*. Houghton, Mifflin, 1880, p. 42

14. Ibid.

Irish barrister, Anglican clergyman, and author, mentions catechizing African American and white children at church in his *Letter Book and Abstract*. Religious instructions to children of both races were common in colonial New England. In Connecticut, Jane De Forest Shelton wrote, "the earlier law at least made the owners teach their slaves to read and attend religious services."[15] In 1660, Samuel Orcutt contended that learning how to read and write in English was an obligatory task for everyone. Those who violated this law were subject to punishment. In 1690, when the court learned that many children and servants in the colony were unable to read religious scripture in English, the grand jury was entrusted with the power to visit each family believed to be neglecting the order of the court. Additionally, the grand jury was ordered to verify whether the children of such families were capable of reading in English and to verify if children were trying to learn. Masters and parents who failed to abide by the education law were charged twenty shillings.[16] This law did not discriminate against people of color. The court intended the law to ensure religious and instructional development in the entire Connecticut colony. Reading the scripture was critical in Connecticut, where church ministers believed in the importance of good moral character.

Reading facilitated African Americans' entrance into the labor market of the time. The employment of free people of color in Rhode Island was noted by William Johnston in 1894. In *Slavery in Rhode Island, 1755–1776*, Johnston elaborated that "with the growth of Providence, many emancipated slaves shared in the increase of general prosperity and left behind effects sufficient to attract the attention of the Town Council."[17] Johnston tells of a Providence resident, Andrew Frank, an African, who lived a comfortable life due to his educational status. Frank left to the

---

15. Jane De Forest Shelton "The New England Negro. A Remnant". *Harper's Magazine*, volume 88. *Making of America Project*. Harper's Magazine Co., 1893, p. 534.

16. See Samuel Orcutt, *The History of the Old Town of Derby, Connecticut, 1642–1880, with Biographies and Genealogies*. Ambrose Beardley Press of Springfield Printing Company, 1880, 106, Connecticut education law of 1660 and 1690.

17. In Providence, Negroes were active in business. Free Negroes enjoyed the industrial developments of the city of Providence. They had assets which attracted the attention of local officials. See William Johnston, "*Slavery in Rhode Island, 1755–1776*", Rhode Island Historical Society, 1894, p. 7.

town 229 pounds and 6 pence when he died in October 1755. Jack Harris left 145 pounds, 11 shillings, and 5 pence in colonial bills upon his death in 1745. Another prominent and successful African American in Providence was Emanuel Bernon, the slave of Gabriel Bernon, a wealthy merchant. After Emmanuel's emancipation, he established the first oyster house in Providence. According to Johnston, the house was located on Town Street, near the site of the Old Custom House of a later day. When Emmanuel died in 1769, he left a house and lot on Stampers Street. His personal estate was valued at 534,105 pounds. In the same town and colony, John Read left 100 pounds after his death.

In Rhode Island, African members of the community prospered well. Caesar Lyndon, the African servant to Governor Josiah Lyndon, was involved in business. Caesar was a commercial agent for his master. While he was conducting his master's business affairs, Caesar had his own commercial deals with the sea captains at Newport and Providence. With his status as a prosperous African, he was able to assist people of his color by lending them money when they were in need.

Massachusetts' history features recorded evidence of the prosperity of Africans and African Americans. Bostian Ken, commonly called Bus Bus [sic], was a landowner who planted wheat on his land. He had four-and-a-half acres of standing wheat in 1656. Also, he owned a house in Dorchester.[18] According to the standard of the time, Ken was a wealthy African American in colonial Massachusetts. Moreover, in Deerfield, Massachusetts, a few African Americans were involved in business. George Sheldon, a Deerfield historian, recorded limited information on African servants who engaged in business transactions during the colonial period. According to his account, in 1750, Pompey, who was a servant to Thomas Wells, had a personal account with Elijah William at the Old Corner Store. In the same town, in 1752, Mesheck, an African, had a business account and another African servant named Cesar maintain a personal account at the Old Corner Store in 1755. Apparently, Major Williams established an amicable relationship with people of African descent.

In New Hampshire, Primus, an African servant to Daniel Fowle, owner of the *New Hampshire Gazette*, was employed as a press man by

---

18. See *The Suffolk Deeds: Liber-1-XIV* [1629–87], 1883, p. 296.

his master. According to Nathaniel Adams (1825), author of *Annals of Portsmouth*, Primus was a good press man despite being an illiterate servant. He worked in the office of his master until old age. Primus was ninety years old when he died. It is possible that he received job training throughout his years of service. Even though he started as illiterate, while working for the press, he acquired knowledge of the printing industry. The *New Hampshire Gazette* was established in 1756 in Portsmouth. It was the first press in the colony. The account of Primus was also noted by Sarah Haven Foster in 1876 in the book titled *The Portsmouth Guide Book*. In this work, Foster writes, "the paper was printed with the assistance of an intelligent negro slave named Primus, who was an excellent pressman. It was the first newspaper published in the province."[19]

Relative to social contributions, William Babcock Weeden, author and Rhode Island historian, wrote that "blacks always played a considerable part in the social life of Rhode Island."[20] The accounts of Johnston and Weeden translate that the labor market in colonial Rhode Island was open to everyone. From this account, it is plausible to note that people of color made fortunes from the labor market. In Rhode Island, Massachusetts, Connecticut, and New Hampshire, Africans and African Americans were socially and economically involved in the fabric of the societies established in these colonies. With respect to language ability a good example of an African American who contributed to a colonial family due to his mastery of the English language was the slave of the president of Yale University. President Timothy Dwight, IV, commended with respect the contributions of a black servant in his family in Connecticut. Fowler notes, "President Dwight spoke of a woman in his house who was often consulted as to the management of his family concerns."[21] Dwight's confidence in his servant gave a great

---

19. Sarah Haven Foster, The Portsmouth Guide Book: Comprising a Survey of the City and Neighborhood, with notices of the Principal Buildings, Sites of Historical Interest, and Public Institutions. Joseph H. Foster, 1876, pp. 31–32.

20. William Babcock Weeden, *Earlier Rhode Island: A Social History of the People*. Crafton Press, 1910, p. 224.

21. Slave of President Dwight of Yale College had a say on the management of his house. She had the ability to communicate well with the family of her master. See William Chancey Fowler, *Historical Status of the Negro in Connecticut*, Charleston, S.C., Walker, Evans & Cogswell CO., 1901, p. 25.

deal of weight to her wise counsel. Another prominent and important African servant in colonial Connecticut was Doctor Primus. This African American practiced medicine with success. He mastered his medical skills while assisting his master, Dr. Alexander Wolcott. James Hammond Trumbull notes that Primus traveled with Dr. Wolcott when he went on his medical outreach. As a bodyguard and medical assistant, Primus helped Dr. Wolcott to compound medicine and perform other medical services. Resulting from assisting his master, Primus acquired sufficient medical knowledge to practice as a physician. After Primus was liberated from bondage, he practiced medicine full-time. Alice Morse Earle (1896) writes that Primus was trained in surgery through helping his master. She went on to note that white patients sought Doctor Primus's medical services, a fact denoting his excellence as a healthcare professional.

Like in other colonies, in colonial Boston, Massachusetts, a prominent female of color was Phyllis Wheatley. This African-born female was sold as a slave in 1761 to John Wheatley, a wealthy Boston merchant and tailor.[22] Due to her ability to master the English language, she gained favor from her mistress, Susanna Wheatley. With the influence of her mistress and her mistress' daughter, Mary, Wheatley excelled in reading and became an iconic female writer of her time. Wheatley was received in England by many influential and honored people of the era, such as Lady Selina Shirley, Countess of Huntingdon; British statesmen, William Legge, Second Lord of Dartmouth, and British philanthropist, John Thornton.[23] These elites were impressed by the poems Phyllis Wheatley penned.

In New England, slaves received their primary education in the house of their first masters. And slaves' education was an eclectic array of professions. For example, in Portsmouth, New Hampshire, Charles

---

22. Phyllis Wheatley was born in Africa and imported as slave in 1761 to colonial New England where she became a poet. See *Memoir and Poems of Phyllis Wheatley, or a Native African and a Slave: dedicated to the Friends of the Africans*, published by Geo W. Light, 1834, p. 9. The information of Miss Wheatley can be found also in *Phyllis Wheatley, Poems and Various Subjects, Religious and Moral*. W.H. Lawrence, 1887

23. See Letter of Wheatley Susanna, 29 March, 1773, to Samson, Als, 2 pages (Samson Occom MSS), Connecticut Historical Society.

Warren Brewster notes that some blacks were good mechanics. Also, he pointed out that "The parlor of the house of the late Richard Hart, on Russell Street, was handsomely finished by Caesar, a house slave."[24] People of African descent were also sometimes trained as seamen in colonial New England. William Johnston notes that blacks were often coerced to go to sea on privateers and merchant vessels, without the consent of the slaves' owners. For the prevention of such behavior, an act was passed in 1757 that commanders of privateers or masters of any other vessels carrying slaves out of the colony without the consent of their masters should be fined twenty-six pounds.[25] Being seamen, blacks were often hired as privateers by colonial officials and private individuals in Rhode Island.

Blacks could go to sea on privateer and merchant vessels with the consent of their masters. In Massachusetts, employment of Africans and European servants was administered according to the law enacted by the freemen during the early years of the colony. When the government of Massachusetts was a corporate body politic, freemen established the pay rate and the protection of servants against unusual treatment. For a time, slavery was not recognized by law in Massachusetts, and persons, blacks or whites, not considered freemen were classified as servants. For the welfare of the servants, freemen and colonial officials enacted humane laws. Massachusetts colonists were against the mistreatment of servants. Nathaniel Ward notes that "the freemen of every township were empowered with making laws for the welfare of their towns."[26] The law enacted by the freemen stipulated that servants who escaped from masters due to intentional evil, and went to the house of a free-

---

24. In Portsmouth, blacks also enjoyed the opportunity of the labor market. They worked as mechanics and as carpenters. Caesar, a house slave, has been credited for finishing the parlor of the house of Richard on Russell Street. On the other hand, Primus, a Negro, worked in the press of Daniel Fowle. See Charles Warren Brewster, *Ramble about Portsmouth: Sketches of Persons, Localities, and Incidents of Two Centuries.* C.N. Brewster & Son, 1859, p. 208.

25. The Act of 1757 prohibited the employment of Negro seamen without the consent of their masters. Those who violated this act were charged according to the law.

26. In Massachusetts, freemen of each town were permitted to make laws for the welfare of their town. See Nathaniel Ward, *The Earliest New England Code of Laws*, 1641. A. Lowell, 1896, p. xiv.

man, constable, or magistrates were entitled to protection. Masters were prohibited from physically abusing their man servant or maid servant. The law required that after seven years of doing faithful and profitable work for the master, servants received recompense for their work at the end of their service.[27]

In colonial Massachusetts, servants and slaves had the right to holidays. During the holidays, African Americans visited their friends and other relatives. It was also during the holidays that African bondsmen in New England elected one of their own as governor of a region for the administration of their social affairs. While New Hampshire was under the jurisdiction of the Massachusetts colony, the holiday law was enforced in the New Hampshire colony, as well. As a result, African Americans were able to elect black governors in the colony. Colonial officials authorized men of color to establish a parallel government because they were not a threat to the colony. Unlike with the establishment of the proxy government, persons of African descent were called upon to perform military and militia services during alarms (danger) or wars against enemies.

In the earlier years of colonial Massachusetts, African Americans were permitted to be trustees of a town. In Worcester, Plymouth, a mulatto and free colored man named Will was among the grantees of Worcester.[28] Though information about Will was not detailed by those who wrote about him, he was a land owner in Worcester. He was among those who witnessed the division of land in 1686 among earlier settlers.

Regarding the maintenance of peace, African Americans worked hand-in-hand with the colonists. The paternal approach employed by the owners of slaves facilitated the integration of colored people into white families. Therefore, when slave owners were attacked, African bondsmen were directly affected. With the affection bondsmen had for their masters, they were often active participants in the common cause

---

27. Ibid.

28. In Worcester, there were free Negroes in the earlier days of the colony. One of them by the name of Will, a mulatto, was a grantee of the town. In colonial New England, many African slaves were freed after serving seven years as was the same for the white counterparts of servitude. See Charles Nutt, *History of Worcester and Its People*. Lewis Historical Publishing Company,1919, vol. I, p. 373.

for the security of the communities where they resided. Additionally, due to the relationship established between the local officials and blacks, black servants were not inclined to acts of insurgency.

In New England, African Americans were fairly treated due to leniency in the local government's approaches to dealing with them. Possibly, blacks were not hesitant to voluntarily defend internal security for the colonies; others were enlisted in the colonial military companies with the consent of their masters. From the data collected, evidence indicates that African Americans were enlisted in all the colonial wars. Likewise in the colonies, everyone participated in communal law enforcement. Edward Hartwell Savage's *A Chronological History of the Boston Watch and Police* (1865) explains that "watches as appears by the order, were to be performed in turn by the inhabitants; they were not 'citizen soldiers' but citizen watchmen."[29] Like other citizens in the colony, African Americans performed watch and guard services because they resided in the same areas with their masters. In New Hampshire, many families had African Americans in their homes. It was impossible for them to disregard watch and guard services while Native Americans attacked them and their neighbors. As in New Hampshire, African Americans in Rhode Island and Connecticut served voluntarily in the French and Indian War. In Massachusetts, Charles Dean states that "Negroes" were enlisted in the army during the French and Indian War. Unlike Dean, Jeremy Belknap noted that many African Americans were enlisted in the colonial army or on-board vessels of war. He also noted that there were many blacks in Massachusetts who perished during the former colonial wars.[30] Furthermore, African Americans served as drummers during the French and Indian War. As an illustration, *James Otis Lyford's History of the Town of Canterbury, New Hampshire, 1727–1912* states that "to protect the earlier settlers of Canterbury against hostile Indians

---

29. Edward Hartwell Savage, *A Chronological History of the Boston Watch and Police: From 1631 to 1865: Together with the Recollections of a Boston Police Officer, or, Boston by Daylight and Gaslight, from the Diary of an Officer Fifteen Years in the Service*, published by the author. The author, 1865, p. 13.

30. See *Queries Respecting the Slavery and Emancipation of Negroes in Massachusetts, Proposed by Hon. Judge Tucker of Virginia, and Answered by the Rev. Dr. Belknap.*" Massachusetts Historical Society Library.

was a business the proprietors and provincial authorities had to consider in a very few years after the first settlement in town."[31] This was true throughout colonial America. As the colonists in New England advocated laws for the administration of their daily affairs, laws were always enacted for safety and security. In Massachusetts, for example, the acts and laws of the colony stipulated "a well ordering of the militia was a matter of great concernment to the safety and welfare of the commonwealth."[32] This Act indicates the emphasis lawmakers put on the security of the people who resided in the colony.

The 1656 Act was legalized by the General Court of Massachusetts. A good example for the Act was performed in Narragansett, Rhode Island. Caroline Hazard's book *Thomas Hazard, Son of Robert, Called College Tom* (1893) comments upon the role of blacks to protect and secure the safety of the colonists. During a wedding, "Negroes" acted as gatekeepers. They were employed as sentinels for the protection of the visitors, the bride and groom, and their families. The best possible speculation is that African slaves manned security at the gate during the wedding to deter Indians from attacking the guests. It was common in colonial New England for Indians to attack the settlers when they had an opportunity. Similarly, settlers were always armed even while in church. A sentinel was also assigned to keep worshipers safe.

It was in 1770 that the Boston Massacre happened. When the inhabitants of Boston attacked the sentinel, who was accused of assaulting a lad, the sentinel returned fire. The incident sparked a riot that resulted in the death of Crispus Attucks, a mulatto rioter. In addition, Samuel Gray, the rope-maker, was shot. James Caldwell and Samuel Maverick, both residents of Boston, were killed during the same incident. Similarly, during the war of the revolution, African Americans were among the militiamen who fought in the battles of Lexington, Concord, and Cambridge, and in other cities at the start of the war. As the Revolutionary War continued, African Americans served their masters' lands without being paid and despite the refusal of some government officials

---

31. James Otis Lyford, *History of the Town of Canterbury, New Hampshire, 1727–1912: Genealogy and Appendix*. vol.2. Rumford, 1912, p. 46.

32. *The Charters and General Laws of The Colony and Province of Massachusetts*. Massachusetts Bay, Printed and Published by T.B. Wait & Co., 1814, p. 157.

to include black men in the military force of the provinces. Interestingly, despite their exclusion as recognized militia, African Americans believed they were obligated to defend freedom and justice against the English. Many of these slaves and servants did not care about their own status, but the security of the land primed their desire for freedom. Hoping to be free, they were determined to perform military duties with courage and loyalty. With this vision, African Americans did many heroic deeds during the revolution.

Even though African Americans owned properties, enlisted in the military, and formed social organizations, they were still under the control of their masters and the colonial government. As early as the 1700s, a string of laws was enacted throughout the New England colonies to manage the behavior of Africans and African American men. These laws addressed such issues as liberty of travel, gathering, and black men's comportment towards their masters. William Johnston (1894) and Edgar Mayhew Bacon noted that in Rhode Island laws were enacted to control slaves. To illustrate, in 1704 when a theft was committed, African slaves and servants and Indians were prohibited from being out of their domicile after nine o'clock at night. Violators of this law were whipped. Similar laws were enacted in Massachusetts and Connecticut, although research did not reveal how strictly the laws of these two colonies were enforced.

In New England, records indicate African Americans were introduced in 1638 in Massachusetts. Accordingly, they were treated as servants as other settlers transported from Europe. Similarly, no restrictions were enforced against them regarding marriage, religion, and holding properties. But with this increase of the population of this race in the colonies, many restrictions were enforced against their movements. Likely, various acts were established for the control of their behavior.

Chapter 2

African Americans in the Government of Colonial New England

People of African descent were employed in the government in colonial New England. Blacks were appointed to judiciary and law enforcement work at local levels, though records of these appointments are scant. Facts about race or about African American people were sometimes omitted from records since, during the Colonial Era, information regarding free Africans was not considered important. Africans born to biracial parents were sometimes identified as white. Persons born under those circumstances had access to education and other privileges throughout their lives. When they were older, their opportunities extended to being appointed as government officials at the local level. They performed watch duties without restrictions and served in the military. Conversely, full-blooded African American slaves and servants performed military duties only during war times. They were not part of the colonial body government, nor were full-blood Africans involved in politics. Throughout the New England colonies, records do not indicate the employment of African American servants as local law enforcement officers.

In New Hampshire, Wentworth Cheswell (sometimes spelled Chiswell) performed law enforcement and government duties in colonial New England. He was born into a biracial family; his father, Richard Cheswell, was a mulatto, and his mother was white. Esq. Wentworth Cheswell was elected justice of the peace and selectman in colonial Newmarket, New Hampshire in 1768.[1] Wentworth was listed

---

1. See data on Wentworth Cheswell was collected from the work of John Ward Dean in *The New England Historical and Genealogical Register*, vol. 39, no. 153, 1885, p. 192.

as white in the United States 1790 census. John Ward Dean, a genealogist in New England, indicated that Wentworth Cheswell was the first colored office holder. Up to the time of the writing of this work, no evidence has been discovered to contradict Dean's acknowledgement of Cheswell as the first African American office holder in New Hampshire.

Additionally, African Americans were employed in colonial government as soldiers and privateers during colonial wars, serving in sensitive military expeditions. Prince, an African American, was included in a secret expedition planned for the arrest of Major-General Richard Prescott, the commanding officer of the royal army in Newport, Rhode Island. In the town of Deerfield, where the French and Indians massacred the English (Americans), Primus, a Negro, was among the soldiers who fought in the war from 1703 to 1704. During the Revolutionary War, Peter Salem, an African American, was credited with killing Major John Pitcairn, a Scottish marine officer. (information regarding military duties performed by African Americans during the Revolutionary War is discussed in chapter seven.) African Americans in the military during the colonial wars are regulated according to the colony from which they hail or according to the colony from which they are most closely associated.

African Americans were also employed in the Continental Navy as sailors and privateers. They performed menial duties or worked as body servants to high-ranking military officers and governors. As body servants of the governors, they acted as official messengers and sometimes as security guards when escorting government officials on trips. A good example regarding a case in which an African American acted as a messenger happened in Rhode Island. Cudjo was a slave and held the trusted position of body servant for Governor Samuel Ward.[2] Frederick Denison, author of *Westerly (Rhode Island) and Its Witness* (1878), notes, "Cudjo brought his master's papers and personal effects safely in his

---

2. Cudjo, Negro body servant and slave of Governor Samuel Ward, served the governor faithfully and was present at the time of the death of his master. Frederick Denison, *Westerley (Rhode Island and Its Witnesses: For Two Hundred and Fifty Years, 1626–1876)*. J.A & R.A Reed, 1878, p. 108.

return to Westerly,"³ thus serving, in this case, as the governor's messenger. In Hartford, Connecticut, Cyrus (sometimes spelled Siras) Bruce was the servant of Governor John Langston for many years in a similar role. He was a waiter at the house of the governor for many years.⁴

In colonial New England, a trusted servant was sometimes consigned the management of the master's estates. For example, in Massachusetts, Mesheck was the servant of Reverend Theodore Hinsdale for eight years, and he was stationed at Fort Dummer. Mesheck's salary was paid by the colonial government. George Sheldon, author of *Negro Slavery in Old Deerfield*, wrote that Mesheck was a mulatto who was attached to his master's family. Due to Mesheck's good behavior, he was charged with the management of his master's commercial transactions.⁵ A similar circumstance of an African American entrusted with the management of his master's estate is noted in the case of Prince Youngey or Prince Johnar. This African American was brought to colonial America when he was about twenty-five years old. According to William Barry, the Framingham local historian of the day, Youngey was first owned by Colonel Joseph Buckminster. It appears that after serving with Buckminster for a time, the colonel handed him over to his son, Dean Thomas. Local historians in Framingham such as Barry, Eliza Buckminster, and Joseph Buckminster wrote that Youngey was a faithful, honest, and prudent servant. Due to these qualities, he was admired by Colonel Buckminster. These authors note that for almost twenty-five years Youngey was charged with the management of a large farm when his master was at the General Court for government meetings. Colonel Buckminster was the owner of several slaves, but he relied heavily on

---

3. Frederick Denison, *Westerley (Rhode Island)*, p. 108. James Thatcher, *Military Journal, During the American Revolutionary War*. Silas Andrus & Son, 1854. Page 86 covers Prince, Negro enlisted in the secret mission for the arrest of Major-General Prescott. For Primus, see George Sheldon, *A History of Deerfield, Massachusetts*, vol.1. Press of E.A. Hall & Company, 1895, p. 298; for Peter Salem, see William Barry, *History of Framingham, Massachusetts, Including the Plantations from 1640 to the Present Time*. J. Munroe and Company, 1847, p. 64.

4. See Charles Warren Brewster, *Rambles About Portsmouth: Sketches of Persons, Localities, and Incidents of Two Centuries, Principally from Tradition and Unpublished Documents*, vol.1 C.W. Brewster & Son, 1859, p. 208.

5. See George Sheldon, *"Negro Slavery in Old Deerfield."* The New England Magazine, 893, p. 51.

the competence of Youngey to manage the affairs at home. Youngey gave the colonel the peace of mind to attend to his several positions of power in Framingham as a selectman, town clerk, and representative of Framingham at the General Court.

The tradition of empowering African American slaves with the management of plantations was also observed in the South. As an illustration, before the Civil War in Mississippi, Benjamin T. Montgomery managed the business of his masters, Joe and Jefferson Davis (who would become the president of the Confederate government.)[6]

Like Mesheck and Prince Youngey other Africans were entrusted with the management of their masters' farms in Deerfield and Framington, respectively, the same holds true in other New England territories. For example, Janes De Forest Shelton recorded pertinent information regarding Quosh, an African American. Quosh belonged to Agar Tomlinson, who resided at Derby Neck, Connecticut. According to Shelton, Tomlinson owned a large estate which was parceled into small houses. This large estate was managed by Quosh whose responsibilities were much like a Southern overseer. The security of the estate and the security of the servants and slaves were under his supervision. Possibly, he enforced rules and regulations at the estates as the Southern overseers did.[6]

African Americans also served in a proxy government affiliated with the colonial government. As early as 1750, colonial officials in Connecticut, New Hampshire, and Rhode Island permitted the establishment of black governments for the welfare of the colonies. The black government was called a modified self-government in *Harper's magazine*.[7] A black person led the African American government. It appears that the election of black governors started in the colony of Massachusetts. *The Diaries of Benjamin Lynde and Benjamin Lynde, Jr.* indicate that the election of a black governor in Massachusetts was conducted in 1741.[8] Conversely, Connecticut historians believe that the office of the black

---

6. Jane De Forest Shelton, "The New England Negro. A Remnant," *Harper's New England Monthly Magazine*, volume 88. Harper & Brothers, 1894, p. 534.

7. Agnes Repplier "The Town That was Strawberry Banke" *Harper's Magazine*, volume 143. Harper & Brothers, 1921, p. 24.

8. *The Diaries of Benjamin Lynde and of Benjamin Lynde, Jr.* Fitch Edward Oliver. Priv. Print, Cambridge, Riverside Press, 1880, p. 109.

CHAPTER 2

governor was functional in 1756. The Hartford Black History Project contends that the office of the black governor emerged in Massachusetts and was introduced to Connecticut and Rhode Island later.[9]

Black governments did not function only for people of African descent; whites utilized their services as well. In the black court, officers tried cases brought before them by whites against their servants or slaves. In addition to judicial services, more than likely white colonial officials requested military services from black leaders. Officials in the black government often belonged to colonial governors or high-ranking military officers. Governor Sam Hun'ton [Huntington], for instance, was one of the black governors, who belonged to Governor Samuel Huntington of Connecticut.[10] (The administration of the black government and the election process and inaugurations are carefully detailed in Chapter 8 of this text.)

The expenses regarding the election process of the black government were supported by slave owners. Several authors—such as Frances Manwaring Caulkins, William Johnston, and Wilkins Updike have documented the contributions made by slave owners during the election process and during the inauguration of black governors. William Chauncey Fowler, the Connecticut local historian, notes that slave owners were accountable to the events of their slaves and their behavior. Slaves were considered like children. This paternal approach was always observed and enforced when dealing with slaves. However, when the decision was made for black people to have the responsibility of exercising a limited government, changes had to be made relative to how black people were perceived. The perception of men of color had to

---

9. William Dilon Piersen, *Black Yankees: The Development of an Afro-American Subculture in Eighteenth-Century New England*. Cambridge: University of Massachusetts Press, 1988, p. 118; he recorded the election of black government by 1756. Same data was noted in the Federal Writers Project, *Rhode Island: A Guide to the Smallest State*, Somerset Publishers, Inc., Jan 1, 1938, p. 205.

10. Frances Manwaring Caulkins, *History of Norwich, Connecticut: From Its Possession by the Indians to the Year 1866*. H.P. Haven, 1874, p. 330; William Fowler Chancey, *The Historical Status of the Negro in Connecticut: A Paper Read Before the New Haven Colony Historical Society*. Walker, Evans & Cogswell Company, 1901, p. 19; see also Wilkins Updike, *History of the Episcopal Church in Narragansett, Rhode Island, Including a History of the Other Episcopal Churches in the States, With a Reprint of a Work Now Extremely Rare, Entitled "America Dissected."* H. M. Ondedonk, 1847, p. 179.

change from seeing them as children who needed close instruction and guidance, to seeing them as competent adults capable of making good, sound decisions.

Black officials' attire became symbolic of their new roles in colonial America. For example, during the election inauguration, slave owners offered military uniforms and other equipment to black officials. As it was common for masters to furnish slaves with military equipment to use on their training days, it is possible that after African slaves received military attire and equipment for the parades, they did not return the belongings to their owners. Likely, horses of wealthy planters were reserved for the use of African Americans during Election Day. In this case, slaves seem to have the same privileges as their masters. The equipment and military attire were provided for the benefit and use of the entire colony in case of emergencies. It was a common custom throughout the New England colonies during the Colonial Era for masters to arm their plantation servants for self-defense and security. In New Hampshire, for security reasons white people were armed while cutting wood. Additionally, guards were assigned for the protection of groups of workers. African Americans were armed just as their white counterparts for the same purpose. It is imperative to note that African Americans received the same protection as their white brethren. In like manner, they were armed for their own protection as were their counterparts.[11]

During the Colonial Era, each plantation was like a military fief or estate. Every inhabitant grabbed a weapon and responded immediately at the sound of an alarm, usually when there was an Indian attack. To Illustrate, in 1676, due to Indian attacks, African Americans were permitted by law in Rhode Island to perform watch duties which are equivalent to police services in our modern era. In a like manner, in 1704, trusted slaves living in South Carolina were required to bear arms for the defense of the colony in case of an Indian attack. In 1708, slaves were included in the militia of Charleston, South Carolina, with the same responsibility as their white brethren. They were armed for the

---

11. See *Report of . . . for the year Ending June 1, 1866: Contains the Military History of New Hampshire, From Its Settlement in 1623 to the Year 1861*, vol. 2, New Hampshire Adjutant General Office. G. E. Jenks, 1866, p. 58.

defense and the preservation of the province.¹² Conversely, free African Americans were prohibited from carrying arms, except those employed as members of the militia and as housekeepers. In the colony of Georgia, every man was armed and called upon for military emergencies. The colony was like a military fief.

On plantations, intelligent slaves were sometimes selected to take care of others. In this capacity, these slaves acted as overseers. As such, they were enforcers of rules on the plantations and punished those who violated the rules set by the owners. African Americans who held these positions were sometimes disliked by other slaves. In the South, overseers were reputed as violent officers. John Henderson Russell, author of *The Free Negro in Virginia*, notes that Hannah Warwick, who was probably a white woman, testified at the General Court that her overseer was an African American.[13]

Body servants who traveled with their masters enjoyed the privileges of meeting high-ranking military officers and government officials. Prince Whipple of New Hampshire, who travelled with General William Whipple, possibly had the opportunity to enjoy such privileges. General Whipple was a government official during the Revolutionary War. Prince Whipple was a slave imported from Africa at an early age. Charles W. Brewster, a local historian in Portsmouth, New Hampshire, recorded remarkable information about Prince. According to Brewster, Prince and his brother Cuffee, were the sons of an African prince. They were sent to America by their father to be educated, but the boys were captured and enslaved instead. In 1766, they were brought to Portsmouth, New Hampshire. The account of Brewster regarding Prince does not totally agree with the writings of William Cooper Nell, an African American historian. In 1855, Nell recorded that Prince Whipple was sold into slavery in Baltimore. In *The Colored Patriot of the American*

---

12. William T. Alexander, History of the colored Race in America, Palmetto Publishing Company, 1800, p. 134.

13. See John Henderson Russell, *The Free Negro in Virginia, 1619–1865*. Johns Hopkins Press, 1913, pp. 38, 95. For information regarding the arming of Africans, see Thomas Cooper, *The Statutes at-Large of South Carolina: Acts Relating to Charleston, Courts, Slaves, and Rivers*, A. S. Johnston, 1840, p. 347; Samuel Goswold Goodrich, *A Pictorial History of America: Embracing Both the Northern and Southern Portions of the New World*, E. Strong, 1844, p. 432.

Revolution, Nell states that Prince was born in Amabou, Africa. His father sent him with his cousin to be educated in colonial America. His brother was educated in the colony and returned to Africa. When Prince and his cousin arrived in the colony, the ship captain sold them into slavery. Prince was purchased by Captain William Whipple of Portsmouth, New Hampshire. Nell does not explain whether Captain Whipple went to Portsmouth for a business transaction or to buy slaves for his farm. Even though he was a slave, Prince was taken care of by General Whipple, becoming his faithful servant. Possibly due to his manner and his obvious intelligence, Prince became a confidante to the General. Brewster writes that Prince was well built and handsome.

When General Whipple reported to Exeter for a special meeting regarding the war, he took Prince with him. As a member of the council, Captain Whipple was appointed General of the First New Hampshire Brigade. During the expedition against British General John Burgoyne, Prince was General Whipple's bodyguard. Even though Prince was a slave, he was close to his master and served General Whipple for many years.[14] When Prince went to war with his master, he had the opportunity to meet General George Washington. William Lloyd Garrison, a

---

14. On their way to Exeter, General Whipple asked Prince Whipple to be ready for the war. If they were called to fight, Prince would have to fight like a man. Prince challenged his master, reminding General Whipple that he (Prince) did not have liberty to fight. His master was fighting for his own liberty. If he had liberty, said Prince, he would fight to the last of his drop of blood. Prince's argument convinced General Whipple to free his slave from that time on. But according to the documentation of Brewster, it appears that Prince was not free as a result of the statement made by his master. Prince continued to serve him until 1784. After the war, Prince resided in the small house which was provided to them by his master. He lived with his brother Cuffee on near Hight Street. During his life in Portsmouth, Prince was admired by whites as well as people of his own color. He was among civil rights activists. In 1799, under the leadership of Nero Brewster, a number of African Americans petitioned to the New Hampshire Assembly for the liberation of African slaves from bondage. Prince Whipple was also one of the signers of the petition. He died in 1797, and his death was regretted by whites and black people in Portsmouth. He was a leader among his people. Brewster identified him as Caleb Quolen.

Charles W. Brewster, *Rambles About Portsmouth, New Hampshire*, C.W. Brewster & Son, 1859, pp. 152–53. For the petition of slaves in New Hampshire, see George Waldo Browne, *Granite State Magazine*, vol. 4. Granite State Publishing Company, 1907, p. 199. The petition was submitted to the New legislature on November 12, 1779.

prominent American social reformer, abolitionist, and journalist, notes that Prince was a bodyguard to his master. Prince was such an outstanding companion to General Whipple that the slave encountered some of the premiere military men and government officials of his day. Prince is pictured in one of the engravings of General Washington on horseback.

Even though there are minuscule records to the inclusion of African Americans in the government in colonial New England, people of this race made an important impact on the survival of the colonial government against the enemies. First, they created a tranquil environment which helped colonial officials in each colony to concentrate on the fight against the Native Americans and the French. Moreover, they defended militarily the internal territorial integrity of the colonies as requested to all the settlers.

Chapter 3

African Americans as Militiamen and Soldiers in the Colony of New Hampshire

Historians have agreed that since the New Hampshire colony was small, the need for African slaves and servants was not as urgent as in the Massachusetts and Connecticut colonies, where many officials and clergymen employed domestic help in their houses and on their farms. According to the census results of 1716 and 1767, collected by Erick R. Tuveson (1995), the Methodist Church, and Charles Brewster, the population of African Americans was minuscule. Collecting the census of free African Americans and slaves was difficult because the names of African Americans appeared only in bills-of-sale and legal documents. For this reason, it was difficult to collect information regarding the subjects in question in some New England towns. Exceptions to the inaccuracy of census-taking occurred when local historians documented the enlistment of African Americans in public service. With respect to their numbers in New Hampshire, below is the census data collected by the authors previously mentioned.

> Population of African Americans in New Hampshire:
> Erick R. Tuveson (1767) 633
> Methodist Church (1767) 623
> Charles Brewster (1767) 24 (Portsmouth only). Brewster did not collect the data of African Americans in the entire colony. Of this number, 24 were males and 63 were females.

The first Africans appeared in New Hampshire, according to many sources, in 1645 when Captain James Smith and Thomas Keyser, his shipmate, kidnapped two black men from Africa and brought them to

CHAPTER 3

New Hampshire.[1] The first slaves brought by Captain Smith were sold to a Mr. Williams of Piscataqua (Portsmouth) which was under the jurisdiction of the Massachusetts Bay.[2] Officials of the Massachusetts General Court detested this kidnapping. In 1646, the court ordered the return of the Africans to their country. The law prohibited slavery except for prisoners-of-war or those sentenced to servitude by some judicial court for an offense lawbreakers had committed.[3] According to the *New England Historical and Genealogical Register*, the will of Robert Cutt—dated June 18, 1674—listed eight black slaves. Cutt lived sometimes in Barbados and moved to Kittery in the Province of Maine after his short stay in New Hampshire.[4] The *Register* does not mention when Cutt became the owner of African slaves. Contrary to the record of that publication, Charles Brewster, author of *Rambles about Portsmouth*, states that in the will of Richard Cutt, which Brewster dates at May 1675, five black servants were mentioned.[5] From these records, there is evidence that blacks were servants and slaves in New Hampshire during the earlier years of the colony.

The New Hampshire colony was formed by immigrants from towns of the Massachusetts Bay, area where many settlements were created during the earliest days of the province. To illustrate, Reverend John Wheelwright, a resident of Boston, and other English inhabitants of the vicinity established the town of Exeter in 1638. A Puritan, Wheelwright

---

1. Captain James Smith and Thomas Keyser were the first English sanctioned in the colony for kidnapping and slavery. Even though these two persons listed above were not punished by law, the Africans were returned to their home country and a law was passed prohibiting slavery in 1646. John Winthrop, *The History of New England from 1630 to 1649, with Notes* by J. Savage, Printed by Phelps and Farnham, 1825–1826, pp. 243–45.

2. Samuel G. Drake, *The History and Antiquities of the City of Boston: The Capital of Massachusetts and Metropolis of New England, from Its Settlement in 1630 to the Year 1670...Also, an Introductory History of the Discovery and Settlement of New England*, vol.1, L. Stevens, 1854, p. 288. For the account of Negro sold to Mr. William of Piscataqua (Portsmouth, N.H.) see also The Essex Institute Historical Collections, 1888, p. 92.

3. For the law of 1646 prohibiting slavery with some exceptions, see Nathaniel Adams, *Annals of Portsmouth*, Portsmouth: The author, 1825, p. 32.

4. For Information about the slaves of Robert Cutt, see *The New England Historical and Genealogical Register*, vol. 44, 1890, p. 112; and Joseph Foster, *Soldier's Memorial*, Portsmouth, New Hampshire, 1893–1921, 1893, p. 20.

5. Charles Brewster, *Rambles about Portsmouth*, C.W. Brewster & Son, 1859, p. 29.

was banished from Massachusetts based on his religious beliefs. Previous to the establishment of Exeter, Hampton was settled by the inhabitants of Massachusetts Bay in 1637. Jeremy Belknap wrote that some planters in the Massachusetts colony planned to settle in Portsmouth where David Thompson built his house in 1623. During the earlier years of the New Hampshire province, no central government existed. The security of the settlement depended on the inhabitants of each district. Since the settlement of Hampton was within the limit of Massachusetts Bay, according to the *Laws of New Hampshire* (1904), from 1639 the Hampton settlement was under the jurisdiction of the Massachusetts Bay Colony. The territory expanded as settlements joined the colony. In 1641, the settlements of Portsmouth and Dover voluntarily joined the Massachusetts Bay Colony.[6] In 1642, Exeter also joined the colony.[7] However, in 1679, New Hampshire separated from Massachusetts Bay and became a royal government, led by a president and council appointed by England's King Charles II. John Cutt, the brother of Robert and Richard Cutt, was appointed president of New Hampshire.[8] From 1679 to 1688, the colony was under the protection of the English crown. In 1688, Sir Edmund Andros was appointed governor of the Massachusetts, New Hampshire, Maine, and the Narragansett (King's Province) colonies. During the Andros administration, arbitrary rules were enforced against the colonies. As a result, the inhabitants of Massachusetts revolted and arrested the governor. In Massachusetts, the general court appointed another governor. However, the colony of New Hampshire remained without a governor from 1689 until 1690.

---

6. In 1641, the settlements of Portsmouth and Dover were part of the colony of Massachusetts as noted in *the Laws of New Hampshire: Province Period*, 1679–1702, pp. 774. As these settlements did not have a central government and could not come to terms in forming a unity government, they joined the colony of Massachusetts. From 1641 until 1679, the laws of Massachusetts were observed in the settlements of New Hampshire.

7. Exeter became part of Massachusetts in 1642, and Hampton was under the jurisdiction of Massachusetts before Portsmouth and Dover. See Edwin Aizro Charlton, *New Hampshire As It Is . . .* A. Kenney, 1857, p. 19.

8. John Cutt, an eminent merchant at Portsmouth, New Hampshire, was appointed by the king to become president of the royal government. See *The New England Historical and Genealogical Register, vol. 44*, The Society, 1890, p. 112.

CHAPTER 3

In 1690, Indians and their French allies from Canada began incursions into New Hampshire. As the colony was without a government, some inhabitants petitioned the Massachusetts General Court for a re-unification of the settlements in New Hampshire Colony. The request was approved, and the two colonies were re-united.[9] In 1692, the union between Massachusetts Bay and New Hampshire was discontinued by order of the King of England. On March 1, 1692, Samuel Allen, a merchant of London, was appointed governor of New Hampshire, and John Usher of Boston was appointed his lieutenant governor. Allen remained in London while the colony was governed by Usher for six years.[10] By 1697, the colonies of Massachusetts and New Hampshire were under the administration of Richard Coote, Earl of Bellomont (sometimes spelled Bellamont). Also, Coote was appointed the governor of New York by the commission of the King. From 1697 until 1741, the Massachusetts and New Hampshire provinces were always united under one governor. The final separation of New Hampshire from Massachusetts occurred in 1741, and Benning Wentworth was appointed governor of the colony the same year.

When Governor Wentworth came to power, New Hampshire was frequently under attack by the French and their Indian allies. From time-to-time, inhabitants of the province were killed and taken as prisoners by Indians. At the time, the colony was not able to defend itself. Being a small and poor province, it was difficult for the colony to support the war effort; therefore, the government of Massachusetts dispatched soldiers for the protection of New Hampshire.

From the very earliest days of the settlements, Native Americans often attacked New Hampshire colonists. During the wars of King Philip (1675), Queen Anne (1702), and King George (1713), and the French and Indian War (1756–1763; sometimes called the Seven Years War), the inhabitants of New Hampshire fought their enemies.

---

9. See *Report of . . . for the year ending June 1, 1866: Containing the military history of New Hampshire from its settlement in 1623 to the year 1861*, vol. 2, New Hampshire. Adjutant-General's Office. G.E. Jenks, 1866, p. 14. In 1690, Nathaniel Fryer was the governor of the colony of New Hampshire. The military laws of Massachusetts were also observed in New Hampshire.

10. Ibid., p. 15.

In 1675, during King Philip's War, business activities in New Hampshire were paralyzed due to Indian attacks, so everyone in the colony was obliged to perform communal policing. The heads of households provided for the security and safety of their families. It was during this war that sentry boxes were placed upon the roofs of houses to monitor the enemies who attacked inhabitants in New Hampshire.[11] Inhabitants were assigned patrol duties under the leadership of brave and experienced men. The names of men assigned for patrol duties were not recorded. During the Colonial Era, sometimes officials did not document the names of men who served during military conflict. For example, the rolls of men who served during King Philip's War were not preserved in New Hampshire, as noted in the *Report of the New Hampshire Adjutant-General* of 1866. From the account of this report, it is sound reasoning to realize the names of New Hampshire men who served in colonial wars cannot be found due to lack of data that would give this information.[12]

In 1745, Governor William Shirley of Massachusetts organized a secret expedition for the attack of Louisburg on the Island of Breton where the French fort was built. In this expedition, African Americans were included. In 1756, when the French and Indian War was officially declared, African American militiamen from New Hampshire were among the fighters who defended the New England colonies. Edwin David Sanborn and Channing Harris Cox wrote how "during the wars that followed with the Indians and the French, every man became a soldier and every house was made a garrison."[13] The colonists, black slaves, servants, and free colored people were enlisted to defend the colony and to guard the frontiers.

African Americans in the ranks of the military in New Hampshire have been noted by many writers. Glen Knoblock, author of *Strong and*

---

11. See Report of Adjutant- General of New Hampshire for the year ending June 1, 1866: Containing the military history of New Hampshire from Its Settlement in 1623 to the year 1861, vol.2, 1866 p. 7.

12. Ibid.

13. Males in New Hampshire were always called upon to serve in the militia of the colony during the French and Indian Wars. See Edwin David Sanborn and Channing Harris Cox, *History of New Hampshire, from Its First Discovery to the Year 1830*. J. B. Clarke, 1875, p. 111.

CHAPTER 3

Brave Fellows: *New Hampshire's Black Soldiers and Sailors of the American Revolution, 1775–1784*, notes the enlistment of African Americans in colonial military companies. Similarly, Charles Henry Bell (1888) mentions the enlistment of an African American man in the expedition of Crown Point. According to Constance Brickwell Ward (1969), slave owners requested the governor to allow military services to be performed by slaves during Queen Anne's War. In the *Report of the New Hampshire Adjutant-General* of 1866, the names of African American soldiers fighting during the French and Indian War are listed. Moreover, in the Provincial and State papers of New Hampshire, names of African Americans who served as active defenders of the colony in 1748 and 1757 are recorded.

From 1645, when African bondsmen first appeared in the settlements of New Hampshire, there were no laws prohibiting their enlistment in the militia. Some African slaves were volunteers like their white brethren. Sanborn and Cox provide information about New Hampshire in the colonial war and how most of the troops were volunteers and others were enlisted by the order of the King according to old English custom.[14]

In 1718, a law was enacted for military services for the first time in New Hampshire. This law provided that "every male person, from sixteen to sixty years of age, except blacks and Indians, should perform military services."[15]

During the Colonial Era, it was common for the generals to take their black servants and slaves with them on expeditions and to enlist them in the militia to complete the quota or requested number of active military men required from each New England colony. The New Hampshire Colony was under populated; therefore, employing blacks in the militia was beneficial to both the colony and to the white soldiers.

---

14. During the French and Indian War, and other colonial wars, voluntary enlistments and the English system of impressments were in force to meet the quota requested by their Majesties the King and the Queen during Queen Anne's War. See Sanborn and Cox, *History of New Hampshire*, pp. 111–12.

15. For the military law of the colony of New Hampshire enacted in 1718, see the *Report of the Adjutant-General of the State of New Hampshire, for the Year Ending June 1, 1866*, vol. II, Concord: George E. Jenks, State Printer, 1866, pp. 37–38.

To illustrate, in 1757, Major John Gilman was with his servant Caesar Nero when Fort William Henry was captured by the French and their Indian allies. More on Caesar Nero will be explored in detail later in this chapter. Lorenzo Johnston Greene, author of *Negro in Colonial New England*, recorded, "Greatest efforts were put forth by the black soldiers in the French and Indian War (1756–1763)"[16] and "recruiting officers admitted black slaves and free blacks in colonial ranks."[17] Similar indication on the enlistment of blacks in the militia of the colony of New Hampshire was recorded by Laura Eliza Wilkes (1919), who notes that "slave masters in New Hampshire did not hesitate to call upon their bondsmen to render assistance in the shouldering of arms, and this call

---

16. During the French and Indian War of 1756–1763, generals made a great effort to recruit Negroes into the ranks of white soldiers. Greene (1969) noted that free Negroes and slaves were enlisted in the ranks of the army. The war of 1756–1763 was too long, and the colony of New Hampshire was exposed to the enemies. William Douglass (1755), the author of *A Summary, Historical and Political of the First Planting, Progressive Important, and Present State*, notes that "in the late French and Indian War, the colony of New Hampshire and Maine were neither capable nor willing to protect their own frontiers, and the colony of Massachusetts Bay took them under protection." From the account of William Douglass, we can conclude that every capable man in the colony was sometimes impressed for military service of the king. During the colonial wars, the incursions of the Canadian French and Indians were common in New Hampshire. Jeremy Belknap recorded pertinent information on the destructions of lives and properties by the French and Indians during the wars. During the colonial period, military men received bounties for their military service.

African slaves and servants were also victims, like their white brethren. In this case, they were eager to defend themselves when the French and Indians attacked. The victimization of African slaves and servants was recorded by New England writers. Samuel Gardener Drake (1870) and Jeremy Belknap (1831) wrote on May 4, 1746, when Indians attacked the settlement of Contoocook, five white men and an African American by the name of Caesar were fired at. In the same area, Elisha Cook, an English man, and the African slave of Reverend Phinehas Stevens of the same settlement were killed. By witnessing such massacres, African Americans had no choice but to fight the enemies. In such cases, they had to join forces with their masters fighting the enemies. African Americans and their masters had an amicable relationship. Possibly, when family members of their masters were attacked, able African and white men capable of bearing arms did not hesitate to defend their community against the enemies. In colonial New Hampshire, men capable of carrying weapons were few and colonists would not afford to exclude African Americans from military service.

17. Lorenzo Johnston Greene, *The Negro in Colonial New England*, Atheneum, 1969, p. 188.

was received positively by them."[18] Luke Gridley recorded in his 1757 diary that African Americans were enlisted in the militia of the colonies and were fighters in the earlier colonial wars.[19] The involvement of African Americans in the fight for the defense of the colony and the interests of their masters was patriotic. They fought also for their own protection. They were not rebellious to their masters; they responded without complaint. In fact, due to the attachment some African Americans had to their masters, the slaves felt as strongly about defending the colony as they did about protecting their masters.

Before and after the law of 1718, which excluded African Americans from performing military services, evidence showed that some masters hired slaves to serve in the wars that plagued the colonies repeatedly. As a result, the masters petitioned the court for money to pay for the militia services performed by slaves and/or servants. In 1713, the New Hampshire provincial government paid Joseph Jackson £4.6 for the military duties performed by his black servants at Fort William and Mary. Apparently, Jackson enlisted several of his African slaves. In the provincial papers of colonial New Hampshire, the number of African slaves belonging to Jackson is not identified. Additionally, military duties performed by his slaves were not mentioned. Another person who received an allowance for the military duties of his servant was Edward Toogood. A record in the *Journal of the General Assembly of New Hampshire* indicates that Toogood signed an account for himself and his servant.[20] Since Toogood's African servant was his "property," Toogood was the only person who possessed the power to sign the servant's name. During the French and Indian War, those who enlisted

---

18. Laura Eliza Wilkes, *Missing Pages in American History: Revealing the Services of Negroes in the Early Wars In the United States of America*, 1641–1815. Press of R.L Pendleton, 1919. In 1919 Wilkes tells us that slave masters called their bondsmen to defend the colony in New Hampshire. Slave owners more likely called upon slaves to fight for the defense of the colony before the enactment of the law of 1718 which prohibited the enrollment of Negroes in the militia of the colony. After the passage of the law of 1718, high-ranking officers took with them their Negro servants to the war field., p. 7.

19. Luke Gridley's *Diary of 1757* While in Service in the French and Indian War, The Case, Lockwood, Brainard Company, 1906, p. 21. This account of Gridley supports that African Americans were among the defenders of peace, security, and safety in colonial wars.

20. Ward, *Negro Slavery*, 1969, p. 19.

were paid a bounty. Because bondsmen were enlisted in the names of their masters, the owners of bondsmen received the bounty allocated for slaves. Even though in New Hampshire slavery was not recognized by law, the General Court believed in individual ownership of slaves. Ward (1969) confirms that slaves were considered personal property in New Hampshire. When slave owners enlisted their property for military duty, the court did not prohibit masters from following through with their decision. In other words, the court did not sanction owners for enrolling their servants and slaves into the military. Because the court did not sanction enlisting slaves and because of the bounty awarded to military men, slave owners were motivated to enlist their men for the public service.

With respect to the servant of Edward Toogood, it is possible that Toogood's servant was enlisted in 1722 during the expedition commanded by Captain John Lovewell when Indians attacked the inhabitants of Maine. According to the New Hampshire Adjutant-General, in 1723 when the Indians began attacking the English, militiamen were sent to scout in search of enemies.[21] The war which Lovewell executed against the Indians was called Lovewell's War. This was an on-going fight in New Hampshire and Maine when Indians attacked many towns that included such places as Brunswick, Dover, and other towns along the Piscataqua River that divides the two states. During the incursions, many people were killed. Herbert Millon Sylvester (1910) notes war was proclaimed on July 25, 1722.

In 1726, during the continuation of attacks by Indians and the French on the settlements in New Hampshire, men in the colony were assigned military duties. Data from the *New Hampshire Provincial Papers* (1870) indicate Captain William Bowen went with his African servant to Casco Bay on a military expedition. For the service of his servant and the renting of a brigantine (ship), he was paid £22. Apparently, the African American belonging to Captain Bowen worked on a ship. It is not known whether or not Bowen was a privateer.

In 1757, African slaves and servants were enlisted in the New Hampshire military to protect Fort William Henry. When the fort was

---

21. See *the Report of the New Hampshire Adjutant-General, 1866*, p. 41.

attacked by the French, many New Hampshire men, African slaves, and African servants perished. Others were captured and taken to Canada as prisoners-of-war. A petition for an allowance or compensation for the damage to slaves, servants, or family members harmed in the act of military service was common. Parents claimed an allowance for their children, slave owners for their servants or slaves, and wives for their husbands. Fort William and Mary was the only large fort built in the New Hampshire colony. According to *Report of the Adjutant-General of New Hampshire* (1866), soldiers began building Fort William and Mary in 1699 during the Earl of Bellomont's administration when he was governor of New England provinces. The construction estimate of the fort was £6,000 as noted in the report of the *New Hampshire Adjutant* in 1866. The fort was completed in 1705.[22] During war, soldiers were always dispatched to the forts for protection. The forts were where settlers took shelter when they feared the possibility of enemy attack. As early as 1739, Governor Jonathan Belcher of New Hampshire wrote that Fort William and Mary was in poor condition and repairs were needed to maintain it. Additionally, he ordered capable men to be enlisted for the protection of the people and trade of the province.[23] It is possible Governor Belcher feared that in case of an attack from the French, the forts would be overrun without resistance if unprotected. Additionally, forts would not serve their purposes well due to dilapidation. When the French attacked Fort William and Mary, few soldiers were stationed there to protect the citadel.

James P. Taylor (1899) describes August 9, 1757, when Louis-Joseph de Montcalm, the French commander, attacked Fort William Henry in New York with 7,606 soldiers. Lieutenant-Colonel George Monro, a Scotch-Irishman serving in the British military, eventually had to surrender the fort because he could not resist Montcalm's military force. After resisting for a day, Monro surrendered on August 10th. Monro had only 2,264 military men—a strident imbalance of power between foes. When he called for assistance from General Daniel Webb, help did not arrive.

---

22. Ibid., p. 21. Report for the year ending, June 1, 1866: contains the military history of New Hampshire, from its settlement in 1623 to the year 186., vol 2. G. E. Jenks, 1866.

23. *Provincial and State Papers, vol. 5, New Hampshire (Colony) Probate Court*, 1871, p. 12.

After the surrender, many soldiers were killed or taken as prisoners by the Indians. Other prisoners-of-war were taken to Canada by the French.[24]

The capture of Fort William Henry and the loss of so many soldiers were blows to the colonies of New Hampshire, Massachusetts, Connecticut, and Rhode Island. After the defeat of Monroe in New Hampshire, men were enlisted for the defense of Fort William Henry, which was under French control. In 1757, Captains Thomas Tash of Durham and Richard Emery were assigned to protect the fort. Captain Tash was the commander of men recruited in New Hampshire for the defense of that fort, and Captain Emery commanded men from New Hampshire. Soldiers under Captain Tash were garrisoned at Number Four (Charlestown) in the Western part of the New Hampshire province as noted by Charles Henry Bell (1888). Africans were included among men enlisted under these two captains.[25] According to *Acts and Resolves, Public, and Private, of the Province of the Massachusetts Bay* (1910), there are records that indicate slave owner, Jacob Biglow of Waltham, requested a payment for the captivity of his black man Caesar who was in public service at Fort William Henry in 1757.[26] Like Biglow, Major John Gilman petitioned the New Hampshire colonial government for an allowance in payment for the service of his black servant who was taken to Canada as a captive. Gilman's slave was captured during the expedition of the surrender of Fort William Henry.[27]

The *New Hampshire Provincial Papers* (1885), the *Report of the New Hampshire Adjutant-General* (1866), and books written by local historians list the names of blacks who served in expeditions during the French and Indian Wars. Jeremy Belknap, a New Hampshire local historian and former president of the Massachusetts Historical Society, recorded that in 1706, among the sixty-four men selected for Colonel Hilton's expedition was a mulatto. Belknap writes he was captured with other soldiers

---

24. James P. Taylor, *The Cardinal Facts of Canada History*, Hunter, Rose Company, Limited, Printers, 1899, p. 64.

25. See *Report of the New Hampshire Adjutant-General*, 1866, p. 187. Caesar Nero was enlisted in the company of Richard Emery. Per page 202, Nero was listed under Captain Thomas Tash.

26. *Provincial and State Papers*, 1872, p. 765.

27. Lois Brown, *Pauline Elizabeth Hopkins: Black Daughter of the Revolution*, Charlotte: UNC Press, 2008, p. 20.

such as Edward Hall and Samuel Mighill. Hilton did not complete the expedition because he and his soldiers did not have provisions.[28] The *New Hampshire Provincial Papers* report that the men in Hilton's expedition were from Exeter, New Hampshire; therefore, the mulatto likely was from Exeter. In all the documents consulted, little was mentioned about the mulatto soldier. His family history and status were not recorded, so it is unknown whether he was a slave, servant, or a free man.

In 1745, when Massachusetts Governor William Shirley planned an expedition for the capture of Louisburg (or Louisbourg), Governor Benning Wentworth of New Hampshire ordered militiamen from his colony to join Massachusetts soldiers. There were several African Americans among this troop of militiamen. John Gloster, slave of Theodore Atkinson, was killed in the expedition. The petition filed by Atkinson indicated that John Gloster enlisted voluntarily in the militia and was among the first persons who marched against Louisburg in the company of Captain Mason. After Gloster's enlistment, his master bought a gun for Gloster which cost £12. This same gun was shot to pieces with a cannon ball, and Gloster was killed. For the loss of his servant, Atkinson petitioned His Excellency Benning Wentworth, Esq., the Honorable Major Council, and the House of Representatives for the colony of New Hampshire in General Assembly to pay an allowance to compensate for his losses.[29] With respect to his petition claim filed on July 19, 1746, Atkinson was paid £3.

In King George's War of 1748, according to the muster roll of Captain Job Clements, Peter, a black man, was among the recruited soldiers. He was a servant of Major Greenleaf.[30] Peter's enlistment was secured by order of the governor of New Hampshire, Benning Wentworth, when

---

28. Jeremy Belknap, *History of New Hampshire*, G. Wadleigh, 1862, p. 172.

29. The Provincial and State Papers of New Hampshire, vol. 18, recorded the petition filed by the Honorable Theodor Atkinson for the incident of his slave John Gloster. The petition was filled out July 19th, 1746. On the Roll of New Hampshire men at Louisburg, Cape Breton, 1745, is the recorded death of the Negro slave of Honorable Theodore Atkinson. See Roll of New Hampshire Men at Louisburg, Cape Breton, 1745, New Hampshire Commissioner at Louisburg Celebration, 1895. Concord, N.H.: E.N. Pearson, 1896, p. 35.

30. Peter, Negro belonging to Major Greenleaf, was enrolled among the soldiers who protected the garrison and people at Rochester and Barrington in 1748 by the order of Governor Wentworth. He was enlisted in the Company of Job Clements. See *Report of the Adjutant-General of the State of New Hampshire*, 1866, p. 108.

he requested men for the protection of the garrison. Peter assumed the duties assigned by Governor Wentworth to secure the garrison and to protect the people of the community. The governor empowered the militia with scouting and patrol duties. Like modern police, the officers patrolled both the neighborhood of Rochester, and surrounding areas. For the services which the soldiers performed, they were paid £2.15 monthly. For the four months of his term of service, Peter received the same pay as Caucasian soldiers.[31]

After the 1748 treaty ended the war, Indians in Canada and the French continued attacking the English in New England. The attacks were instigated by the French, who furnished Native Americans with weapons. Despite the treaty to end the war, men were still enlisted to fight for the protection of the colony, and African Americans were enlisted alongside their white brethren. According to the *New Hampshire Provincial and State Papers* (1885), Scipio, a servant to Dr. Joseph Atkinson, and Caesar Durham were African Americans who fought against the Indians and French. This information was recorded in the *Report of the New Hampshire Adjutant General of 1866*.[32] In the *Provincial Papers*, the name of Joseph Atkinson's servant is recorded as Sippo. It appears the two names represent the same person, despise the different spellings. According to the muster roll of 1757, Scipio enlisted as a soldier on April 8, 1757, and was discharged on October 21 of the same year. In April 6, 1758, while in the military force, Scipio was twenty-six years old, as recorded in the *New Hampshire Provincial and State Papers* (1885). Similarly, Caesar Durham was enlisted in the military on April 29, 1757, and discharged on October 30 of the same year.[33] He was forty-five years old in 1758. Both Scipio and Durham were enlisted in the company of Captain Thomas Tash.

Another African American by the name of Scipio was enlisted in the company of Captain Johnson from March 31 until November 27, 1760.[34] In the same year, an African American by the name of Scip Martin was

---

31. Ibid., pp. 108–110.
32. In the Colonial Era, the spelling of Roman names given to African Americans was not consistent. The name Cesar was sometimes written Ceasar. In the same period, many Africans were named Ceasar, Nero, or Scippio. Similarly, others were named Jupiter.
33. *Report of Adjutant-General of New Hampshire*, 1866, p. 203.
34. Ibid., pp. 189–203.

in the company of Captain Ephraim Berry. Martin enlisted on March 12 and was discharged on November 18. During Martin's time of service, he was at Station Number Four (Charlestown).[35] Possibly, his first name was misspelled; instead of *Scip*, it should have been written as *Scipio*. These previously identified African Americans fought unjust wars that blacks and Englishmen were subjected to by the French and their Indian allies. In 1757, Caesar Nero, servant of Major John Gilman, was taken captive among the New Hampshire soldiers who surrendered Fort William Henry to French commander, Louis-Joseph de Montcalm. Caesar's master escaped, but Caesar was taken to Canada where he spent three years, according to Charles Henry Bell (1888). When Gilman presented inventory for his losses to the government, he listed the belongings of his African American servant. The inventory made by Major Gilman on May 5, 1758, is as follows: "To my Negro boy's gun & clothing he [sic] being taken & carried to Canada £30."[36] Caesar Nero was in the company of Captain Richard Emery at Fort William Henry. During the Colonial Era, it was common for superior officers to take their slaves as body servants. In addition, the slaves were armed and listed as militiaman of the colony. Caesar Nero, a native of Africa, was born in 1741, according to the account of one of his descendants, Pauline Elizabeth Hopkins,[37] and he was imported to Exeter, New Hampshire, when he was fourteen years old in 1755. Upon his arrival in Exeter, he was bought by Major John Gilman and assigned domestic duties. In other words, Nero was a house servant. After liberation from his master, Caesar Nero added a surname. He became known as Caesar Nero Paul in 1760, and he was a soldier who fought during the American Revolutionary War.[38]

Another slave named Caesar, belonging to Jacob Biglow of Waltham, New Hampshire, was captured during the 1757 French takeover of Fort William Henry. According to Biglow, Caesar was taken prisoner while

---

35. Ibid., p. 249.

36. Charles Henry Bell, *History of the Town of Exeter, New Hampshire*, Press of J.E. Farwell & Company, Boston, 1888, p. 235.

37. Lois Brown, *Pauline Elizabeth Hopkins: Black Daughter of the Revolution*, Charlotte: UNC Press, 2012, pp. 20–21.

38. Ibid. Brown tells readers how Caesar Nero accompanied his master to one of the expeditions during the battles of the French and Indian War. In the same book, a possible date of birth is given for Caesar Nero.

he was in the public service of the colony. Due to the captivity and suffering Caesar endured, the colony paid Biglow £8.00, money withdrawn from the public fund. Caesar was kept in captivity until 1760.[39] Other men of color were victims of the Fort William Henry attack. Massachusetts men such as Caesar, Cuggo Canada, and Jacob Lindsey were captured and taken to Canada. Moreover, Lyn Jock, a Negro belonging to Nathaniel Whittemore, Boston alias (Boston Burn), and James Bristol (a mulatto) were captives during the same incident.[40] According to Hopkins, Prince Light and Samuel Freemen, both African Americans, were taken to Canada and held as slaves because they were in bondage in New England. Captives who were slaves in New England held the same status in Canada, where they could be sold. Like African slaves and servants, many English in the United Colonies of New England were kept as prisoners-of-war in Canada. According to John Quincey Adams (1843) confirms the New England Confederation was formed May 19, 1643 and was comprised of the Massachusetts, Plymouth, Connecticut, and New Haven colonies. The objective of the organization was to protect the Confederation against enemies.

During the continuation of the French and Indian War in 1760, Scipio re-enlisted into the company of Captain William Johnson. Scipio was recruited on March 31, 1760, and discharged on November 27 of the same year. He was called upon eight times to serve during the war.[41] The re-enlistment of Scipio indicates that he was a good soldier

---

39. See the petition of Jacob Biglow of Waltham. Biglow argues his Negro man, Caesar, was taken prisoner at Fort William Henry in 1757 while employed in public service. Caesar remained in captivity until 1760 and did not return home until October in that year. Biglow asked to be paid an allowance for the Caesar's services and capture. The petition was approved, £8.00 were paid to Biglow from the public treasury. See *The Acts and Resolves, Public, and Private, of the Province of Massachusetts Bay*, published in 1910, p. 144.

40. *The New England Historical and Genealogical Register*, vol.14, 1860, pp. 271–74. Boston, alias Burn, a Negro, was taken captive with Robert Rogers, nearTiconderoga in 1756. *The Library of Universal History*, vol. XI, 1899. Note that during the capitulation of Fort William Henry, mulattoes, African Americans, and friendly Indians were subjected to the same conditions as the English (p. 53). The same information was noted by David Dobson, *The French and Indian War from Scottish Sources*. Genealogical Publishing Com., 2003, p. 27. The journal was published by S.G. Drake, 1860, pp. 271–72.

41. *Report of the New Hampshire Adjutant-General*, 1866, p. 246.

and performed admirably during his service terms, despite the poor and feeble condition of the colony, as noted by political economist Arthur Latham Perry.

Under the pressure of war, in 1754 a law was passed that ordered officers of the troops and companies to call out their troops at least four times each year for military exercise. Failure to obey the order was a punishable offense. According to the law, a penalty of £5 was charged for each day of neglect. The same law stipulated that parents or masters should pay the fines for minor children or servants, respectively. Furthermore, commanding officers of troops or companies had the authority to order men liable to do military duty in time of war and to carry arms and munitions with them. No man was to be exempt from doing military duty in time of war except with certification from two surgeons. Military law extended to all plantations. In addition, constables and clerks of companies were given the power to attach the goods or estate of delinquents and sell them at auction, with only a four-day notice, and after subtracting all fines and costs.[42]

African Americans in Law Enforcement in Newmarket, New Hampshire

In 1742, Pomp, a black man who belonged to Lieutenant Samuel Gilman, appears as an appointed constable in the historical records of Newmarket, New Hampshire. It is unclear whether Pomp was a constable in colonial government or the "black government." In whichever government he served, Pomp performed law enforcement duties. During the Colonial Era, constables assumed the responsibilities of the police.

If the information regarding the employment of Pomp is correct, Wentworth Cheswell was not the first black person to occupy a government position in New Hampshire as some have said. Pomp was appointed constable four years before Cheswell's birth in 1746. The authors who identified Cheswell as the first black man to hold a government seat may be mistaken due to lack of information regarding Pomp's

---

42. For the additional act passed in 1754 that ordered everyone to serve in the militia, see the *Report of the New Hampshire Adjutant-General*, 1866, pp. 114–15.

employment in the colony. It is difficult to conduct research concerning Pomp and his employment as constable due to his single-name reference. Sylvia Fitts Getchell and others who wrote about Pomp did not document enough information about their sources for this researcher to track additional confirming evidence.

Conversely, scholars and historians have recorded outstanding data about the employment of Wentworth Cheswell Wentworth, a mulatto African American in the government of colonial New Hampshire. Local historians—such as James Hill Fitts, the author of *New Fields, New Hampshire*, and Charles Wyllys Elliott, author of *New England History*, have mentioned the accomplishments and law enforcement work performed by Justice of the Peace Cheswell. In addition, Nellie Palmer George, author of *Old Newmarket, New Hampshire*; Mark J. Sammons and Valerie Cunningham, authors of *Black Portsmouth: Three Centuries of African-American Heritage*; and Jeremy Belknap, author of *History of New Hampshire*, have noted all the governmental duties performed by Wentworth Cheswell in Newmarket. Fitts and George listed and detailed several governmental positions Cheswell held. He was the symbol of honor for people of African descent residing in New England. In an era when African slaves and servants were considered inferiors unfit for government duties, the appointment of Esq. Cheswell as justice of the peace and other positions of power was proof that he was capable of performing duties entrusted to him. In 1820, during the debate on the admission of Missouri to the United States as a free state, a representative from New Hampshire commented on the accomplishments of Cheswell. Senator David Lawrence Morril noted Cheswell as a responsible man with good character. Morril went on to elucidate that Cheswell held several first offices in the town where he lived. As to his work abilities, the senator said that Cheswell was competent and performed his various duties promptly and accurately.[43]

Charles Wyllys Elliott notes what Jeremy Belknap says about Wentworth Cheswell. He was a clerk in one of the country towns and had a

---

43. Thomas Hart Benton, *Abridgment of the Debates of Congress, from 1789 to 1756: Dec. 1, 1817–March 3, 1821*. D. Appleton, 1858, p. 691.

CHAPTER 3

good education. Belknap acknowledged Cheswell's status as a mulatto and attested to the fine quality of Cheswell's writing.[44] Belknap, founder of the Massachusetts Historical Society, credited Squire Cheswell for collecting critical information regarding massacres of the English in New Hampshire by Indians when they attacked plantations. According to Belknap, Cheswell collected the information regarding the Indian massacres from surviving victims and witnesses of the scenes.[45] Nellie Palmer George notes that Cheswell held the esteem and confidence of community members in Newmarket and stands prominently in the history of that small town.[46]

Wentworth Cheswell was biracial. He was born in 1746 from the union of Hopestill March Cheswell, a mulatto, and Catherine Keniston, a white woman,[47] both residents of Newmarket, New Hampshire. When Wentworth was born, his father was a housewright (mason). With money he made from building houses, he sent his son to Dummer Academy, a prestigious, but free grammar school for boys in Byfield Parish in Newbery, Massachusetts.[48]

Hopestill March Cheswell was a prominent man in Newmarket. He petitioned for a bridge over Squamscot River on November 21, 1746.[49] White people had a good relationship with the Cheswell family, but it is unknown whether or not other African Americans received the same or comparable privileges.

---

44. Charles W. Elliott, *The New England History, from the Discovery of the Continent by the Northernmen, A.D. 986, to the Period when the Colonies Declared Their Independence. A.D. 1776*, 1857, p. 182.

45. Jeremy Belknap and John Farmer, *The History of New Hampshire*, vol.1, S.C. Stevens and Ela & Wadleigh, 1831, p. 203.

46. See *The Granite Monthly: A New Hampshire Magazine Devoted to History, Biography, Literature, and State Progress*, vol.48, J.N. Metcalf, 1916, p. 203. "Mansion House of Wentworth Cheswill" written by Nellie Palmer George.

47. George, 1916, p. 203, in the *Granite Monthly*, vol. 48–49. see data on Wentworth Cheswell.

48. Cushing Caleb, *The History and Present State of the Town of Newburyport*, E.w. Allen, 1826, p. 67. William Dummer was among the oldest and most respected men in Massachusetts and was lieutenant governor in 1716. See also Nehemiah Cleveland, *The First Century of Dummer Academy*, Nichols & Nayes, 1865, p. 5.

49. James Hill Fitts, *History of Newfield, New Hampshire, 1638–1911*. Rumford Press, 1912, p. 468.

After completing his education, Wentworth was employed as a teacher in Newmarket. In 1768, at twenty-two years of age, he was then appointed justice of the peace (1768–1769), according to James Hill Fitts (1912). Cheswell's teaching experience and his stellar reputation in the community were probably reasons for the appointment. It was noteworthy in Newmarket that a descendent of the African race performed judiciary duties so proficiently. Also, Cheswell was appointed because of his exceptional education, outstanding moral character, and the respect he had earned from both white and black members of the town. Africans did not usually have access to local politics, but Cheswell's unique posture in the community put him at an advantage for people to know him well and for him to know others well. He was recognized as a person with impartial views about members of his community. In addition to duties as justice of the peace, Cheswell performed the obligations of a lawyer for people in Newmarket. Joseph Harvey, in "An Unchartered Town on the Lampey–Historical Newmarket," notes, "before any regular attorney was settled in the town, he [Cheswell] drew deeds, leases, agreements, contracts, wills, and other instruments for his townsmen and acted as justice in examination of civil and criminal cases." Harvey also lists Cheswell's occupations as lawyer, judge, and soldier.[50] Based on Harvey's account, Cheswell was familiar with legal proceedings and processes, and his election to the justice of the peace officer was justified.

As a judiciary officer, Cheswell executed deeds, wills, and other legal papers, confirms Nellie Palmer George. Fitts (1912) identifies Cheswell as executor of the will of Deacon Joseph Judkins in 1770.[51] In addition, Cheswell acted as a judge for civil and criminal cases. As justice of the peace in town, his judicial services were of benefit to both whites and blacks. In 1782, Cheswell was appointed coroner for the county of Rockingham. As county coroner, more than likely he took the inquest (a judicial inquiry to indicate the cause of an accident or sudden death of a person). By June 10, 1791, New Hampshire law required every coroner to be sworn and bonded before discharging the duties for that

---

50. See Joseph Harvey, "An Unchartered Town on the Lampey–Historical Newmarket," *Granite Monthly*, vol. XL, no. 2003 (February and March), 1908, pp. 50–51.

51. Fitts, 1912, p. 103.

office. By law, the coroner was authorized to take inquests of violent deaths or those deaths that happened within the county. It was also the duty of the coroner to certify the body of a person who died by accident. The coroner was the official who investigated sudden deaths, homicides, and suicides. Likely, witnesses might be summoned by him, since he was empowered by law to act the same as any other person trained in this capacity. He continued to serve in the same employment in 1783. After two years as a coroner, Cheswell took a hiatus, and, years later, was re-assigned as the coroner of Rockwell County in 1795. He was the first African American to hold the position of coroner in the United States.

In 1783, Cheswell was appointed selectman in New Hampshire. The number of these officers varied. Daniel Thomas Worcester (1879) notes a town could appoint three, five, seven, or more selectmen to the office. In 1785, Cheswell was re-assigned to the same position. In 1795, records show that he was selectman in Newmarket. In his capacity as selectman, Cheswell regulated town affairs, such as, building roads and bridges, overseeing the concerns of the poor, assessing taxes, building public schools, and employing and paying teachers, as noted in a law passed in 1719 in colonial New Hampshire. When New Hampshire became a state, selectmen performed the same duties as they did during the colonial and provincial eras.

In addition to law enforcement and administrative duties, Cheswell was appointed regulator of the town as assessor in 1784. He served in this position for almost three terms (1786–1789), according to Fitts. Two years later, he was appointed to the same position due to his stellar ability to perform the duties entrusted to him. As town regulator, he served as auditor for many years. In 1786, he was auditor in Newmarket. After thirteen years, he was re-assigned. In the 1800s, Cheswell served more two terms as auditor. Records indicate that he was auditor in 1801 and 1804–1806. In 1801, he was recorded as representative in Newmarket. Fitts writes that Cheswell was a lot-layer in the same town.

As administrator, Cheswell was often a moderator; he was a presiding officer during town meetings because he regulated these gatherings. He had the power to evict anyone who disrupted the meetings. Those who resisted eviction were fined according to New Hampshire law. John

Norris McClintock (1888) wrote that the law of 1718 ruled a person to be fined for being disruptive at a meeting. The cost of the fine was £20.[52]

In addition to his law enforcement services, Cheswell was politically involved in community affairs and meetings regarding the Revolutionary War. On October 20, 1775, when the inhabitants of Newmarket organized a meeting to prepare for war, Cheswell was selected as an envoy to attend the provincial committee meeting at Exeter. From this meeting, he received important instructions that were to be communicated to the local committees at Newmarket. Unfortunately, that information does not seem to have been recorded. The selection of Cheswell as an envoy of the local government to the provincial committees shows that he was respected and valued by town citizens and local officials.

When the war against England was imminent, Cheswell was among the signers of the Association Test in 1776,[53] even though Africans in Newmarket were prohibited from signing. The Association Test had been organized in many towns throughout New England before the Revolutionary War. New England inhabitants who signed were enrolled in the militia and committed to defend the provinces against any attacks by the army of the English crown. Stationed in Boston, Cheswell was enrolled in the Continental Army. On September 29, 1777, he marched under Colonel John Langdon with other men at Saratoga.

Cheswell also contributed to the development of his city. In 1780, an act granted liberty to set up and carry on a lottery to raise money to repair and support Strantham and Newmarket Bridge. When the

---

52. Cheswell is noted as the first black office holder, and he was appointed to many positions of trust in Newmarket, New Hampshire. See Nellie Palmer George, "Mansion House of Wentworth," *Granite Monthly*, 1915, p. 203. James Hill Fitts, author of the *History of Newfield, New Hampshire*, discussed the accomplishments of Wentworth Cheswell, Esq.. In his book, on pages 103, 124, and 140, the information of Wentworth Cheswell was well recorded. Also see Nellie Ida Palmer George, *Old Newmarket, New Hampshire: Historical Sketches*, New-Letter Press, 1932, pp. 38, 55. In the *Provincial and State Papers*, vol. 20, New Hampshire, 1871, p. 558, Wentworth Cheswell of Newmarket is mentioned as coroner. Charles Whyllys Elliot, author of *New England History*, says, "Wentworth Cheswell was a town clerk, and had good education. He was town clerk of Newmarket. He was a mulatto." See page 182.

53. See Nellie Palmer George, "Mansion House of Wentworth Cheswill," *Granite Monthly*, vol. 48–49. Also see Nellie Ida Palmer George, *Old Newmarket, New Hampshire*, pp. 56–57..

Act passed on November 9, Cheswell was appointed manager of the lottery under an oath administered by a justice of the peace. Along with Cheswell, Josiah Adams, Major Mark Wiggin, and Simon Wiggin, all white men, were appointed as managers for the lottery.[54] In 1786, Cheswell was on the Newmarket committee, with Samuel Gilman and Joseph Young, whose members were selected by the people to petition the General Court for the repair of the bridge in that town as recorded by James Hill Fitts (1912).[55]

Researchers do not know if Wentworth Cheswell was trained under an experienced justice of the peace, but based on Harvey's description of Cheswell's legal duties, it is plausible that he was a brilliant, knowledgeable, self-educated man. There is no indication in the records that he went to law school or trained under a judge. During his legal services, he possibly served his townsmen without regard to color or race. As the only lawyer in town, he was respected for the services he rendered to clients. As there is no record concerning how satisfied his clients were, a look at his election to justice of the peace and later appointments to other administrative positions—coroner, moderator, assessor, selectman, and auditor—speak to his talents as a lawman. If he had been incompetent, local leaders would have objected to his inclusion in the government, and complaints of incompetence surely would have been recorded. A variety of records, though, document positive notices regarding Cheswell's work ability. His long years in local government indicate that educated, talented Africans, when given opportunity, were able to perform their duties as well as, if not better than educated white citizens.

Wentworth Cheswell was a businessman and property owner along with his government duties. Nellie Palmer George, who wrote about Cheswell's mansion, tells us he had a house near Piscassic, later called Moonlight Bridge. This house was occupied by his son, Thomas Cheswell.[56] Wentworth owned other lands, one on the border of Wod-

---

54. See *Laws of New Hampshire: Revolutionary period, 1776-1784*. New Hampshire, Henry Harrison Metcalf, New Hampshire, Secretary of state, New Hampshire Committee of Safety. John B. Clark Company, 1916, p. 333.

55. Fitts, 1912, p. 184.

56. George, "Mansion House of Wentworth Cheswell," The Granite Monthly: A Magazine of Literature, History and State Progress, vol 48, p. 203.

ley's Fall Road and the other in the town of Durham. Also, with Benjamin Meade, Wentworth was joint-owner of the Brick House Estate and property near the town landing.[57] George comments that "the house where Arthur Dearborn was residing was [Cheswell's] property."[58] Cheswell was a family man, and his son, Thomas, continued his legacy of community involvement, service, and leadership. Wentworth Cheswell had thirteen children with his wife, Mary Davis of Durham, New Hampshire. Thomas was the eldest son. Cheswell sent Thomas to Phillips Exeter Academy, a prestigious school located in Durham, New Hampshire. Thomas, who spent his life in Newmarket, served as selectman (1816–1817) like his father. In addition, he was assessor in 1823 and overseer of the poor in 1815.[59] Like his father, Thomas was active in town and church affairs.

In colonial New Hampshire, the population of African Americans was small. Therefore, few acts were established for the control of their behaviors. During colonial wars, they were always included in the security apparatus.

---

57. Ibid., p. 59.
58. Ibid., p. 204.
59. Nathan Franklin Carter, *Native Minister of New Hampshire*, Mumford Printing Company, 1906, p. 563.

Chapter 4

African Americans as Militiamen and Soldiers in Colonial Connecticut

According to many Connecticut historians, Africans were present in Connecticut around the 1620s, when laws for administering the institution of slavery did not exist in the colony. Four towns in the Connecticut colony were once part of Massachusetts Bay; therefore, the laws of Massachusetts were enforced in those towns. According to historians Clarence Winthrop Bowen (1886) and William Robertson (1859), Woodstock, Somers, Suffield, and Enfield were towns that followed the laws which governed Massachusetts Bay. Woodstock has been part of Massachusetts Bay since 1692. It was not until 1713 when the line was officially drawn between Massachusetts Bay colony and Connecticut that the towns—Somers, Suffield, and Enfield—became part of Massachusetts. It was in 1749 that these towns were joined to the Connecticut colony after petitioning voluntarily to the general court. Records show that African slaves were present in Woodstock at the time that town was under Massachusetts Bay's jurisdiction. Lucy Sessions Wallace conducted research on the Wallis Family, residents of Woodstock. Wallace discovered that the David Wallis family had four African servants. One of them, Samuel Dearing, served with his master in the French and Indian War in the company of Captain Ebenezer Moulton of Brimfield. While Wallace identified the Africans as slaves, Samuel Dearing was identified as an African servant on his marriage record.[1]

After many years, the population of African bondsmen was higher in Connecticut than in New Hampshire. Frances Manwaring Caulkins

---

1. Lucy Sessions Wallace, "The Wallis Family," in *The History of the Town of Holland, Massachusetts*, Tuttle Company, 1915, p. 686.

wrote that "in Norwich, there were more ... blacks than [in] other towns."[2] In 1756, there were 223 colored people in Norwich.[3] Charles Wyllys Elliott notes that in 1756 "as appears by the colony census of that year, there were 3,019 blacks."[4] Elliott estimates was the same as that of William Dillon Piersen and Lorenzo Johnston Greene, who noted that there were 3,019 blacks in Connecticut in 1756, not including the population of Norwich.[5] In contrast to the estimate of Elliot, Greene and Piersen, William Chauncey Fowler records that in 1756, the population of blacks was 3,636 and the population of whites was 976,000.[6]

In Connecticut, Africans were well-integrated into the community due to the colony's liberal political system. Frank London Humphreys writes that "people in Connecticut for a century were under the liberal charter granted by the British crown. They enjoyed free representative government."[7] African servants and slaves benefitted from the system implemented in colonial Connecticut. During the early years of the colony, men of color had the same militia privileges as the English. The notion of liberal government in Connecticut is noted by Edward Rodolphus Lambert, author of *History of the Colony of New Haven*. Lambert posits that "the early colonists in Connecticut were men of intelligence, abating some of their religious views, and the Connecticut intelligentsia understood those principles of liberty which have resulted in the establishment of those institutions which distinguished them among sister states of the union."[8]

---

2. See Frances M. Caulkins, *History of Norwich, Connecticut: From Its Possession by the Indian to the Year 1866.* H.P. Haven, 1874, p. 328.

3. Ibid, p. 26. The population of Norwich in 1756 was 5,540, of whom 223 were colored.

4. See Charles W. Elliott, *New England History*, 1857, p. 448.

5. See William Dillon Piersen, *Black Yankees*, Cambridge: University of Massachusetts, 1988, p. 163; Lorenzo Johnston Greene, *The Negro in Colonial New England*, Atheneum: New York, 1969, p. 9.

6. William C. Fowler, *The Historical Status of the Negro in Connecticut: A Paper Read before the New Haven Colony Historical Society.* Walker, Evans & Cogswwell Company, 1901, p. 36.

7. See Frank London Humphreys, *Life and Times of David Humphreys: Soldier—Statesman—Poet, "belov'd of Washington,"* vol.1, G. Putnam & Sons, 1917, p. 38.

8. See Edward Rodolphus Lambert, *History of the Colony of New Haven Before and After the Union with Connecticut*, Hitchock & Stanfford, 1838, p. 38.

CHAPTER 4

The liberal, democratic system of colonial Connecticut was politically beneficial to African bondsmen. The Africans elected one of their own as governor of the black proxy-government. In addition, the governor appointed his own lieutenant. The bondsmen had a court of justice and law enforcement officers. There were no other colonies like Connecticut in which African slaves elected black governors throughout the colony. The election process, the inauguration of black governors, and the functions of black law enforcement officers in the proxy black government are discussed in Chapter eight.

Lambert's account relates accurately the comportments of the early leaders who governed Connecticut and the types of leaders who held religious positions in churches. According to a variety of documents consulted, the relationship between Africans and their masters was friendly from the early years until 1660, at which time blacks were excluded from communal maintenance of law and order. Government officials and the inhabitants of the colony were approachable, to some extent, to African bondsmen. Lambert's perception of African relations in Connecticut is confirmed by Herbert Baxter Adams in *Labor, Slavery, and Self-Government*. Adams notes that in towns such as Norwich, New Haven, Hartford, and New London, Africans were large in number and were approved as fellow members by their white counterparts.[9] But in 1717, the freemen in the town opposed Robert Jacklin, a free African American, from purchasing land in New London. In addition, in May 1717, the inhabitants of New London petitioned their representatives to ask the General Assembly to take measures to prevent any person of African descent from ever having any possessions or free real estate within the municipal area.[10] In *African Americans and People of Color Collection, 1701–1854*, data indicate that the petition of the inhabitants of New London regarding Jacklin was unsuccessful.[11]

---

9. Herbert Baxter Adams, *Labor, Slavery, and Self-Government*, vol. 2, John Hopkins University Press, 1893, p. 390.

10. Fowler, 1901, p. 5.

11. See State Archives Record Group No. 003. New London Court, African Americans Collection, New London County African Americans and People of Color Collection, 1701–1854. Judicial Department. State Archives Record No. 003, p. 3.

Even though the lower house passed a bill prohibiting Africans from purchasing land in New London, there are no records indicating the bill was enforced. In the record of New London County gathered in the State archives, data indicates that Jacklin owned land in New London and Colchester, and he rented land in both towns. At one point, Jacklin was taken to the probate court because he was not able to pay the bills for the land he owned. Jacklin was emancipated in Newbury, Massachusetts. After becoming a free man, he moved to New London in 1711. In the same town, slave and eventual freedman, Adam Rogers was a land owner. Rogers received a deed of gift from his father-in-law, Thomas Jones. These illustrations prove the Act of the General Assembly prohibiting African Americans from owning land in New London was not always enforced.[12]

In 1721, Jacklin was still in New London, according to diarist, Joshua Hempstead. Hempstead, who daily recorded a plethora of information regarding New London, says that year Jacklin lost a child.[13] However, the cause of death is not noted.

From the time the first African servants and slaves were imported into the colony, they were free to attend military and militia training. William Chauncey Fowler wrote in 1901 that blacks had some military training on a lower level, which he referred to as "military musters on a small scale."[14] The military training of African slaves was also recorded in *Connecticut Magazine* in 1899, when the editors affirmed that "in colonial days blacks held regularly military training on a greatly reduced scale."[15] Military training occurred frequently throughout the colonies of New England, a tradition which was observed for many years. Henry Reed Stiles (1858) notes, "blacks training was also common at one time subsequent to the Revolu-

---

12. Joshua Hempstead, *Diary of Joshua Hempstead of New London.* New London Historical Society, 1901, p. 114.

13. Ibid.

14. Ibid., p. 21.

15. *The Connecticut Magazine*, vol. 5 notes that "Negroes had training days of a rather uncertain character and a greatly reduced scale. These trainings were regularly held." See *The Connecticut Magazine: An Illustrated Monthly*, vol.5, edited by George C. Atwell, A. Phelps Arms and Francis Trevelyan Miller. The Connecticut Magazine Co., 1899, p. 322.

tion. Training was held at Pickett's Tavern, about half a mile above Hayden's Station."[16] Stiles talks about Ti, a slave who belonged to Captain Jona Ellsworth. Called General Ti, the soldier trained his black militiamen. General Ti had his own uniform which he received from his master, a captain of the cavalry.[17] During the Colonial Era, it was common for the owner to give military equipment to his servants and slaves. In Massachusetts, Connecticut, Rhode Island, and New Hampshire, slave owners did not have any fear of equipping bondsmen because they did not pose a danger to the colony, in general, nor to their masters, in particular.

When General Ti trained people of African descent, he sometimes became frustrated with them. Under pressure and out of frustration, he rebuked them expressing sharp, derogatory remarks, "A niggar [sic] always will be a niggar, don't know anything and will always be a niggar."[18] A similar illustration indicating the training of African bondsmen was shown by the training directives given to them by General Ti. The orders before the training are as follows: "You nigger who got no white stocca, and no rocker shoe, stand out of the way."[19] From this quote, the militia trainer emphasizes the attire of his men. Militiamen without proper attire were separated from the other group who were well-dressed. If the slave of Captain Ellsworth was a person of African descent, he enforced rigidly the rules regarding militia uniform and appearance.

With respect to training Africans, it was wise to train them because every man who was trained militarily added to the security of the colony. As historians have recorded, Connecticut and her sister colony New Hampshire were frontier colonies, so Indian attacks were frequent. Therefore, training blacks to serve in the militia was important for the protection and defense of inhabitants. Alarms or enemy attacks occurred at any time without notice. It was a custom to call upon citizens, servants, and slaves to fight in times of war. During wars against the French and

---

16. See Henry Reed Stiles, *The History of Ancient Windsor, Connecticut*, C.B. Norton, 1858, p. 492.
17. Ibid.
18. Ibid., p. 494.
19. Ibid., p. 493.

Indians, there was no time to train militiamen. So, for preventive measure, Africans and persons of African descent received training continually. Regularly established training days were enacted for black soldiers as had been established for their white brethren. The history of "Training Day" in Connecticut can be traced to September 8, 1653, from the order of the General Court stipulating that "the court doth grant the soldiers of these four towns on the River [Harford, Windsor, Wethersfield, and Middletown] and Farmington one day for a General Training together, and they have liberty to send for Captain John Mason to desire his presence and to give him a call to command and to appoint the day; provided that each town shall have power to reserve a guard at home, for the safety of the towns, as occasion shall serve."[20] In addition to military training, training day was a time to transact town affairs. Many civil and criminal cases were adjudicated. Likewise, social events were held that day. When the number of Africans in the communities increased, Africans were allowed to have their own training day.

In 1637, colonial officials in Connecticut appointed Captain John Mason as the officer to train men for military duty on each plantation. As historian Jane De Forest Shelton (1894) notes, Africans resided under the roof of and close to their masters. It is sound to speculate that they received the same military training as the English. Therefore, in 1653 when the training day became mandatory, Africans were probably involved in the same militia training. It does not appear that Africans had a separate training day in the earlier years of the settlements. According to the military regulation of 1650, the law required that "every male person above the age of sixteen years shall have in readiness a good musket or other gun, a sword, rest or bandoleers [i.e., ammunition pouches], also powder, match and bullets; shall be trained six times yearly in March, April, May, September, October, and November, by appointment of the chief officer in the several towns, to meet at 8 o'clock in the morning."[21] The regulation of 1650 and 1653 called for Africans to have the same military obligations as white colonists.

---

20. James Hammond Trumbull, *The Memorial History of Hartford County, Connecticut, 1633–1884: Town Histories*. E.L. Osgood, 1866, p. 509.

21. Allen B. Lincoln, *A Modern History of Windham County, Connecticut: A Windham County Treasure Book*, vol. 2, S.J. Clarke Publishing Company, 1920, p. 1007.

Moreover, as the safety and security of colonial Connecticut depended on the efforts of volunteers, blacks carried the same military obligations as the volunteers in the colony. In 1866, James Hammond Trumbull, author of *The Memorial History of Hartford County*, affirmed that in 1643 due to the threat of the incursion of the Indians against the settlers, everyone in the settlements was ordered to keep watch and ward every night, from sunset to sunrise.[22] The watch and ward were communal, and no one group of people was selected to serve in that capacity, so African Americans were obligated to participate. In 1653, when the Dutch and English were in conflict, the inhabitants of Connecticut were troubled, fearing that the Dutch would incite Indians to a massive insurrection in the colony. From this threat, colonists in Connecticut could not afford to exclude their African slaves and servants from military training. In the *Connecticut Public Records of 1636–1776*, data shows that in 1653, the governor of Connecticut called a session regarding the danger of his colony being attacked by the Dutch.[23]

In 1660, colonists enforced a military policy which was not inclusive. In this year, Africans were excluded from keeping watch and ward, nor did they receive the same militia training as the English. It is unknown whether the law of 1660 was observed throughout the colony. In Connecticut, each town or settlement was locally governed. The General Assembly did not interfere with how local governments were managed. For example, in the watch policy of Hartford, African Americans were not excluded. Isaac William Stuart, the Connecticut local historian, tells us that "in Hartford, every male inhabitant over sixteen years of age, with exception in favor of certain magistrates and church officers, was to take his turn as watchman."[24] Stuart shows how settler's communal defense was in force in Hartford. Due to the Indian attacks, it would be pointless to marginalize colored people from militia duties. The intensity and frequency of the Indian attacks on Hartford County have been noted by many writers. Hartford was consistently under the menace of French and Indian attacks from the beginning of the settlement.

---

22. Trumbull, 1866, p. 508.

23. Ibid., p. 509.

24. Isaac W. Stuart, *Hartford in the Olden Time: Its First Thirty Years*, F.A. Brown, 1853, p. 57.

Even though the law of 1660 prohibited the participation of African Americans in the defense and maintenance of public order, the enforcement of such law would be difficult because many high-ranking military officers were slave owners.

With respect to law enforcement, the 1660 law reads as follows: "it is ordered by this Court, that neither Indian nor Negro servants should require training, watch or ward, in this colony."[25] This was the first law enacted in the colony denying black people the responsibility of police duties and militia training. *The Public Records of the Colony of Connecticut* does not explain the reason for this exclusion, nor do Connecticut historians such as Stiles, Fowler, and Trumbull discuss why colonial officials enacted the law. Interestingly, scholars have not revealed any incident that accounts for enforcing the exclusion law. In Connecticut, leading men such as the clergy and deacons held slaves in their respective families. Theophilus Eaton, first governor of the New Haven Colony, was a slave owner; Edward Hopkins, second governor of Connecticut, had slaves.[26] In 1761, Captain John Perkins of Hanover Society, Norwich left fifteen slaves in his will.[27] It is difficult to believe that the 1660 Act was observed by these important, powerful men. If their African slaves were employed as laborers on the land, it is more than likely that they carried weapons and were trained in their use. Connecticut local historians and modern colonial American historians have not recorded measurable data revealing how the Act of 1660 was executed. The effect of that law with respect to Africans and Indians has not been found among documented sources. During the Colonial Era, it was common for government officials to overlook militia law due to frequent attacks from enemies, such as the French and their Indian allies.

In 1741, a military law was enacted in the colony of Connecticut that did not exempt blacks from the militia. This law ordered the participation of all male persons from sixteen years of age to fifty to carry arms and attend the military musters and exercises of the troops that

---

25. See *The Connecticut Public Records of the Colony of Connecticut Prior to the Union With New Haven Colony*, J. Hammonds Trumbull, Hartford, Brown & Parsons, 1880, p. 349.
26. Fowler, 1901, p. 4.
27. Adams, 1893, p. 391.

comprised the residential military company.[28] The mandatory training of all able-bodied males in the colony was likely in preparation for King George's War, which lasted from 1744 to 1748. Lincoln notes that "the Act of 1741 was passed in view of the hostile attitude of the French and their Indian allies, especially in Maine. These hostilities erupted into war in 1744 and resulted in the capture of Louisburg from the French."[29]

African Americans as Defenders of Public Safety and Order in Connecticut

Due to the volunteer system employed for the enlistment of soldiers and the militia in the French and Indian War, African Americans were included in the quotas of the colony. They joined their masters and the white soldiers in expeditions against enemies. In the records of the Massachusetts Historical Society, there were few African Americans who deserted during the war, and many re-enlisted in other expeditions. In addition to being soldiers, some African Americans were enlisted as trumpeters and sailors.

One of these soldiers was Prince Goodin, a free African American who was enlisted in 1754 as a sailor from the town of Canterbury. His military missions were conducted on Lake George. It is unknown whether Goodin was still in the military in 1755 and 1756 during the French and Indian War. But in 1757, he was listed as captured at Fort William Henry and taken to Canada by the French. In Montreal, Canada, Goodin was sold into slavery and remained there until the fall of Montreal in 1760. The Connecticut Historical Society reported that through the efforts of his company Goodin was freed, but the report fails to note just how he was emancipated.[30] *The Public Records of the*

---

28. See Lincoln, 1920, p. 1007. The Act of 1741 stipulated that "All male persons 16 to 50 years of age shall bear arms and duly attend all musters and military exercise of the respective troops and companies where they are listed. Every listed soldier to be provided with a well-fixed firelock barrel not less than three and one-half feet long, or other good firearms, a good sword or cutlass, a warm, primer and priming wire fit for his gun, and 12 flints."

29. Ibid.

30. See *Rolls of Connecticut Men in the French and Indian War*, vol. 2, Connecticut Historical Society, 1905, p. 378.

Colony of Connecticut (1890) show that Goodin was enlisted in the company of Colonel Israel Putnam, and Goodin was stationed at Fort Edward with Putnam's company when the Fort William Henry capture occurred. After the fall of Montreal, Goodin rejoined his company. In 1761, he petitioned the General Assembly to pay for the damage of his captivity. As a result, he was paid £10 out of the treasury of the colony. For the treasury to grant Goodin's request indicates that free African Americans were entitled to the same privileges as their white counterparts. He did not have dual status as would be the case if he were a slave. If Goodin had been a slave, the recompenses for the captivity would have been paid to his master.[31]

In 1744 during the reign of King George II in England, France, with Spain as its ally, declared war against England. In the North American colonies, the war was called King George's War. The war was fought between the English and the Canadian French. While the news of King George's War reached Boston in June the same year, the French governor of Cape Breton had received intelligence about the war three months earlier, on March 29, 1744. Consequently, he ordered a preemptive attack on the English at Canso, Nova Scotia. French militiamen captured the English and burned Fort Canso. Captives were carried to Louisburg, the powerful French fort in Cape Breton.[32]

In response, William Shirley, governor of Massachusetts, planned a secret expedition for the destruction of the French fort. The Connecticut colony furnished 1,000 men under Lieutenant-Governor Roger Wolcott.[33] In Massachusetts, Sir William Pepperell was appointed commander of the expedition, and Wolcott was named his second-in-command.[34] Africans were included in the expedition against Louisburg. The colonies requested military assistance from the king in England, but the king was occupied with the war in Europe and unable to assist the colonists in

---

31. *The Public Records of the Colony of Connecticut [1636–1776]*, Brown & Parsons, 1890, pp. 539–39.

32. Epaphras Hoyt, *Antiquarian Researches: Comprising a History of the Indian Wars in the Country Bordering Connecticut River*, Ansel Phelphs, 1824, p. 229.

33. Edward Rodolphus, *History of the Colony of New Haven Before and After the Union with Connecticut*, Hitchock Stafford, 1838, p. 37.

34. Theodore Dwight, *History of Connecticut: From the First Settlement to the Present Times*. Harper & Brothers, 1840, p. 272.

America. So, the colonists took Louisburg from the French without any assistance from the Crown.

The capture of Louisburg on June 17, 1745, was a blow to the French but heartening to the English colonies. After the French defeat, the English were motivated to take more territories from the French, while the French and Indians increased attacks on the frontiers in 1746.[35] In 1747, when the Indians attacked St. George and Saratoga, more militiamen were enlisted for the execution of the war. The Island of Cape Breton, where Louisburg was established, was ceded back to the French in 1748 with the Treaty of Aix-La-Chapelle.

Regarding the enlistment of men in Connecticut, two regiments were formed to execute war in 1755. After the formation of the regiments, General Phineas Lyman was assigned to command the First Regiment, and Elizur Goodrich, Esq., was in command of the Second Regiment.[36] Nathan Whiting was appointed lieutenant colonel under Goodrich. On the other hand, John Pitkin was lieutenant colonel under Lyman.[37] In the regiment of Lyman and the regiment of Goodrich, Africans were enlisted as were the English.

On the 18th day of May, 1756, England declared war against the French, and it was in June of the same year that the king of France declared war against England.[38] When the war was formally declared, Sir Henry Fox was the principal secretary for England. He was appointed in 1755 as successor to Sir Thomas Robinson. Upon the declaration of war by the King of England, John Campbell, sometimes called the Fourth Earl of Loudoun, and a friend of Lord Halifax, was appointed as the commander-in-chief of His Majesty's forces in America.[39] In addition to the military rank, Campbell was appointed governor of the Virginia colony. General James Abercrombie was appointed commander of the soldiers of the Northern colonies when Governor Shir-

---

35. Hoyt, 1824, p. 234.
36. Trumbull, 1898, p. 303.
37. Ibid.
38. Dwight, 1840, p. 291.
39. Lady Madilda Ridout Edgar, *A Colonial Governor in Maryland: Horatio Sharpe and His Times, 1753–1773*, Longmans, Green and Company, 1912, p. 94.

ley of Massachusetts was removed from the command. While General Abercrombie continued to serve in colonial America, Lord Loudoun was recalled to England in 1758. His recall was due to his failure in several expeditions organized in 1756. According to many historians, he was not productive as a military commander. He was recalled to England after the capture of Fort William Henry under his command of the army. He was accused of antagonizing colonists in America, as recorded by Lawrence Shaw Mayo. After the departure of the Earl of Loudoun to England, the command of His Majesty's soldiers was entrusted to Major-General James Abercrombie.[40] Under the command of Abercrombie, the Connecticut colony furnished 2,000 men even though the Earl of Loudoun requested only half of the raised number. From the account of Benjamin Trumbull, Connecticut raised 2,500 men for execution of the war.[41]

In 1757, Connecticut soldiers were under the command of the Earl of Loudoun. In the same year, Major David Whitney and Chauncey Whittlesey of New Haven were under the same leadership. With respect to the war, few Connecticut soldiers remained in action when the Earl of Loudoun requested soldiers to return to their respective towns. According to James Hammond Trumbull and Charles Jeremy Hoady, 280 soldiers were selected to act as rangers to secure frontiers and to deter enemies.[42] Colonel Phineas Lyman was dispatched to Fort Edward, whereas Nathan Whiting listed men for three companies who were stationed at Fort Edward.[43] But after the departure of the Earl of Loudoun to England, the policy and the conduct of war were readjusted. The king's ministers in England advocated an aggressive military approach for the defeat of the French in North America. The defeats the English witnessed in the Southern and Northern expeditions from 1754 to 1757 affected the English military men.

---

40. Lawrence S. Mayo, *Jeffrey Amherst: A Biography*, Longmans, Green and Company, 1916, p. 55.

41. Trumbull, 1898, p. 314.

42. James H. Trumbull and Charles J. Hoady, *The Public Records of the Colony of Connecticut*, Press of the Case, Lockwood & Brainard Company, 1880, p. 61.

43. Ibid., pp. 22, 61.

CHAPTER 4

Secretary William Pitt set an aggressive policy aiming for the capture of Canada and other French territories in the western world.[44] He indicated clearly in his letter to the governors of Massachusetts Bay, New Hampshire, Connecticut, Rhode Island, New York, and New Jersey that the King was disappointed about the military defeat of the English against the French and the failure of many previous expeditions against them. As the English were determined to oust the French from the American colonies, the King requested Governor Campbell to raise men for the attack against the French in Canada via Crown Point.[45] Unlike the King of England, colonial officials in Connecticut were concerned about the protection of the frontiers to their own colony. Therefore, increasing men in the rank of the military was critical for the safety of the frontier inhabitants.

In 1758, the English government decided to capture the French fort at Louisburg, which the French used to attack the English in New England. To execute the campaign against Louisburg, Jeffrey Amherst was appointed Major-General. In addition, 11,000 men were raised to be under his command.[46] In the same year, British Secretary of State William Pitt stressed to British parliament that the war was to be fought with increased vigor, as noted by Charles MacFarlane and Thomas Thomson.

---

44. Charles MacFarlane and Thomas Thomson, the comprehensive history of England, from the earliest period to the suppression of the Sepoy revolt, and continued to signing of the treaty of San Stefano, 1792. Place of publication not identified.

45. For the letter of Secretary William Pitt to the governors of New England colonies, including New York and New Jersey, see *The Public Records of the Colony of Connecticut, [1636–1776]*, edited by James Hammond Trumbull and Charles Jeremy Hoady, published by the Press of the Case, Lockwood & Brainard Company, 1880, p. 92. Secretary Pitt's letter read to the Assembly was dated December 30th, 1757.

See also the work of Francis Thackeray, *A History of the Right Honourable William Pitt, Earl of Chatham*, C. and J. Rivington, 1827, p. 419. Secretary William Pitt was the son of Robert Pitt, of Boconooc in Cornwall. William was born in November 15, 1708.

According to John Hill, he was educated at Eaton, and he also attended Trinity College, Oxford, but never graduated. His family was wealthy, and through their influence, he became a member of the parliament representing the Old Sarum. During his years in the government, he was reputed as the greatest orator in England. The king and other officials disliked William Pitt due to his political approach. He advocated a war policy against the enemies of England compared to officials such as Premier Walpole. Pitt was appointed secretary of state during the administration of the Duke of Devonshire. *Facts and Features of English History, a Series of Alternating Reedy and Memory Exercised*, John Hill (Principal of the Normal Call, Colombo), 1873, p. 218.

46. Mayo, 1916, p. 3.

The new policy advocated by Secretary Pitt was due to the failure of Lord Loudoun in 1757. Apparently, the manner in which Loudoun executed the war was not intensive enough. Therefore, under the leadership of General Amherst, Pitt wanted a different approach and a vigorous intensity in the execution of war. As a result, the Connecticut colony was obligated to enlist more men. Similarly, the defeat of the English against the French at Fort William Henry resulted in the increase of Connecticut men in the rank of the army. Theodore Wright wrote that the Connecticut Assembly ordered the enlistment of 5,000 men who were formed into four regiments of twelve companies. Colonel Nathan Whiting, Eliphalet Dyar, Joseph Read, and General Phineas Lyman commanded the newly formed companies.[47] Africans were included in the regiments formed in 1758 and served in Connecticut from 1754 to the fall of Canada in 1760.

The information regarding colonial militia services performed by African Americans can be found in the documents of the New Haven Historical Society. In 1888, Rev. Elijah C. Baldwin, who read a paper before the New Haven Historical Society, noted that in the earlier years of North Brandford history, there were many blacks and Indians who resided in the neighboring Branford. Most of them were enlisted as soldiers during many expeditions in the French-Indian War, and few ever returned.[48] Those who did not return from the war were either killed or captured by the enemy and taken to Canada, as was the custom at the time. Some of the captured Africans and Indians may have been sold into slavery. It is difficult to ascertain how many black soldiers perished in Branford or who they might have been since the New Haven Historical Society did not record the census of Africans in Branford.

For information regarding the enlistment of people of color in the Connecticut militia, this researcher consulted volumes of muster rolls (1755–1762) and records from the Connecticut Historical Society, 1903 and 1905, volumes 1 and 2. These collections reveal some people of color were paid for their services during the French and Indian War.

---

47. Trumbull, 1818, p. 385.
48. See Elijah C. Baldwin, *Branford Annals* Read April 7, 1886 before the New Haven Historical Society, Papers of the New Haven Colony Historical Society, vol. 4. New Haven Colony Historical Society, New Haven, 1888, p. 317.

Regarding fighting, people of color did not fight only for the welfare of the colony, but for the interests of the Crown as well.

In the African American Collections of the Connecticut State Archives, there is a section entitled "New London County, African Americans and People of Color Collection 1701 to 1854, Judicial Department, State Archives Group No. 003." The researcher recorded that Wait Wright, son of Hagar Wright, a free black woman, was not paid for military service during the French and Indian War. According to the disposition of the court, Hagar's son served onboard the sloop *Reference* under the command of Captain John Prentice. When Wright made a formal complaint to the selectmen about his military services during the colonial war, Captain Prentice was deceased. According to Wright, he served in the 1745 expedition to Cape Breton that ended with the capture of Louisburg (Louisbourg). During the colonial wars, government sailors and privateers employed to defend the colony divided the prize—merchandise commandeered from enemy ships—among themselves. The decision to pay the military by dividing booty was ordered by the crown of England through the king's representatives. During war time, privateers who fought on the water highways were men of war, the same as any other soldiers who fought on the battleground in villages and towns. According to Wright, the expedition he participated in was supported by 101 men, and he did not receive his share of £5,000 prize money. It appears that there was no verdict in the petition of Wright.[49] As a result, he sued the government for his share. Through the language of the deposition, clearly Wait Wright was a privateer or a sailor aboard the sloop, so he had the right to receive the prize money. The outcome of the case was not noted in the Connecticut archives. The evidence indicating that Wright was a privateer or a sailor supports the fact he deserved his share of the prize. In colonial New England, goods confiscated or taken from enemy ships were divided by the fighting crews. Non-fighting crew members such as the cooks and utility men working on board the warship did not receive prize money from goods taken from enemy ships.

---

49. See the New London County, African Americans and People of Color Collection, 1701–1854, Judiciary Department, Connecticut State Archives Record, Group No. 003, p. 4.

Ben Dawson was an African American who served in the French and Indian War. His account as a soldier is documented in the Connecticut archives. His name is listed on the petition filed by the selectmen of Lebanon, Connecticut. Dawson also served in the American Revolutionary War. A petition was filed on behalf of Dawson who wanted recompense for his military service. It appears that after serving time in the military, Dawson was sold and freed.[50] Additionally, the records in the Connecticut State Archives show that Dawson was poor and was supported by the New London selectmen. As a result, after filing a petition, the selectmen of New London were ordered to be paid for their support of Dawson. It was not uncommon for those who did not receive their bounty following military duty to petition for their share after the war. Often generals, colonels, and captains petitioned for their servants or slaves who served in the conflicts between the English and the French in colonial New England. After King George's War ended with the signing of the Treaty of Aix-La Chapelle in 1748, the French continued to attack New England settlers.

The French and Indian War was officially declared by the crown of England in 1756, but the Indians and the French commenced attacking New England before the official declaration. In fact, the French secretly armed the Indians who attacked the New England colonies. By 1755, African Americans were enlisted in many military companies, including the Third, Fifth, and Seventh. Among those who served in 1755, records show that Richard, a black man, enlisted in the regiment of Major General Phineas Lyman. Richard was a soldier in the Fifth Company commanded by Captain John Patterson of Farmington. According to the Connecticut Historical Society, Richard enlisted as a soldier on April 9, 1755 and was discharged on October 1, 1755. His military record can be found in the Connecticut State Library in the Adams papers.[51]

The re-employment of people of African descent in the French and Indian War was prevalent. The Connecticut colony was not highly

---

50. Connecticut Archives, Miscellaneous papers. Second series 1686–1820, in two vols. and index. Harford, Connecticut State Library, 1957, pp. 9, 12, 20.

51. See *Rolls of Connecticut Men in the French and Indian War, 1755–1762*, vol. 9, Connecticut Historical Society, 1903, p. 13.

populated during this period. Every man of sound mind and body was enlisted in the militia or the military. There were also those who accompanied their masters on several expeditions against the French and Native Americans.

A number of Africans were enlisted in Connecticut companies in 1755 because the colony needed a large number of men for the construction of forts, for garrisoning the forts, and for scouting. In the Seventh Company, commanded by Captain Nathaniel Peck of New Haven, Jack, a black man, was among the Connecticut men enlisted either for scouting or guarding the forts against the French and Indians. He enlisted on August 28 and deserted on October 27, 1755. Jack was enrolled in the Connecticut militia in accordance with the law of 1755, which required the enlistment of Connecticut men for the execution of war. In the third regiment, led by Colonel Dyer Eliphalet, three African Americans were enlisted as drummers. These soldiers were listed as Negro Ceasar, Negro Catto, and Benjamin Paul, Negro. It is unknown whether or not the Africans who were enlisted as drummers did scouting or worked on the construction of the forts.

In the Fourth Regiment commanded by Colonel Elihu Chauncey in 1755, in the Company of Major William Whiting of Norwich, Prince, Negro and Jupeter [sic], Negro were enlisted. Prince served from September 6 to December 13, and Jupeter was in service from September 8 to December 13. These two African Americans are listed on record as soldiers. In the same regiment, in the Eighth Company of Captain Thomas Hobby, Simon, Mulatto was enlisted from September 3 to December 6. Simon was biracial, which is why the epithet "mulatto" follows his name—for added identification.[52]

In 1755, Prince, the servant of Captain Lomis, was enlisted among the soldiers from Colchester. Similarly, Peter, the servant to widow Lomis, served in the expedition. African Americans were also enlisted in the military companies formed in Farmington, Norwich, New Haven, and Hartford.[53]

---

52. See *Rolls of Connecticut Men in the French and Indian War, 1755–1762*, vol. 9. Connecticut Historical Society, 1903, pp. 49, 60–61.

53. Ibid., pp. 13, 15, 30–31, 36, 38.

In the campaign of 1756, several African Americans were enlisted for the attack of Crown Point. Payne Kenyon Kilbourne writes that the campaign of Crown Point was abandoned, and the attack of Louisbourg was unsuccessful. African Americans served under many Connecticut military officers. According to the records consulted at the time of this writing, black men served under Captains Israel Putnam of Pomfret, Aaron Hitchcok of Suffield, and Noah Grant of Windsor. According to "A Roll of Sundry Men," in the expedition led by Captain Israel Putnam, Cato, a Negro, was one of the soldiers who fought in the war. He enlisted for military service on April 13, 1756 and ended his service October 14, 1756. Caesar, Negro was named in the same regiment. In the Sixth Company commanded by Captain Aaron Hitchcock of Suffield, London, "Negro" was listed as a private. This person of African descent was enlisted on April 20, 1756, until December 1, 1756. Captain Noah Grant of Windsor, who commanded the Seventh Company, had black men serving under him. One of them was named Prince, and he served from April 14 until October 30, 1756. In the same company under Captain Grant, the name Jupitur [sic] Negro was listed.[54] This name was probably a misspelled version of Jupiter. In the record of the Connecticut Archives Index No. 61, Jupitur, Negro, was listed serving the military as a private.

Major Patterson, who commanded the Third Company in 1756, had two black men in his company, Ambo and Bristol. Ambo enlisted on March 30, 1756, until November 1, 1756, and Bristol enlisted on April 5, 1756, until December 1, 1756. In the Eighth Company of Captain John Jeffrey, two soldiers were enlisted named Fuller and Newport, both black men. Colonel Andrew Ward, Jr. had African Americans in the Fourth Regiment. Among the black men who served in these regiments were Backos with Captain Eliphalet Whittlesy of Newington, Connecticut; Sipio, a Negro, was killed in 1756 for unknown causes. In addition to Fuller, Newport, and Sipio, other black men fought in 1756.[55]

In 1757, the Connecticut colony voluntarily doubled the number of troops required by His Majesty's military commander in America.

---

54. Ibid., pp. 100–101, 103, 122–23.
55. Ibid., pp. 129, 130–31, 141–43, 152, 160.

CHAPTER 4

Some military men who had enlisted in 1757 were stationed at Fort William Henry under the command of the Scot, Colonel George Monro. Fort William Henry was doomed when the troops which guarded were taken prisoner by nearly 8,000 Indian and French soldiers. At the time of the attack, Fort William Henry was guarded by 3,000 colonial soldiers. Fort George was guarded by General Daniel Webb with 4,000 or more, as noted by Theodore Dwight, a Connecticut local historian. Among the men recorded by the Connecticut Historical Society (1903), Walpole, William, and Joseph, all three of African descent, were enlisted in the First Regiment of Colonel Phineas Lyman of Suffield. Moreover, in Lieutenant Nathan Whiting's company, Jeffrey, a Negro, was enlisted. He served from March 2 until November 24, 1757. In the same year, Ned Odell and Toby Boston, both black men, were enlisted in the company commanded by Samuel Hubbel of Fairfield. In the Seventh Company, commanded by Captain Adonijah Fitch, was listed a black man named Tobey whose military rank was private. Joel, a Negro from Colchester, served under the command of Welles Edmund of Hebron. Also, African Americans were enlisted in the militia of the Connecticut colony during short alarms, as was the case of Zekera and Petro, two Negroes under the command of Captain Ammy Frumble of Windsor in 1757. [56] In Captain Johnathan Buell's company, Fuller, a Negro, served with the militia in time of alarm for relief for eleven days. Gooff, a Negro, served seventeen days as a militiaman during the time of alarm for relief. Jeffrey, a Negro, served in the Second Company of Lieutenant Nathan Whiting of New Haven, Connecticut.

In 1758, when William Pitt was appointed Premier, his war policy was aggressive toward the interests of the French in America. He was determined to deny the king of France any territory in colonial America. With that vision, he was prepared to capture the entire territory of Canada from the French. Each New England colony was obligated to raise militiamen for that cause. In Connecticut, the Assembly ordered the enlistment of 5,000 men who were formed into four regiments of

---

56. See *Rolls of Connecticut Men in French and Indian War, 1755–1762*, vol.2, Connecticut Historical Society, vol.1, 1903, pp. 188, 211.

twelve companies each. The companies were under the commands of Colonel William Whiting of Norwich, Eliphalet Dyer of Windham, and John Read. In the 1758 campaign, Negro Cuff and Negro Cesar were enlisted under Captain John Durkee of Norwich in the Third Regiment of Connecticut Troops. Mark, a Negro, served as private, as noted in the Connecticut Archives Index No. 61 of the Colonial War. In addition to these names, African Americans who served from 1755 to 1757 were re-enlisted in 1758.[57]

In 1759, the English executed a fierce strategy which led to the capture of Crown Point and Ticonderoga. In the same year, the English and provincial men marched against the French and Indians in Quebec and Niagara. In the campaign that captured Crown Point, Quebec, and Niagara, Africans were included in the fight. Among enlisted soldiers in 1759 are Primas, Newport, Asa Affrica, Cesar, and Asher. Asher was a resident of the town of Goshen, and he was listed on the muster roll of Captain Tarball Whitney in the Third Regiment. Primas was enlisted in the Second Company in General Lyman's regiment of Connecticut Troops.[58]

Theodore Dwight noted that due to the loss in battle of so many Connecticut men, the Assembly was determined to enlist another 6,000 men. In Windsor, Connecticut, Henry Stiles (1859) wrote that John Joseph (colored) served as a soldier in Connecticut in 1759. In addition to Newport, Stiles believed that the old black man, Dr. Primus, was a Windsor man who served in the campaign of 1759.[59]

In 1760, Hazard was in the company of David Hubbard, Jr., and he was enlisted from March 25 to November 25. In 1761, when the General Assembly requested additional soldiers to protect the fortress, African Americans Ceasar, London, Theophelus, Prince, William, and Jupeter were enlisted as soldiers.

During the Havana expedition in 1762, Cato and London, both African Americans, re-enlisted. In the same campaign, Frank, a Negro,

---

57. See *Rolls of Connecticut Men in French and Indian War, 1755–1762*, vol. 2, Connecticut Historical Society, 1905, pp. 9, 13, 26–29, 52, 86, 93.

58. Ibid.

59. Henry Stiles, *The History of Ancient Windsor, Connecticut*. C.B. Norton, 1859, pp. 346, 349.

CHAPTER 4

enlisted in the company of Samuel Whiting of Stratford from April 1 to November 5.[60]

In 1760, the King of England executed a different plan for the war. He ordered General Jeffrey Amherst to attack Montreal. During this expedition, the Connecticut men called to arms included Negroes who fought under General Amherst.[61] Hazard, a Negro, served in the company of Captain King from March 25 until November 25, 1760. After the fall of Canada, American soldiers were entrusted with the repairs of forts and fortifications. In 1761, the Connecticut General Assembly voted to enlist 2,300 additional men. On the payroll of Captain Hierlihi's company in 1761, Caesar, a Negro, was among those who served in the militia. His date of service was from April 10 to December 20. Jupiter and William were African Americans who served in the company of Captain Oliver Wolcott. On the muster roll of Captain Walter Pearce's Company, a Negro named Theophelus was listed in 1761. In 1762, Cato was listed on the payroll of General Lyman's company of Connecticut soldiers. Charles, Peter, and Frank were Negroes among the soldiers who enlisted in 1762.[62] In 1762, after the fall of Canada, King George II requested the American colonies to furnish men for the attacks of the French and Spanish territories in the West Indies. In this expedition, Major-General John Paterson was accompanied to Cuba by London, his African body servant.[63] London, who served in the military from March 15 to December 5, 1760, was enlisted in the company commanded by Roger Enos.[64]

The Connecticut colony was second to Massachusetts in terms of population and wealth. This colony furnished large numbers of military

---

60. Ibid., pp. 104, 164, 191, 246, 277, 304.

61. William Farrand Livingston, *Israel Putnam: Pioneer, Ranger, and Major-General, 1716–1790*, G.P. Putnam's Sons, 1901, p. 107.

62. *Rolls of Connecticut Men in the French and Indian War, 1755–1762*, 1905, pp. 322–23, 329.

63. Thomas Egleston, *Life of John Paterson: Major-General in the Revolutionary Army*. G.P. Putnam's Sons, 1894, pp. 4–5.

64. See *Rolls of Connecticut Men in the French and Indian War, 1755–1762*, vol. 10, 1905, p. 322. In the colony of Connecticut, prior to 1660, African Americans were entrusted with the maintainance of order as their European counterparts. But in 1660, the law prohibited them from performing watch and ward. On the contrary, during the colonial war especially the French and Indian War, they were always enlisted for the defense

men during the French and Indian War. During war times, African Americans were included in the security apparatus like their white brethren. Data shows that Africans and African Americans numbered in many companies and regiments, and these black men were participants in many expeditions. This was not the same in the colonies such as Rhode Island, where the numbers of Africans and African Americans were not large. In the following chapter, data will indicate that the Rhode Island Colony had fewer African Americans than the Connecticut Colony, and that the bondsmen-slave association forged a different relationship than the relationship between bondsmen and slaves in the other colonies.

Chapter 5

African Americans in the Militia of Colonial Rhode Island

The history of Negroes in the Rhode Island Colony is quite different from the history of Negroes in colonial New Hampshire, Connecticut, and Massachusetts. In Rhode Island, the majority of African bondsmen lived on large farms in Narragansett Bay. In Newport, as in Narragansett, the population of African descendants was sizeable. There African Americans worked as shipbuilders. Contrary to Rhode Island, in Massachusetts, African Americans resided in towns throughout the colony where their employment was diversified. They worked in factories, industries, and on the docks, and they did carpentry and iron work. Some were masons and seamen. Farming was not as large an industry in Massachusetts, New Hampshire, and Connecticut as in Narragansett. In Narragansett, North Kingston, and South Kingston, the farms where Negroes and Indians did most of the labor belonged to high-ranking officials and the most influential political elites of the colony—the family of Deputy Governor Robert Hazard, Governor William Robinson, Colonel Christopher Champlin, and Colonel Daniel Updike, attorney general of the colony for twenty-four years.[1] This was not the case in other New England colonies. Due to the large number of slaves who worked on Rhode Island farms, a different relationship existed between them and their owners. To avoid revolts and insurrections, a close relationship was established between slave owners and their bondsmen, so that slaves felt as if they were free. Thomas Williams Bicknell, the premiere Rhode Island historian, commented, "Slaves, their untutored

---

1. Wilkins Updike, *History of the Episcopal Church, in Narragansett, Rhode Island.* H.M. Onderdank, 1847, pp. 18, 179.

mind, their free, social dispositions, their willing and obedient spirit, made them the object of familiar approach and of easy control." The same observation was mentioned by Edward Peterson, author of *History of Rhode Island*. Peterson posited that due to the healthy treatment from their masters, African slaves in Newport were not conscious of being in bondage. It seems that the paternalistic approach utilized by slave owners was healthy to their relationship with their slaves.[2]

The Narragansett landholders were law makers who considered their slaves' interests. The farms were inhabited by many slaves, yet the owners did not hesitate to permit the slaves to bear arms. This circumstance was different from the political situation in the Massachusetts Bay colony where the government allowed Negroes in the militia to bear arms—only under the pressure of war. During times of peace, any laws authorizing militia training of Negroes and Indians were repealed; whereas, in Rhode Island, there were no laws prohibiting black people from militia duties.

Rhode Island operated as an isolated colony, unlike the United Colonies (Massachusetts, Connecticut, New Haven, and Plymouth), which depended on each other for security and safety. The confederation of the United Colonies was formed on May 19, 1643, for mutual defense among the member colonies. Early colonial historian, Elisha Reynolds Potter, records that Rhode Island did not join the United Colonies because of a petition by Massachusetts. According to Potter, there existed a continual jealousy between Massachusetts Bay and Rhode Island.[3]

The security of Rhode Island depended solely on its own inhabitants. Therefore, colonial officials were obligated to avoid marginalizing any percentage of the residents, such as Negroes and loyal Indians. Moreover, the Massachusetts colony disliked the political principles of Rhode Island because Indians were treated as owners of the land. Military options employed by the United Colonies against the Indians were detested by colonial Rhode Island political elites. This difference

---

2. Thomas Williams Bicknell, *A History of Barrington, Rhode Island*. Snow & Famham, Printers, 1898, p. 402; Edward Peterson, *History of Rhode Island*, J.S. Taylor, 1853, p. 104.

3. See Elisha Reynolds Potter, *The Early History of Narragansett: with an Appendix of Original Documents, Many of Which Are Now for the First Time Published*, vol. 3, Marshaw Brown, 1835, p. 37.

in the way the two colonies treated Native Americans was another political disagreement between the Rhode Island and Massachusetts colonial officials. During the early years of the establishment of colonies in Rhode Island, members of the Massachusetts General Court claimed the Warwick territory. On the same island, Pawtuxet residents were under the authority of the Massachusetts Bay colony, an agreement that lasted sixteen years.[4] Officials in Massachusetts Bay and Plymouth opposed the establishment of Rhode Island as a colony. To illustrate, in 1643, when the four towns in Rhode Island (Providence, Portsmouth, Warwick, and Newport) applied for admission to the United Colonies, the application was denied upon condition. To be accepted as a member of the United Colonies, the Rhode Island towns had to agree to be incorporated into the Massachusetts or Plymouth colony. In reality, some of the small colonies which formed Rhode Island were established by people banished from Massachusetts due to their religious beliefs. Such was the case of Roger Williams. He was banished from Salem, Massachusetts, because he was a separatist and a non-conformist. He opposed the interference of the civil authorities in the administration concerning matters of conscience.[5] It appears that the inclusive militia policy observed in Rhode Island was accepted by everyone in that colony who feared outside military attacks. As the number of Negroes in Rhode Island increased, the colonial government took them into consideration as a force for the defense of the colony.

It is difficult for present-day researchers to decide upon a reasonable census estimate for the number of Africans in Rhode Island. Authorities in the colony were inconsistent in their collection methodologies of data about the African population. For example, historian William Babcock Weeden noted that on December 25, 1707, Governor Cranston said that "no Negroes were imported into Rhode Island from the coast of Africa from the 24th of June 1693, to the 25th of December 1707."

---

4. Samuel Greene Arnold, *History of Rhode Island*, 1859, p. 11. See also William Read Staples, *Annals of the Town of Providence: From Its First Settlement, to the Organization of the City Government to June 1832*, 1843, p. 75.

5. See William Read Staples, *Annals of the Town of Providence*, Providence, Printed by Knowles and Vose,1843, p. 11.

Weeden called this "a technical statement."[6] Possibly, the governor was attempting to avoid a conflict with the Royal African Company, which was deeply involved in slave trade. The account of Wilkins Updike supports this notion. In 1847, Updike recorded that the collection of the 1730 census of the population of the colony, Kings County, reported a lower number of African slaves than the more than 1,000 slaves who were really living in Rhode Island. He explains that it was common to conceal the number of slaves in the colony from the knowledge of the royal government in England.[7] According to the 1730 census, there were 1,648 Negroes in all of Rhode Island, but Newport, Rhode Island, had 649.[8] The number of African slaves recorded in Newport seems to be an estimate. Weeden says these numbers "do not agree in themselves."[9] He believed that the estimates were incorrect because the slave traders in Rhode Island operated aggressively. He also believed that the slave trade conducted by the Providence merchants sometimes was not recorded by colonial officials. As Weeden noted, it is difficult to give weight on the Rhode Island census taken in 1730 regarding the number of Africans in the colony because Rhode Island officials did not want to cooperate concerning the census ordered by the Board of Trade in England. It appears that the listed census was just an estimate because there is no record indicating how the census was conducted and data was collected. Consequently, as is other colonies it does not look as though the government kept accurate records on the African slave trade.

Were the many African bondmen who lived on farms excluded from watch and ward duties? Rhode Island law required that every person on the farms receive militia training. Before the formal prohibition of slavery in Rhode Island in 1652, there is no indication that people of color, including African slaves, were restricted from watch and ward duties or from military training and service. Furthermore, there were

---

6. See *Records of the Colony of Rhode Island and Providence Plantations, in New England*, 1859, p. 54; and Weeden, 1910, p. 187.

7. See Wilkins Updike, *A History of the Episcopal Church in Narragansett, Rhode Island: Including a History of Other Episcopal Churches in the State*. H.M. Onderdank, 1857, p. 174.

8. Weeden, 1910, p. 219.

9. Ibid.

no laws to regulate the behaviors of black servants or slaves before 1652. Masters and slaves worked on the farm together before slavery was prohibited. On May 18, 1652, the commissioners of Providence Plantation and Warwick passed a law prohibiting the enslavement of Africans. At the time, the island had two governments. One was formed of Providence and Warwick, and the other government was under the authority of Newport and Portsmouth. The union between the four towns was dissolved in 1651. From this period to 1654, the two governments functioned separately. In 1652, the commissioners at Warwick and Providence enacted laws for the management of the colony, including an Act to abolish slavery. It seems that after the unification of the four towns in the colony, the Act of 1652 prohibiting slavery did not have an effect. Despite the Act, slavery flourished in the colony.[10]

The Act and order of 1652 passed in Providence and Warwick reads as follows:

> Whereas, there is a common course practiced amongst English men to buy Negroes, to that end they may have them for service or slaves forever, for the preventing of such practices among us, let it be ordered, that no black mankind or white being forced to covenant bond, or otherwise, to serve any man or his assignees longer than ten years, or until they come to be twenty four years of age, if they be taken in under fourteen, from the time of their coming within the liberties of this colony, and at the end or term of ten years to set them free, as the manner is with the English servants; and that man that will not let them go free, or shall sell them away elsewhere, to that end that they may be enslaved to others for a long time, he or they shall forfeit to the colony £40.[11]

---

10. See Benjamin B. Mussey, *Facts Involved in the Rhode Island Controversy: With Some Views Upon the Rights of both Parties*. B.B. Mussey, 1842, p. 6. Also, John Pitman, *A Discourse Delivered at Providence, August 5, 1834: In Commemoration of the First Settlement of Rhode Island and Providence Plantations. Being the Second Centennial Anniversary of the Settlement of Providence*. Providence, R. Cranston & Company, 1836, pp. 48–49.

11. *Records of the Colony of Rhode Island and Providence Plantation in New England*, 1856, vol. 1, p. 243. See also *Proceedings of the Rhode Island General Assembly*, vol.1, 1649–1669, p. 25.

The Act of 1652 did not only prohibit slavery of Africans, but also enslaved white people were protected under this law. In *History of the State of Rhode Island,* Samuel Green Arnold (1859) stipulates that the 1652 Act was framed as a prevention measure against the enslavement of Africans and whites, a prevalent practice during the 17th century.[12] The same Act gave African servants privileges comparable to white servants. It is unknown whether in Providence and Warwick African slaves had the same privileges as the English after the passage of this Act. When the 1652 Act was enforced, Africans who resided in the Providence and Warwick settlements were more likely to be free and therefore liable to militia duties. African slaves who acquired the status of servants were subject to the same obligations as white servants with respect to the defense of the colony. Whatever assignments colonial laws ordered white servants to perform, black servants would be subject to the same mandates, including militia, watch, and ward duties.

In 1665, Rhode Island made it mandatory for every person to keep weapons in his or her house. This requirement was observed throughout the American colonies. Like the English, free Africans had the same privilege. Arnold (1859) wrote that in Rhode Island in 1665, "Every man was required to keep on hand two pounds of powder, and four of lead. Each town was obliged to maintain a public magazine [or a store for arms, ammunition, and provisions for use during military operations] for its defense." Colonists took the protection of their citizens seriously as the American government officials do in our modern era. Sometimes towns which did not store weapons for defense were fined.

Colonial Order for African Americans to Perform Law Enforcement Duties

Before the discussion of the colonial authorization of African Americans in law enforcement, it is pertinent to relate the circumstances preceding this event. In 1675, all New England colonies except Rhode Island were under major territorial conflicts with Native Americans. Metacom, also

---

12. See Samuel Greene Arnold, *History of the State of Rhode Island*, D. Appleton & Company, 1859, p. 240.

known as Pometacom and Metacomet, was called Philip or King Philip by the English. He was the second son of Massasoit, a member of the Wampanoag Indian tribe and sachen (or chief) of the tribe. King Philip created a hostile relationship between his government and the English government in New Plymouth. As a result, the Indians made many incursions into the land occupied by the English in Plymouth colony. During these attacks, many English perished, so the United Colonies—Massachusetts, New Haven, Plymouth, and Connecticut—were forced to defend their subjects and friendly Indians from King Philip's aggression. At the time when the United Colonies were at war against King Philip, the Rhode Island colony maintained a friendly relationship with the Narragansett Indians. Government officials in Rhode Island decided to be neutral, avoiding any confrontations with Native Americans. In fact, the colonial officials in Rhode Island were against the war of 1675. In *History of the State of Rhode Island and Providence Plantations*, Samuel Greene Arnold notes that "Rhode Island was not a member of the New England Confederacy and therefore not bound to take part in hostility provoked by the other colonies."[13] Arnold insinuates Rhode Island colonial officials blamed the United Colonies for the hostility with Indians. Like Arnold, William Read Staples believed that the English in Rhode Island were not involved in the fight against Indians in 1675.[14]

The neutrality of the Rhode Island colony did not produce a tangible result. The Narragansett Indians, after being attacked by soldiers of the Connecticut and Massachusetts colonies, made many incursions in some towns in colonial Rhode Island. Arnold notes that South Kingston was attacked, and Indians killed fifteen persons. The attack on South Kingston was the first of that kind in Rhode Island from the Indians during King Philip's War. Warwick was also attacked and destroyed, except for one stone house that could not be burnt.[15] The pressure of the war was also felt in Providence. The inhabitants deserted the city, fearing Indian attacks. Eventually, colonial officials were forced to establish a mandatory watch and ward.

---

13. Ibid. p. 399.
14. See Read, 1843, p. 161.
15. Arnold, 1859, p. 408.

In 1676, the Rhode Island Assembly established an Act ordering Negroes to perform watch duties. The law stipulated that "A Negro man capable of watch ... shall be liable to that service as the English."[16] The watch duties at this time were equivalent to some of current law enforcement duties. In colonial time, militiamen in the position of watchmen guarded churches during worship hours, patrolled the city for the presence of enemies in town, and prevented attacks from unfriendly Indians. The rounds made by watchmen deterred enemies from ransacking towns. Sometimes, the watchmen made arrests of enemies who attempted to destroy property or kill people. Watchmen had the power to detain Indian suspects, and during war times they acted as military police.

In the same year, data shows that African Americans were counted as people expected to guard the colony. The order of the Assembly of Rhode Island voted in 1676, which was recorded in the *Records of the Colony of Rhode Island* (1857), reads as follows:

> That person be empowered in the town of Newport and Portsmouth, to take an exact account of all the inhabitants in this island, English, Negroes and Indians, and make a true list thereof, the proper inhabitants in one list, the English now come amongst us in another list, and the Negroes in another list, and Indian in another list; and also to take account how all persons are provided with corn, guns, powder, shot, and lead, and make return thereof to the next sitting of this Assembly.

The Assembly chose people empowered to do the same in Newport and Portsmouth. John Coggshall and Jireh Bull were the representatives assigned to take the census in Newport. In Portsmouth, census-taking was entrusted to Robert Hazard and John Sanford.[17] Caroline Elizabeth Robinson writes, "In 1676, town leaders in Portsmouth were empowered to take exact account of all the inhabitants on the island, English, Negroes, and Indians, and make a list of the same, and also take exact

---

16. *The Record of Rhode Island and Providence Plantations in New England, vol. II, 1664 to 1677*, 1857, p. 536.

17. See *Records of the Colony of Rhode Island and Providence Plantations*, 1857, p. 536.

account how all persons were provided with corn, powder, shot, and lead."[18] The same account was noted by Wilkins Updike. In 1847, he recorded that "in 1676, when an enumeration of people was made, for the purpose of establishing a watch guard, the blacks were of consequence to be ordered to be numbered separately."[19] This order of the Assembly shows that Negroes and Indians were able to carry arms and other military necessities in Rhode Island. Carolina Elizabeth Robinson, author of *The Hazard Family of Rhode Island, 1635–1894*, notes that Robert Hazard and three other officials were charged with collecting the census as well as overseeing the distribution of guns, powder, shot, lead, and corn.[20]

In colonial Rhode Island, blacks were not excluded from the militia in legal terms. There were no Acts or proclamations excluding people of African descent from performing militia duties. Governor Samuel Cranston revealed pertinent information to questions relating to African slaves in the colony when the Board of Trade in England inquired on April 17, 1708. The board ordered Cranston to collect data on the numbers of African slaves imported by private traders into the British colonies. Cranston sent a circular to the governors requesting the same. When the Board of Trade asked Cranston how many militiamen were in the colony, on December 5, 1708, the governor responded: "It is to be understood that all men within this colony, from the age of sixteen to the age of sixty years, are of the militia. So that all freemen above and under said ages are excluded in the above said number of the militia."[21] In his response, Governor Cranston did not exclude Negroes. African

---

18. The census was required by the commission formed of Deputy Governor Captain John Easton, Captain John Cranston (son of Governor Samuel Cranston), Mr. Robert Hazard for Portsmouth, and others. See *the Narragansett Historical Register*, vol. 7, Rhode Island Citizens Historical Association, Narragansett Historical Publishing Company, 1889, p. 312.

19. See Wilkins Updike, *A History of the Episcopal Church In Narragansett, Rhode Island*, New York, 1847, p. 171.

20. Caroline Elizabeth Robinson, *The Hazard Family of Rhode Island, 1635–1894*, published by the author, 1896, p. 3. In Arnold's *Rhode Island*, the information can be found on page 410. Arnold called the census a "classified census."

21. See *Record of the Colony of Rhode Island and Providence Plantations, in New England: 1707–1770*, 1859, p. 59. In this year, 426 black servants resided in the colony. The population was divided as follows: Providence 220; Portsmouth 7; Warwick 40; Westerly 20; New Shorehan 6; Kingstown 85; Jameston 32; Greewich 6; the total was 426 people.

slaves and free men aged sixteen to sixty years who resided in Rhode Island served in the militia like their Caucasian counterparts. Historically, in Rhode Island the law required every man to perform militia duties. However; the number of African slaves was not listed. In 1701, the Act for better regulation of the militia stipulated

> all persons within this colony above the age sixteen years, and under the age of sixty years, as well as housekeepers and others, shall be obliged to watch or ward or find or procure a sufficient man to watch or ward upon legal notice given to any of them by the captain or commander in chief to watch and by the governor, deputy governor, assistant conservator, and wardens of the respective towns to ward, the warders to be such persons as are not in the captain's list: And the said persons appointed to watch do at all times and upon all accessions observe and follow such orders and instructions as they shall from time to time receive from the respective head officer, as aforesaid. And if any person shall refuse or neglect to watch and follow such orders as upon legal notice given as aforesaid, he or they so neglecting or refusing, shall pay as a fine the sum of 5s in money to be taken and imprisoned in manner and forth as the fines for neglecting of training or alarm are taken and proceeded in.[22]

This law ordered the involvement of specifically designated members of the community to become engaged in law enforcement when the need arose. According to the language of this law, "all persons within this colony [Rhode Island]" certainly made Africans obligated to perform law enforcement duties.

In 1706, seven years before the end of Queen Anne's War, the enlistment of the militia in Rhode Island took on a different magnitude. During this particular year, the defense of the colony became the work of almost every citizen. Men who were incapable of serving in the militia

---

22. *Records of the Colony of Rhode Island and Providence Plantations, in New England*, 1859, p. 432; *Laws and Act of Her Majesties, Colony of Rhode Island*. S.S. Rider and E. Rider, 1896, p. 48.

assisted in the defense however they could. Arnold (1889) recorded that "the exigencies of the war demanded vigorous efforts. Everything in the colony was placed upon a war footing, and almost every man became a soldier, or in some way assisted in the common defense."[23] In 1665, a law was passed that required "six trainings a year, under a heavy penalty, and allowed nine shillings a year for the pay of each enlisted soldier. Additionally, every man was required to keep on hand two pounds of powder and four of lead. Each town was obliged to maintain a public magazine for its own defense."[24] Negroes were not exempted from the requirement to store powder and lead in their houses. Moreover, there were no objections for the maintenance of public magazines for the defense of plantation towns where Negroes resided. They benefited from the same access to the public magazine as their white and Indian brethren.

Samuel Greene Arnold articulates the protocol for community soldiering and law enforcement during wartime. In *The History of the State of Rhode Island and Providence Plantations*, Arnold notes that almost every man was obligated to become a soldier for the defense of the colony. The Coast line was covered with scouts."[25] It is pertinent to note that during wars in colonial Rhode Island, people of African descent were included among the defenders of freedom and peace. Rhode Island in 1708 was sparsely populated; the entire population was 7,181 inhabitants, which included 1,015 freemen (whites), 56 white servants, and 426 black servants. It appears that the rest of the people were slaves. During the early years of the settlement in Rhode Island, Connecticut, and Massachusetts Bay, African Americans were identified as servants or Negro men of their respective owners. The term "slave" was sometimes omitted when referring to people of African descent. When Negroes were called servants, they had the same privileges as the servants of people whose origins were of European extraction. Additionally, Negro servants had the same obligations as European-born servants to defend the colonies. The enumeration of black servants in the 1708 census as the same as

---

23. Arnold, 1889, p. 25.
24. See Arnold, 1859, p. 319.
25. Arnold tells us that communal law enforcement became very critical in the colony of Rhode Island due to the pressure of war. He notes also that every man became a soldier. See Samuel Greene Arnold, *History of the State of Rhode Island*, 1860, p. 25.

white servants is an indication that both groups were valued the same relative to militia responsibilities to the colony.[26]

In 1718, colonial officials in Rhode Island repealed the laws exempting people from performing military service. This law was passed to force the Quakers to perform military duties because they always rejected participating in military services due to their religious beliefs. The pressure of the war was so exorbitant that government officials could not afford to exclude Negroes and other able men from military service. The law of 1718 reads as follows:

> Whereas, the body of laws for the settling and regulating the military forces within this colony are increased to so great a number by reason of the many wars, which, from time to time this colony hath been engaged in against the French and Indians, and other enemies, which hath rendered many of them [the laws] useless, and may be for the future prejudicial, if not repealed;
>
> Be it therefore enacted by the General Assembly of this colony, and by the authority of the same, and it is hereby enacted that all acts heretofore made; relating to the militia, or appointing officers for the same, be hereby fully and absolutely repealed and declared null and void; and that for the future, the following orders, regulations and rules relating to the same, be kept and observed by all persons in this colony.[27]

This law was proactive legislation for the protection of the colony. As the colony was so frequently attacked by enemies, it was not in the best interest for colonial officials to exclude Negroes, Quakers, and friendly Indians from the militia. Colonial officials anticipated the possibility of more attacks from the French and Indians who were determined enemies against British interests in the American colonies.

---

26. See *Records of the Colony of Rhode Island and Providence Plantations, in New England*, 1859, pp. 53–59.

27. Samuel Greene Arnold, 1859, p. 415. He states that "the law exempting Quakers from bearing arms or paying military fines, now required every citizen to do his part in personally defending the state. The exemption act was restored when the war was ended."

CHAPTER 5

African American Privateers in Colonial Wars in Rhode Island

Historically, privateer work has been conducted by pirates and other seamen who inflicted commercial pain on other ships for personal gain. People who were engaged in this enterprise were punished severely by colonial government officials. But during the conflict between France and England in colonial America, officials in Rhode Island enacted a law which authorized privateers to serve under the direction of officials during the war as coast guards as well as patrolling the sea to destroy any enemy ships nearing the Rhode Island coast. The Crown of England authorized colonial officials to employ privateers during war time. The Duke of Newcastle wrote and sent a letter to the governor of Rhode Island dated March 31, 1744. In the letter, His Majesty requested the governor to do everything in his power, to encourage His Majesty's subjects to fit out ships to act as privateers against the enemy.[28] Moreover, His Majesty ordered that Rhode Island's privateers distress and annoy the French in their settlements, trade, and commerce. These strategies were employed as deterrents to war and to drain the financial capability of the King of France to support the war. In our modern era, this strategy is similar to commercial sanctions and freezing money.

The French and Indian War had also an effect In the Rhode Island colony. Like other colonies of New England, Rhode Island sent men to defend other colonies. On January 27, 1744, Governor William Shirley of Massachusetts wrote a letter to Rhode Island relating to officials that Rhode Islanders were exposed to the attacks of the enemy due to the colony's proximity to the sea. Governor Shirley was specific in his letter to Governor William Greene, listing salient reasons to explain why it was important for New England colonies to attack the French fort at Louisburg on the island of Breton. In his letter, Governor Shirley noted:

> Sir: Though I doubt not that the interest of the common cause of New England will sufficiently animate your government to exert themselves rigorously in the intended expedition against

---

28. See the proclamation of his Majesty King of England sent to the governor of Rhode Island in the letter written by the Duke of Newcastle. See *Records of Rhode Island*, 1860, p. 89.

Louisburg, yet I would beg leave to add that the exposed situation of your colony by sea, and the resentment of the enemy against it, on account of the activeness of your privateers, make it probable that you may have a sudden visit from the French, this summer if Cape Briton [Breton] is not reduced.

Governor Greene knew that the New England colonies were vulnerable to the attack of the French along the Rhode Island sea coast. Therefore, for better execution of the destruction of the French fort at Louisburg, many men were needed. Thus, the Rhode Island Assembly ordered the enlistment of five hundred men at the expense of Massachusetts Bay. Further, Rhode Island developed a vigorous privateer system in New England. Howard Chapin, historian, recorded that the colony had twenty-one privateers.[29]

Governor Shirley's military strategy was advocated by the Duke of Newcastle, as well. In his letter to the governor of Rhode Island, the Duke advised Governor Greene to take precaution to avoid enemy attack, an act which would make His Majesty's subjects suffer.[30] Further, the Duke sent a proclamation issued by King George II of England authorizing the use of privateers in the war. According to the proclamation, "officers, noncommissioned officers, and crew members in a privateer ship were entitled to a prize." The proclamation also ordered the governor to use his power to encourage the inhabitants of the colony to act as privateers against enemies. The objective for employing privateers was to inflict pain on the commercial interests of the French, including settlements."[31] The Rhode Island government took the proclamation

---

29. *Records of the Colony of Rhode Island and Providence Plantations, in New England*, 1859, p. 74. See also *Records of the Colony of Rhode Island*, 1860, p. 105; Howard Chapin, *Rhode Island Privateers in King George's War, 1739–1748*, 1926, p. 11.

30. The Letter from the Duke of Newcastle to Governor Greene was written on March 3, 1744. In the letter, the Duke advised the governor to protect His Majesty's subjects from the French attacks. See *Records of Rhode Island and Providence Plantations*, 1860, p. 80.

31. The proclamation of His Majesty ordered the Governor to encourage his subjects to fit out ships for privateer services against the enemies. See *Records of Rhode Island*, 1860, p. 80. Privateers were employed as a military strategy to inflict commercial and psychological pain to the enemies.

into consideration, and the Assembly enacted laws legalizing the use of privateers during wartime.

Privateers in colonial Rhode Island acted as coast guards for the security of maritime trade. The employment of privateers as water patrol officers reached its peak during King George's War. William Babcock Weeden, in his *Early Rhode Island*, notes that when France joined Spain in the war of 1744, commonly called King George's War, the Rhode Island privateers punished the French economy.[32] Edgar Stanton Maclay, author of *A History of American Privateers*, says that "it was in the war of 1744 that American privateers began seriously to assert themselves as a distinctive sea force expedition against Louisburg."[33] England's King George's proclamation advocated the enlistment of privateers for the common good and as a distinct military force for the colony in times of war.

The Rhode Island Historical Society publication says from the period of 1748 to 1756, Negroes were often induced to go to sea as privateers (aboard a private ship, persons commissioned to perform a variety of duties when war has been declared) without the consent of their masters. Lorenzo Johnston Greene recorded the account of Negroes employed as privateers for Rhode Island. According to him, in 1742 five African Americans were among the thirty-seven privateers sent during the war in Providence, Rhode Island. Each privateer received a full share of the prize money.[34] Strong speculation asserts that in cities such as Newport and Bristol, which were close to water highways, there were many Negroes assigned as privateers.

In 1740, Howard Chapin recorded that Ben Courant, an African American belonging to widow Courant, served on the *Virgin Queen* under Captain Thomas Wyatt, John McCarty, Samuel Robins, and John Brown. Since widow Courant resided in Providence, Ben was enlisted as a privateer from that city. During this expedition, two Indians were

---

32. See Weeden, *Early Rhode Island*, 1910, p. 227. The privateers were attacking every French ship that came across. In addition to the French ships, it is possibly that the Rhode Island privateer attacked also the Spanish's ship because the French joined Spain during the war of succession.

33. See Edgar Stanton Maclay, *A History of American Privateers*, London, 1900, p. 39.

34. For the five privateers of Providence in 1742, See Green, 1968, p. 189.

enlisted as privateers, as well. Chapin identifies them as Samuel and Joshua who served as privateers on the same ship as Ben Courant. In 1741 when Captain Benjamin Norton of Newport and the owner of sloop *Revenge* was commissioned as privateer by Governor Ward, Norton employed African Americans. Among his crew were Samuel, an African American belonging to Mote, and Daniel Walker, also an African American. In addition, Captain Norton's African American man served on the same sloop. During this period, when seven men were enlisted in Providence to serve as privateers, James Jennings, an African American, was included.[35]

During Captain James Cooke's expedition, the French captured nine Negroes who patrolled the water highway, according to historian Edward Field.[36] Additional historical evidence suggests that blacks were enlisted as privateers, and the prizes paid for their services went to their masters. For example, Ann Lippit signed for a Negro man on the crew of the *Tartar* in 1748.[37] Her signature strongly suggests that the Negro belonged to her, and he acted as a privateer on his mistress's account. For this reason, it is highly probable that Lippitt collected any prize received from her slave's privateer work. In 1757, Scipio, an African man, served on the privateer, *George of Newport*, to assist in a mission.[38]

The inclusion of African Americans as privateers in Rhode Island during the French and Indian War was documented by Rick Stattler in 2004. Organized by Stattler who is employed at the Rhode Island Historical Society, the *Guide to Manuscript* catalogues pertinent information on African American privateers and militiamen. Each manuscript

---

35. See Howard Chapin, *Rhode Island Privateers in King George's War, 1739–1748*, Providence, Rhode Island Historical Society, 1926, pp. 33–34.

36. For the captured nine Negroes in the company of Captain Cooke, see Edward Field, *State of Rhode Island and Providence Plantations at the End of the Century: A History*, vol. 1, Mason, 1902, p. 584. Privateers were always subject to capture during their missions. The missions were dangerous because each side in the war employed privateers for the destruction of to commercial interests.

37. William Babcock Weeden, *Early Rhode Island*, Grafton Press, 1910, p. 227. Many slave owners signed their slaves, giving them permission to serve as privateers so the owners could claim money for their slaves' services.

38. Howard M. Chapin and The Rhode Island Historical Society, *Rhode Island in the Colonial Wars: A List of Rhode Island Soldiers & Sailors in the Old French & Indian War 1755–1762*, printed for the Society in Providence, 1918.

is numbered and identified. To illustrate, in the Champlin Papers numbered as MS30, the names of African Americans who served on the privateer *Brigatine* in 1757 are recorded: Joseph Hull, Cuff Godfrey, and Prince Lillibridge were crew members. Additionally, "Negro Amas and Scipio, a Negro belonging to Thomas Atwood were included as crew members." Christopher Champlin's records (MSS20) identify African Americans among the crew members on the privateer brigantine *George*—Ben Negro, Cezar Steven, and Boston Molborne. On November 8, 1762, Samuel Chace claimed shares in the privateer *Speedwell du Chace* for his servant Cesar Chase or Cesar Fry.[39]

African Americans in the Militia during the French and Indian War in Rhode Island

In 1744, colonial officials in Rhode Island ordered protection for Fort George and enlisted ten men in addition to the soldiers already stationed at the fort. In 1745, the Rhode Island Assembly ordered the enlistment of one hundred and fifty men for the expedition against Cape Breton, where the city of Louisburg was located. At Louisburg, the French built a powerful fort from which they attacked the English in New England. According to the *Records of the Rhode Island and Providence Plantations*, George Taylor and Lieutenant William Smith were entrusted with raising soldiers in Providence for the expedition to Cape Breton. Captain Joseph Champlin was engaged in the expedition of Louisburg in 1745. In the collection of militia lists (1739–1747) recorded at the Rhode Island Historical Society, the names of African Americans who served during the Louisburg expedition are included. In the manuscript numbered MSS 673 Sg, data shows that Simpson Quimons served in the company of Captain Champlin in 1745. Stattler believed that other African Americans served with Quimons in the same company. Newport Coffin, an African American, served in the company of Captain Calis in 1745.[40]

---

39. See Rick Stattler, *Guide to Manuscript at the Rhode Island Historical Society to People of Color*, June 24, 2004, Rhode Island Historical Society.

40. See Rick Stattler, *Guide to Manuscript at the Rhode Island Historical Society to People of Color*, June 24, 2004.

The records of local historians such as Samuel Greene Arnold, William Babcock Weeden, Howard M. Chapin, William Johnston, and William Rice provide the names of Negroes who served during the French and Indian War. Moreover, *The Records of the Colony of Rhode Island and Providence Plantations* lists the names of Negro soldiers who fought during the wars. *The Nine Muster Rolls of Rhode Island Troops* identify the names of black soldiers who fought during the French and Indian War. Lorenzo Johnston Greene, author of *The Negroes in Colonial New England*, listed a few names of those who served in colonial Rhode Island. Rick Stattler, compiler of the *Guide to Manuscripts at the Rhode Island Historical Society to People of Color*, lists names of Negroes who served in expeditions during the French and Indian War. Moreover, he recorded names of Africans who served onboard the war ships and names of others who worked to construct military forts. Phoebe Bean, a librarian at the Rhode Island Historical Society, provided information on the companies and the regiments with which these Africans served. She was able to bring to light the ethnicity of each man of color who served in the colonial war. According to Bean's work, there were Indians, Negroes, and mulattoes who sacrificed their lives in the name of freedom.

All the authors who recorded the names of Negroes who served in Rhode Island during the colonial wars deserve credit. It is not easy to find the names of black soldiers because in the Rhode Island Colony, militia men, soldiers, and privateers sometimes were not listed by race or ethnicity. In the same colony, there were also many people of color who had Christian names, making it difficult to distinguish them from European subjects. In New Hampshire, Connecticut, and Massachusetts, Negroes had peculiar names reserved only for them to some extent. Names such as Scipio, Caesar, and Pompey were common. In Connecticut, the ethnicity of African American colonial soldiers was mentioned in the list recorded by the Connecticut Historical Society in 1903 and 1905. In Massachusetts, local historians recorded the ethnicity of African American soldiers. Conversely, the names of the soldiers listed on the muster rolls were not identified by races, however, there were different lists for Negroes and Caucasians. Throughout New England, the names of African Americans and the names of friendly Indians were listed on the same muster rolls as whites. Therefore, researchers who listed the names of Negro soldiers in Rhode Island had to conduct intensive investigation across various documents for accurate identification. In the work of Howard Chapin, a former librarian at the Rhode Island Historical Society, soldiers of Indian descent were listed as such, but he failed to identify Africans. In his *Rhode Island in the Colonial Wars: A List of Rhode Island Soldiers & Sailors in the King George's War: 1740–1748*, there are many soldiers listed who served during the French and Indian War, but few are identified as Negroes. William Babcock Weeden identifies Andrew Frank, an African American who served in one of the colonial wars. Weeden writes that Frank left a gun after his death. According to Weeden, the gun was purchased for the war. The monetary value for the gun was £5.[41]

In *The Nine Muster Rolls of Rhode Island Troops*, Benjamin Negro was listed among soldiers who served in Captain Daniel Walls' company in Providence, January 12, 1758, in the French and Indian War.[42] According to Edward Field, there were nineteen names on Captain Walls' company roll.[43] Rick Stattler's *Guide to Manuscript at the Rhode Island Historical Society Relating to People of Color* identifies Benjamin, Negro as a soldier under Captain Compey, along with Ceasar, Jacob, Peter Cheese, and Sambo.[44] Historian Lorenzo Johnston Greene, in *The Negroes in Colonial New England*, lists James, Sambo, Ceasar, and Benjamin Negro as soldiers from Providence who fought during the colonial wars.[45] Phoebe Bean identified Nero Bosworth of Bristol as someone who marched on alarm in August 1757. Fortin Browen, a colored man of Smithfield, was also among those who marched on the alarm. Obe-

---

41. William Bocock Weeden, *Early Rhode Island: A Social History of the People*, Crofton Press, 1910, p. 261.

42. Benjamin Negro was listed in the *Nine Muster Rolls of Rhode Island Troops* as a soldier.

43. Edward Field, *State of Rhode Island and Providence Plantations at the End of the Century: A History*, vol. 1, Providence: Mason Pub.. Co., 1902, p. 430.

44. Rick Stattler, compiler of the *Guide to Manuscripts at the Rhode Island Historical Society*, lists Benjamin Negro, Peter Cheese, Jacob Ceasar, Ceasar, and Sambo as soldiers on the roll of Captain Daniel Walls' company. See MSS 673 in the guide.

45. Lorenzo Johnston Greene, *The Negro in Colonial New England*, Atheneum, 1968, p. 188.

diah Caesar, a colored man of North Kingstown, served with the Fourth Company under Captain Jeremiah Greene in 1757.[46] Bean lists Joshua George, a mulatto, as being in Captain Greene's company. She noted also that Negro Hanley Phillips of North Kingstown marched on the alarm.[47] It is noteworthy that in 1757, many Africans were enlisted as military men due to losses the English suffered. The armies of the king of England and Americans lost Fort William Henry in the North, and during that battle George Mew, an African American serving under the command of Captain John Whitting[48] and was taken prisoner. In 1757 the Rhode Island Assembly entrusted Captain Whitting with the command of the Third Company.

In 1760, during the invasion of Quebec and Montreal, the Rhode Island Colony furnished its quota of military men. After the fall of Canada, the British government ordered the invasions of Cuba, the domain of the Spanish king, and the French colony of Martinique. For the English, the invasion of Cuba and Martinique were critical to deny the French any access from attacking the English subjects on the sea highway. Phoebe Bean provided many names of African Americans who served in the expedition against Canada and Havana, including Joel Lewis, a colored man who served in Colonel Harris' company in 1760 and in Captain Hawkins' company in 1762.[49]

---

46. Phoebe Bean, *R.I. Colonial Patriots of Color*, Rhode Island Historical Society, 2004; *Records of the Colony of Rhode Island and Providence Plantations in New England: 1757–1769*, A.C. Greene and Brothers, State Printers, 1861, p. 26.

47. Bean, 2004.

48. Ibid.

49. Chapin and The Rhode Island Historical Society, 1918, pp. 29, 36, 38, 45, 74, 95, 104, 111, 122. In Rhode Island, no restrictions were enforced against the enlistments of African Americans in the militia during the colonial era. Throughout many colonial wars, they were enrolled as militia men or privateers.

Chapter 6

African Americans as Officers and Militiamen in Colonial Massachusetts

In 1638, Captain William Pierce imported Africans to colonial Massachusetts aboard the *Desire*. He originally intended to dock at the Bahama Islands. The account of Africans being imported to colonial New England has been well-documented by early New England historians: Governor John Winthrop, Joseph Barlow Felt (1827), and Governor Thomas Hutchinson of Massachusetts (1760). All acknowledge that upon the return of Captain Pierce from the island of Providence he brought with him Africans to Massachusetts Bay. Even though these authors admit Africans were introduced into the colony, they failed to mention what course Captain Pierce took with the Africans. Did he give them to the authorities? Were Africans shared among government officials? While early New England historians do not have pertinent responses on the fate of the first imported Africans from New Providence, George Washington Williams believed Africans belonging to Samuel Maverick in 1638 were brought by Captain Pierce. Except for Maverick, it seems there are no authoritative records revealing the names of New England inhabitants who held Africans from the ship *Desire* in their houses.

Contrary to many New England historians, in the *History of New England* by John Winthrop, data show that Captain William Pierce brought Africans to colonial Massachusetts Bay in 1637. The date of the arrival mentioned by New England historians contradict Governor John Winthrop's date who governed the colony at the time apparently, Massachusetts was somewhat actively involved in the slave trade. In addition to importing Africans to the colony, Captain Pierce was sent to the West Indies to sell Pequod prisoners. According to Winthrop, 13 children and two Pequod women were being transported by Pierce to the West Indies, but the transport ended at the island of Providence. The slave trade in colonial Massachusetts was authorized by government officials even though they failed to enact a law for slave trading at the time.

Slave trade was a monopoly for the government. Because the colony needed workers, in 1633, wages were increased excessively. John Winthrop notes that the increased wages called for carpenters to be paid three shillings for a day and a laborer was to receive two shillings and six pence. After wages increased, the General Court regulated wages. According to the order of the General Court of 1633, the daily pay rate for carpenters, masons, and others was two shillings per day. Laborers were paid eighteen pence a day. From this illustration, it is sound to note that Captain Pierce's trip was financed by government officials to solve the problem of a shortage of workers. In early colonial New England, servants were employed only by government officials, church ministers, and wealthy company officials. To illustrate, Samuel Roads, the author of *History and Traditions of Marblehead*, stipulated that in that city, almost every wealthy family held many Africans as slaves. He pointed out that Captain Lee employed many Africans for loading and unloading ships at the port of Marblehead. Clergy in Marblehead also had African servants in their houses.[1]

Throughout the historical records of New England, Samuel Maverick of Noddle's Island has been noted as the first person to hold Africans as slaves in the colony. The same information was noted by Thomas Hutchinson in 1795. Like Governor Hutchinson, Beatrix Creswell recorded that when Samuel Maverick returned from his trip to Virginia in 1636, he brought with him ten black people in addition to eighty goats and fourteen heifers.[2] According to Creswell, "the ten Af-

---

1. For information on selling Pequot prisoners, see John Winthrop, *The History of New England from 1630 to 1649, with Notes by J. Savage*, vol. 1, Boston: Phelps and Farnham, 1825, pp. 234, 254. See also William Bradford, *History of Plymouth Plantation*, published for the Massachusetts Historical Society, 1856, p. 360. In his book, the letter sent to Bradford by Governor Winthrop relates the accounts of the Pequod prisoners sent to Bermuda by Captain Pierce. See Samuel Roads, *The History and Traditions of Marblehead*, Boston, Houghton, Osgood, 1880, p. 11.

2. Beatrix Cresswell, *The Mavericks of Devonshire and Massachusetts*, James G. Commin, Exeter, 1929, pp. 43–44.

ricans were some of the first imported to New England."³ The account of Creswell contradicts by two years the popular date that Africans were first imported to the colony of Massachusetts Bay in 1638.

John Josselyn, a Scottish traveler who visited the colony of Massachusetts Bay, discovered Africans in the house of Samuel Maverick. In 1638, when Josselyn reached the colony, he was housed by Maverick. Josselyn did not document any information on the Africans held at the house of Maverick. Thomas Hutchinson, governor of Massachusetts, and George Washington Williams, an African American historian, have quoted the account of Josselyn on the existence of Africans in Boston. Williams believed the record of Josselyn on slavery is more authoritative than others.⁴

In Josselyn's book, *An Account of Two Voyages to New England, Made during the Years, 1638, 1663*, Josselyn mentions that Maverick desired to have biracial children with the African woman who resided in his house. His attempts to have a sexual relationship with her were rejected by the African woman, whom Josselyn believed had been a Queen in Africa. Additionally, two African men resided in Maverick's house during Josselyn's stay. One of them was the butler of the African woman. It is unknown if the unnamed African man was assigned as a butler by Maverick. Josselyn describes Maverick as a hospitable person who welcomed visitors to his house free of charge. A similar view of his good manners was noted by Edward Johnson, one of the settlers in the colony and a government official. He recorded in his book, "Samuel Maverick was of a very loving and courteous behavior, very ready to entertain strangers." As the authors listed above, Edwin Monroe Bacon writes that Maverick held the Africans as servant before making them slaves.⁵

---

3. Ibid.

4. See George Washington Williams, *History of the Negro Race in America from 1619 to 1880*, 1882, p. 176. Also see Thomas Hutchinson, *The History of the Colony of Massachusetts Bay, from the First Settlement. Thereof in 1628, Until . . . 1691 . . .*, 2nd ed., 1760, p. 444.

5. See John Josselyn, *An Account of Two Voyages to New England, Made during the Years 1638, 1663*, Boston: William Veazie, 1865, pp. 13–26; Edward Johnson, *Wonder-Working Providence of Sion's [sic] Savior in New-England*, vol. 2, 1867, p. 37; Edwin Monroe Bacon, *The Book of Boston: Fifty Year's Recollections of the New England*, 1916, p. 84.

Since 1638 when African Americans were introduced to the Massachusetts colony, laws enacted for the administration of servants applied to African Americans, as well. In many legal records, men and women of color were mentioned as servants. Initially, there were no laws enacted for the control of the behavior of any inhabitants during the early years of the Massachusetts colony. However, in 1641 when the officials enacted the Massachusetts Body of Liberties, slavery was legalized. Slavery became a legal status for strangers, prisoners of war sold to the English, or persons punished by the court. It is not known if this law aimed to legalize Africans or Indians as slaves. However, Indians who had been captured during the Pequod War had become slaves in the houses of many high-ranking officials. People of African descent had been brought from the Bahamas, but they were not treated as slaves. There is no evidence indicating that the earliest subjects of African descent were slaves in Massachusetts Bay.

The article of the Body of Liberties which legalized slavery stipulated as follows:

> It is ordered by this court, and the authority thereof; that there shall never be any bond slavery or captivity amongst us, unless it be lawful captives taken in just wars, as willingly sell themselves or sold to us, and such shall have the liberties and Christian usage which the law of God established in Israel concerning such persons do morally require; provided this exempts none from servitude, who shall be judged thereto by authority.[6]

This article clarifies the meaning of the law. It is noteworthy that interpretation of the Body of Liberties regarding slavery has been subjected to different opinions. Some historians believe that the Body of Liberties article prohibited slavery, and others note that this Act legalized the institution of slavery. As an illustration, Emory Washburn in 1869 recorded that in 1641, slavery was legalized in Massachusetts as an

---

6. For the section of the Body of Liberties prohibiting slavery, see the *Charter and General Laws of the Colony and Province of Massachusetts Bay*. Printed and Published by T.B. Wait and Co., 1814, p. 63.

institution. According to him, the law was enacted by "the judgment and the will of the freemen of the colony to regulate and limit slavery as it existed." Contrary to Emory, Governor Thomas Hutchinson of Massachusetts recorded that slavery in Massachusetts was prohibited, except for prisoners taken in war. Even though in Hutchinson's opinion slavery was not legal in Massachusetts, he noted that some inhabitants regarded the institution of slavery as a public mischief.[7]

The slavery of Africans was advocated by a powerful and an influential man of the colony. In 1645, Emanuel Downing, wrote a letter to his brother-in-law, John Winthrop, the governor of Massachusetts Bay. Downing's letter stressed the need for African slaves in the interest of the colony. He believed that capturing Indians in a just war was a deliverance from God. He went on to stipulate that in such war, Indians (men, women, and children) kept as prisoners may be exchanged for Africans who were beneficial for the English in the colony. He noted that the colony would not be populated by the English only without the importation of Africans. In his opinion, Africans would be used to enhance the business of the colony, and they would be on hand to continue their work for the next generation of Englishmen—their children. According to Downing, the expense of caring for twenty blacks was equal to that of one white. He had doubts about whether the country could be populated without the importation of African slaves.[8] Downing's opinions about enslaving Africans were based on commercial profits and valuable services slaves could perform on the plantations. A careful examination of Winthrop's journal indicates a correlation between the reasons for the pro-slavery stance. Emanuel Downing argues in his letter and conditions within the colony regarding the need for workers and reasons for financial shortages. In 1645, Winthrop wrote that "the war in England kept servants from coming to the colony.... It was dif-

---

7. Emory Washburn, *Slavery as It Once Prevailed in Massachusetts*, Press of John Wilson and Son, 1863, p. 3; Hutchinson, *The History of the Colony of Massachusetts Bay, from the First Settlement Thereof in 1628, Until . . . 1691 . . .* 2nd ed., 1760, p. 444.

8. For the letter of Emanuel Downing encouraging the slavery of Africans, see Lilian Brandt, "The Massachusetts Slave Trade," *The New England Magazine*, vol. 21, Making of America Project, New England Co., 1900, p. 91. Also see Ulrich Bonnell Phillips, *American Negro Slavery: A Survey of the Supply, Employment and Colonial of Negro Labor as Determined by the Plantation Regime*. D. Appleton, 1918, p. 101.

ficult to pay their wages because money was very scarce." To support his explanation, Winthrop gives the example of Rowley "who was forced to sell his oxen so that he could pay his servant. In addition, Rowley was not able to keep his servant because he was unable to pay him for the following year."[9] This may be one of the reasons importing Africans flourished in the colony.

From the time of the arrival of the first Africans in the colony, there were no laws prohibiting African servants from performing militia duties. In addition, the Massachusetts colonial officials did not enact laws for the control of the Africans' behavior. During the earlier years of the colony, Africans were identified as servants or maid servants. In regard to their well-being, they were protected by laws regarding treatment and management of servants. Due to their status as servants, Africans were allowed to own property, to join churches, to be a guarantee of the town, and to perform militia duties like servants of European descent. Additionally, they had the right to sue and be sued by the English in the colony. There are a number of examples demonstrating the ways Africans in colonial Massachusetts were integrated into the community.

Bostian Ken of Dorchester, commonly called Bus Bus [sic], was a land owner. The Suffolk Deed indicates that Bostian bonded over his house and four and one-half acres of land in Dorchester as a bond to free Angola, a Negro man in service to Anna Keayne, the widow of Captain Keayne. The term of the liberation of Angola was set in 1656. In this case, Anna Keayne did not want to free Angola after he had served her for some years. As a result, she requested payment to free Angola from her service. In colonial Massachusetts, servants were requested to serve a number of years before being liberated from their masters. It is notable that Angola's case went to court for him to gain liberation. In Massachusetts Bay, the Acts Respecting Masters, Servants, and Laborers stipulated, "All servants that have served diligently and faithfully, to the benefit of their masters, seven years, shall not be sent away empty; and if any have been unfaithful, negligent or unprofitable in their service, notwithstanding the good usage of their masters, they shall not be dismissed, till they have made satisfaction according to the judgment

---

9. Winthrop, 1853, pp. 269–70.

of authority"[10] (This law was first enacted in 1630, and was re-enacted in 1633, 35, 36, 41). Throughout the records consulted, Angola was always listed as a servant. To illustrate, in 1653 when Angola married his wife Elizabeth, he was mentioned in the Town Record as the servant of Robert Keayne. Angola bears this same description in the will of captain Keayne. The date set for the Angola's liberation was the year when Captain Robert Keayne died.

Jack Welcome is another black man who owned property in colonial Massachusetts. According to *The History of Malden, Massachusetts*, in 1701 town officials gave Welcome a small piece of land, about a quarter of an acre, near the Boston line on the side of the Great Road. He and his wife built a house and lived there until his death, when his son became the owner of the house.[11]

There are records that show African Americans benefitting from other rights guaranteed to servants. In 1641, Dorcas, a black maid servant to Mr. Stoughton of Dorchester, was admitted into the church and baptized.[12] In the same year, Hope, the son of Mingo, an African, was born in the colony. His date of birth was recorded the same way as the English. Hope was born on March 19, 1641, in Boston. It appears that Hope was the first African born in colonial New England. From documents consulted, there is no data indicating the existence of an African child born before the birth of Hope. The name given to Mingo's son indicates that Africans were, to some extent, treated the same as the English servants. During the early years of the settlement, Africans were not subjected to the indignity of being named after Roman men of great military and political stature such as Caesar, Pompey, and Scipio. In some slave communities, slaves were stripped of their African names and called by names reflective of men of great power. Possibly, it was in the 1700s that Africans were named as such in colonial Massachusetts

---

10. John D. Cushing, The Laws and Liberties of Massachusetts, 1641–1691. A Fascimile Ed., Containing also Council orders and Executive proclamations, vol.1. SR Scholarly Resources Inc., 1976, pp. 38–39.

11. Deloraine Pendre Corey, *The History of Malden, Massachusetts*, Malden, the author, 1898, pp. 400–401.

12. See *Records of the First Church at Dorchester, in New England, 1636–1734*, First Church (Dorchester, Boston, Mass). G.H. Ellis, 1891, pp. xiv, xvi, 5; see also John Winthrop and Savage, *The History of New England 1630–1649*, p. 36.

Bay. The names listed in this book show that Africans were given either Christian or African names.

Another person who joined the church in the early years of the settlement was Matthew of Dorcas. It is unknown whether or not he was the son of Dorcas of Dorchester. Matthew is mentioned as an inhabitant of Dorchester. He joined the First Church on July 12, 1648. In 1657, the death of Richard, an African and servant of John Lowell, was recorded in the town document. The marriages of Africans were also recorded in the same manner as the English. In 1659, Clement, a servant of John Joyliffe, was married to Mary, a servant of the same master.[13]

In Worcester, Massachusetts, Will, a mulatto, was one of the guarantees (town bond insurers) of the town and a landowner. In 1685, he was present to witness when Captain Gookin was given a hundred acres of land, along with Captain Henchman, the son of Nathaniel Henchman; David Fiske, the surveyor; Christopher Reed; and Benjamin Eaton.[14]

There are many cases indicating that blacks were able to sue those who offended them in court. For example, the records of the Courts of Essex County and the files of the Quarterly Courts of Essex County, report that in 1659, Mungaly and Moninah, a black man and his wife, sued Mr. Samuel Bennett when their mare with foal drowned by falling into a pit that Bennett had dug and left open. Mungaly and Moninah had been servants of Captain Bridges, who had liberated them.[15] In contrast, African Americans also were subject to be sued. In Malden, Ebedmelecks, a black man, was sentenced to receive five stripes for breaking the Lord's Day. During colonial days in Massachusetts, breaking religious rules was punishable by law. The illustration of the punishment dispensed to Ebedmelecks for breaking the Sabbath reveals

---

13. See *A Report of the Record Commissioners Containing Boston Births, Baptisms, Marriages, and Deaths*, 1883, pp. 11, 39, 48, 61, 72.

14. See William Lincoln, *History of Worcester, Massachusetts, from its earliest settlement to September 1836: with various notices relating to the history of Worcester County*, Hersey, 1862, p. 35.

15. For the case of Moninah and Mungaly of Lynn, former servant to Captain Bridges of Lynn against Samuel Bennit of Lynn, see *The Genealogical Magazine*, vol. 10–11, p. 129. See also *Records and Files of the Quarterly Courts of Essex, County, Massachusetts, 1656–1662*, 1912, p. 183.

that Africans were subjected to the same laws as the English in the early years of the colony.

The relationship between Africans and their masters and neighbors has been addressed by many writers who have mentioned that African servants were well cared for and treated well.[16] In fact, African servants or slaves were often attached to their masters, and a genuine mutual relationship sometimes existed between them. It is difficult to ascertain when Africans transitioned from the status of servant and acquired the status of slave. Even after the official legalization of slavery under the Body of Liberties, to some extent, Africans were still termed as servants in legal documents.

As both terms *servant* and *slave* were used in the early days of the settlement, it is pertinent to give a brief note on those terms. In New England, English and Indian servants were employed by wealthy inhabitants as well as agents of the companies. Likely, church ministers also had servants in their houses. In regard to slaves, evidence also indicates that Indians were enslaved during the Pequod War in 1637. In addition to Indians, Englishmen sanctioned by the court were also enslaved in Massachusetts Bay. In 1827, Joseph Barlow Felt recorded that in 1638, Lieutenant Davenport was paid £3.8 for his service as superintendent of slaves. The slaves he supervised were those punished by the court. Felt notes that the slavery penalty fit the crime.[17]

With respect to the militia duties, during war time, able-bodied colored men defended their master's land. Similarly, slave owners who were military commanders took their black slaves or servants along with them to war zones to fight for the security of the colony. Some slave owners hired out their black slaves or servants for the defense of the colony, and later received money for services performed by the slaves. Traditionally, in colonial New England the system of hiring out slaves or servants was common.

---

16. For a good example on how Negroes were treated, see Charles Brooks and William Henry Whitmore, *History of the Town of Medford, Middlesex County, Massachusetts*, J.M. Uster, 1855, p. 432. These two authors note that Negroes in Medford, Massachusetts were treated, generally, much after the manner in which parents treat their children.

17. See Joseph Barlow Felt, *The Annals of Salem: From Its First Settlement*, Salem, 1827, p. 113.

Historians such as Lorenzo Greene have noted cases in which African slaves were hired out by their masters for financial gain. Greene writes that in 1679 Mingo, an African belonging to Miles Foster of Boston, was hired out to manage a warehouse belonging to Roger Darby. Sometimes African slaves were entrusted to manage the affairs of their masters. Greene recorded that in 1682 Peter Cross's African man served as seaman by managing the sloop which belonged to his master. Hiring out African slaves and servants was an established practice in other New England colonies. In 1858, Henry Benson noted that Mingo, an African American belonging to Deacon Thomas Clark around 1730, was hired out during the day. He drove a plow and thereafter worked with his master. After his master's death, Mingo was given the opportunity to choose a new master among Cross's sons. First, he stayed with Thomas, a choice that did not last long because Mingo was not happy. He did not like keeping the tavern in which his new master was involved. Instead, Mingo went to live with Cross's other son, Timothy.[18]

The antagonistic relationship between the Indians and the English strengthened the ties between blacks and whites. In colonial Massachusetts and other New England colonies, blacks were often hated by the Indians; therefore, whenever Indians attacked a town, the slave owners or masters had the same obligations to defend blacks as they did to defend English subjects. As there were many Indian attacks on the colony, did colonial officials authorize the enlistment of black men? Did blacks assist their masters to suppress enemies? Were Africans enlisted in the military companies of the colony? The responses to these questions will be based on the laws enacted by colonial officials and the records of colonial wars. Collecting data about the lives of Africans in the Colonial Era is difficult because historical records were hit and miss regarding Africans. Therefore, for the researcher, finding authentic information was comparable to going on a treasure hunt. Many documents were examined to discover the history of blacks in the militia and the military of the colony. Precisely, recorded data from Massachusetts was viewed

---

18. See Lorenzo Johnson Green, *The Negro in Colonial New England*, New York: Atheneum, 1969, pp. 115–17; Henry Bronson, *The History of Waterbury, Connecticut*, Bronson Brothers, 1858, p. 321.

and studied to collect from local historians unquestionable records on the enlistment of African slaves in the militia of the colony. Similarly, Acts of the Massachusetts legislatures revealed pertinent information on the militia services African slaves, servants, and free men performed during the Colonial Era.

Laws of Massachusetts Bay Colony on the Enlistment of Blacks in the Militia

Initially, when Africans were imported into Massachusetts Bay Colony, government officials did not enact any laws including or excluding them from militia or military services. In the earlier years of the colony, towns were less populated and were separated from each other by large distances. Like towns, plantations were also less populated. The same view was noted by Francis Parkman, author of *France and England in North America: Count Frontenac and New France under Louis XIV.* He revealed that "in colonial Massachusetts, houses were isolated in an extensive distance. In little villages also houses were far apart, and enemies were capable of inflicting pain upon the inhabitants."[19] Therefore, in such conditions, every able-bodied male who resided in the colony had a responsibility to defend his domicile towns or settlements. Possibly, if called upon for the assistance by neighboring towns, these men were compelled to respond to the alarm. George Henry Moore, author of *Notes on the History of Slavery in Massachusetts*, agrees that during the earlier years of the colony, due to the survival of the institutions, everyone in the settlements was a citizen soldier. In addition able-bodied men, women and children were bearers of arms.[20] Slaves, such as those belonging to Samuel Maverick, were defenders of the colony. Similarly, Bostian Ken, alias Bus Bus [sic], and Angola were permitted to bear arms. These two African Americans were in the colony possibly before 1656. Angola was in the colony before 1656 because he was married to

---

19. Francis Parkman, *France and England in North America: Count Frontenac and New France under Louis XIV, 1877*, Little Brown, 1891, p. 371.

20. For the community soldiering in the colony of Massachusetts in the early years of the colony, see George Henry Moore, *Notes on the History of Slavery in Massachusetts*. D. Appleton & Co., 1866, p. 243.

Elizabeth, a black maid servant to Edward Hutchinson, on April 20, 1654.[21] Angola's marriage date confirms that he was among the earliest African servants in colonial Massachusetts. In the town of Malden, Ebedmelecks, a black man, bore arms because he was in the colony before 1653. In Essex County, Mungaly, a black man, was one of those who would be able to carry arms because his name appears among Africans who were present in the early years of the colony. He might have been in the colony before his legal case dating 1659. Black Will, who lived in Essex County, was another able man to bear arms during the earlier years of the colony. His name appeared in the Essex County Court in 1657. Among African maid servants, Dorcas, servant of Mr. Stoughton, was able to bear arms. She was baptized, as mentioned in the beginning of this chapter, in the year 1641 according to John Winthrop. She was approved in the church after she had obtained years of experience as a diver in the same year when the Body of Liberties was enacted. John Winthrop, the elder, did not mention when Dorcas was imported to the colony. The only clue about her is that she joined the church after years of experience. In her case, there are no arguments as to whether or not she was among the blacks transported by Captain Pierce or that she was in the colony before 1638. The number of years it took for her to gain her diving experience is unknown. In Boston, according to John Winthrop, in 1641, there was a female servant, possibly the maid of Captain Pierce, who burnt the clothes of her master. She was among those who could bear arms. Unlike Dorcas of Dorchester, Elizabeth, a black maid servant of Edward Hutchinson, was among those women who would have carried arms during the earlier years of the colony.[22] In addition to the blacks noted above, Katharine, a black maid servant of Daniel Rumbale, was in the colony before 1658, as records show that she was punished for moral vices in 1658. The names listed above are illustrations of people of color who were in the colony during the early years when everyone was allowed to bear weapons in case of alarm or enemy attacks. Black servants in Plymouth Colony were included in the militia during the early

---

21. For the date of the marriage of Angola, see Jerry Chamberlain Watts and Massachusetts Historical Society, p. 42.

22. Elizabeth was the wife of Angola. See Watts and Massachusetts Historical Society, 1903, p. 421.

years just as black servants were included in the militia at Massachusetts Bay. John Gorham Palfrey tells us that Abraham Pearse, the Blackmoor, was on the list of men allowed to bear arms in 1643. Palfrey collected the information on the Plymouth Records, vol. III.[23] If there were more African Americans in Plymouth, they were subject to the same military obligations as Abraham Pearse.

In 1652, due to the pressure of war between the English and the Dutch, colonial officials in Massachusetts were obligated to authorize blacks, Scots, and Indians the same training privileges as the English. The enlistment of Africans, Scots, and Indians was ordered as a preventive measure. During the English-Dutch conflict, the Dutch in New Nederland (New York) were well-equipped as a military force. They were competing for the control of territories in North America. On the contrary, in colonial Massachusetts, colonists did not put forth an effort to establish an army for the defense of the colony. George Bancroft, who wrote *History of the United States*, stipulated that the elders in Massachusetts did not want to take part in the Europeans' conflict. He went on to note that the elders in Massachusetts said that "the wars of Europe ought not to destroy the happiness of America. It was safest for the colonies to forbear the use of the sword, but to be in a posture of defense."[24] The decision to enlist Africans, Scots, and Indians proved to be a good strategy. When war broke out, they were immediately called upon to serve the colony. Similarly, the fear of the English colonies in North America was noted by Thomas Francis Gordon. He wrote that "the English feared being expelled by the Dutch with co-operation of the Indians when the war between England and the Dutch broke out in 1652."[25]

The conflict between the Dutch and English, according to Thomas Hobbs, began on May 14, 1652. Unlike Hobbs, Charles Knight related that the war commenced on the 19th of May the same year. The accounts of both authors are supported by Christopher Thomas Atkinson.

---

23. For Abraham Pearse see John Gorham Palfrey, *History of New England during the Stuart Dynasty*, vol. 2, Little Brown, 1876, p. 30.

24. George Bancroft, *History of the United States: From the Discovery of the American Continent to the End of the Late War*, vol. 1, A. Fullarton and Company, 1845, p. 444.

25. Thomas Francis Gordon, *Gazetteer of the State of New York: Comprehending its Colonial History*, printed for the author, 1836, p. 516.

The conflict started when the Dutch military commander Admiral Van Tromp violated the English sea territory after General Blake of Deane warned the Admiral. When the Dutch did not heed the warning, the English shot at the fleet of Dutch ships, thus initiating the war.[26] As in Europe, the American colonies were always affected by the Europeans' wars. Therefore, officials in Massachusetts Bay took legal procedures to include blacks, Indians, and Scotchmen in the militia of the colony. The account of the Massachusetts Militia Act to enlist and train new recruits was recorded by Joseph Barlow Felt, George Henry Moore, and the Massachusetts Historical Society, among others. The May 27, 1652, Act states that "all Negroes, Indians, and Scots inhabiting with or servants to the English from the age of sixteen to sixty years, shall be listed and are hereby enjoyned [sic] to attend training as well as the English."[27] The Scotchmen who were ordered to enlist and train in the militia were those captured in the battle of Dunbar during the administration of Oliver Cromwell. Even though George Henry Moore, Joseph Barlow Felt, William Washington, and the Massachusetts Historical Society mention the authorization of African Americans in the militia, they did not explain the reasons these non-Englishmen were ordered to receive the same training as the English. In contrast, this current work reveals the salient reasons the colonial government included African servants to become legal members of the militia.

In 1652, the Massachusetts Bay colony was not populated by a large number of people of African descent. But the small portion of Africans in the colony was enough to increase the ranks of the colonial militia. Joseph Barlow Felt notes that there were about 200 blacks in the colony.[28] The estimate Felt gives is a probability because there was no formal or systematic census taken at this time. In addition, it was not easy

---

26. See Thomas Hobbes, *The English Works of Thomas Hobbes of Malmesbury*, vol. 6, 1840, p. 383; Christopher Thomas Atkinson and Navy Records Society, *Letters and Papers Relating to the First Dutch War, 1652–1654*, Navy Records Society, 1899, p. 14; Charles Knight, *School History of England Abridged from the Popular History of England [with] Questions*, vol. 1, 1865.

27. George Henry Moore notes that all Negroes, Indians, and Scots residing with the English were ordered to be trained as the English. The law of 1652 was also related by Felt in his *Annals of Salem*, 1849, p. 415.

28. Joseph Barlow Felt, *Annals of Salem*, vol. 2, W. & S.B. Ives, 1849, p. 415.

CHAPTER 6

to collect data regarding the number of Africans living in the colony because the plantations were built a long distance from one another. Furthermore, a central government did not exist in Massachusetts Bay. The Essex Institute notes that before 1763 there was never a resemblance of an attempt at census-taking in Massachusetts. Taking a census was an unpopular measure, and when a census was taken it was not accurate.[29]

While Felt recorded the numbers of black people in colonial Massachusetts in 1652, he failed to give the census of Scots and Indians in the colony. In regard to the Scots, after the Oliver Cromwell War of 1650, many of them were taken prisoner in London. In 1651, three hundred Scotsmen were consigned to Thomas Kemble of Charlestown, a neighborhood in Boston, and transported to Boston, Massachusetts, by John Beex and Robert Rich.[30] On November 11, Sir Arthur Hesilrigge ordered 150 Scotch prisoners to be delivered to Augustine Walker, master of the *United Ship*, to be transported to New England.[31] In 1689, Charles Knight noted the transportation of Scots in New England, as well. From the letter of Cromwell recorded by him, records show that John Colton, minister of Boston, acknowledged the arrival of Scottish prisoners in Boston, Massachusetts. Minister Cotton Mather noted that "they were then kindly used, having been sold for a limited servitude in a country where their labor was welcomed, and ill-rewarded."[32] In the battle of Worcester, Cromwell took many more prisoners. In 1652, 270 Scottish prisoners were sent to Massachusetts.[33]

The militia law of 1652 did not only require military services of blacks, Scots, and Indians, but the law also authorized them to bear the same military burden as the English for the protection, security, and safety of the colony. It is significant to note that this was the first inclusive

---

29. Essex Institute Historical Collection, vol. XXIV, Salem, MA: Printed for the Essex Institute, 1888, p. 100.

30. Walter Kendall Watkins, *The Ochterloney Family of Scotland, and Boston in New England*, Priv. Print, 1902, p. 4.

31. Ibid.

32. See Charles Knight's *Popular History of England*, vol. 4, Brodbury, Evans, & Company, 1689, p. 135.

33. John Adams Vinton, *The Upton Memorial: A Genealogical Record of the Descendants of John Upton, of North Reading, Mass. . . . Together with Short Genealogies of the Putnam, Stone, and Bruce Family*. Private use of the office of E. Upton & son, 1874, p. 6.

act enforced at Massachusetts Bay for militia enlistment. Even though the number of Scots and Indians in the colony at this time is unknown, any enlisted and trained number of Scots and Indians would make an impact in the militia quota of the colony. As the colony was not overly populated, colonial officials welcomed any increase of able-bodied men capable of carrying weapons. The illustrations of the arrival of Scots in Massachusetts were documented in this work to show that upon their arrival, they held the same status as Africans and Indians. They were servants; therefore, they did not have the same privileges as Englishmen. It is unknown whether or not some of them were slaves to the English. Even though the Scots were people of European descent, in the Massachusetts Bay Colony, they were categorized as bondsmen.

On April 5, 1654, England and Holland concluded a term of peace. There were rumors that the Dutch in New Netherland attempted to attack the colonies of New England. Probably, the Anglo-Spanish War of 1654 did not have any effect on the colonies of New England. Perhaps, due to the easiness of the conflict between the English and Dutch, the 1652 Act for the enlistment and training of blacks and Indians was discontinued. In 1656, when a militia was enacted, blacks and Indians were exempted from military training and bearing arms. The law of May 1656 stipulated that "it is ordered and declared by this court and the authorities thereof, that henceforth no Negroes or Indians, although servants to the English, shall be armed or permitted to train."[34] The law did not document reasons for exempting blacks and Indians from military training and bearing arms. This was the first time people of color were excluded from militia training and bearing arms by an Act of the assembly. As for Indians, they were consistently prevented from carrying weapons due to their hostile behavior to whites. As early as 1633, an Act was passed to prohibit selling arms to Indians. The Act also restricted anyone from repairing any gun, armor, or weapon belonging to the Indians. Violators of this Act were doomed to pay £10 for every gun, armor, or weapon sold to the Indians. Similarly, a fine of £5 was charged to persons who sold powder to Native Americans. Additionally, 40 shillings was fined to violators who sold pounds of powder, and 40 shillings

---

34. Moore, 1866, p. 243.

for every pound of shot or lead.[35] The Indians also bought their weapons from the French and the Dutch, weapons the Native Americans used against the English. For this reason, the English accused the French of inciting violence against their interests for many years. Moreover, the French instigated many conflicts between Indians and the English in New England, as well as in other English colonies in North America.

In 1656, when blacks and Indians were excluded from militia training, Great Britain and France signed a peace treaty. William Douglass notes that according to the deal of the treaty, the subjects of the King of France were not allowed to fish, trade, or harbor in the territory of the English. Similarly, the English were ordered to act the same as the French. They were not permitted to fish, trade, or harbor in the French territories, except in cases of distress, to repair, to get wood, or to get water. The exclusion of African Americans from militia training was possibly due to the peace term which the French and the English concluded in 1656. As the colony was not under military threat from the enemy, the exclusion of African Americans and Indians remained in force.

The New England colonists rejected the notion of having a standing army. However, the colonies had militia companies and regiments which were ordered to muster, that is, to assemble for inspection and/or in preparation for battle, every month. Though this exercise was consistent, the militia did not gather as a professional army. According to Samuel Adams Drake, "inhabitants of colonial New England opposed the establishment of a permanent military of any kind whatsoever.' He goes on to note that the fathers set a tradition that a standing army was a standing danger and their sons would have none of it.'"[36] During war time, militiamen were enlisted voluntarily or by order of the Crown of England. Sometimes servants and slaves accompanied their masters to the expeditions to help suppress their enemies. This was the case for African servants and slaves. Sometimes local officials enlisted African servants and slaves to furnish the quotas requested by colonial officials. For

---

35. See *Laws of the Colonial and State Governments, Relating to Indians and Indians Affairs, from 1633 to 1831 ... with ... the Proceedings, of the Congress of the Confederation, and the Laws of Congress from 1800 to 1832 on the same subject.* United States, 1832, p. 10.

36. Samuel Adams Drake, *The Border Wars of New England: Commonly Called King William's and Queen Anne's War*, C. Scribner's Sons, 1897, p. 129.

the protection of villages and towns, militiamen were enlisted locally. In this case, African servants and slaves were included in the militia to fully participate in the communal security of the towns.

In 1660, England was again in a military conflict with Holland. In anticipation of any attacks to the colony by the Dutch from the New Netherland colony, members of the Massachusetts general assembly did not exclude blacks and Indians from military training. The militia Act of 1660 ordered the attendance of military training and exercising of every person above sixteen years. George Henry Moore believes that Indians and blacks were not exempted.[37] The inclusive militia services regarding blacks were the initial policy observed in the earlier years of the settlement until 1656. With the Anglo-Saxons' system of local control imported from England and observed by the settlers, it is unknown whether blacks were excluded from all the settlements and/or plantations from militia duties. Possibly, high-ranking military men who owned African servants did not comply with the Act, especially if the officers employed to perform military duties to protect their properties and their families. Plantations were small and not densely populated. In addition, the plantations were separated from each other, miles apart. It is questionable to believe that with enemy Indians roving around the colonies blacks would be excluded from defending their masters' plantations. Moreover, colonists lived under the same roofs with their African servants. It would be unwise to deny them weapons which they could use to defend the family or properties of their masters.

In 1675, New Plymouth Colony was attacked by King Philip. As the colony was a member of the United Colonies, New Plymouth's request for military assistance from the other member colonies was rendered without question. The United Colonies were formed in 1643 after the Pequot's War, an armed conflict in New England between the Pequot Indians and an alliance with Massachusetts Bay, Plymouth, and Saybrook colonies, along with their Native American allies—the Narragansett and Mohegan tribes. The intention of the United Colonies was

---

37. Moore says that the militia law of 1660 required the training and military exercise of every person above sixteen, and did not exempt Negroes and Indians.

to protect themselves against the encroachment of the Dutch and the French. Also, they needed to secure themselves against tribes of Native Americans who intended to harm the confederation of Massachusetts, Plymouth, Connecticut, and New Haven. Interestingly, Providence Plantation and Rhode Island Colony refused to join the union upon request. And the settlement of Piscataqua (New Hampshire) was not admitted because the inhabitants of that colony did not have the same Puritan beliefs as Massachusetts Bay and other colonies.[38]

The Indian King Philip, also known as Metacomet, waged war against the English colonies. The war, which began on Saturday, June 20, 1675, was devastating to Plymouth Colony. When the Indians attacked the Swansea Village, they plundered all the houses of the English in their absence. During the battle, between 600 and 800 English were killed. The city of Taunton in New Plymouth was King Philip's target. Because he disliked the English so much, King Philip's intention was to exterminate the entire population in Taunton. Four days following the initiation of the war, Indians killed five English men in Swansea and wounded two others. As a result, government officials in Plymouth requested military assistance from other New England colonies. In Massachusetts Bay, a company of 70 mounted men were dispatched to Plymouth. Similarly, local officials in Boston sent military men to the same cause. On June 26, 1676, Captain Hezekiah Willett was captured and killed by Indians. According to George Madison Bodge, when Captain Willett was killed, his head was delivered to King Philip. The 25-year-old was the son of Captain Thomas Willett. During Hezekiah's capture, he was accompanied by Jethro, an African servant belonging to Hezekiah's father.[39]

When his master was killed, Jethro was taken hostage. During the time of his captivity, Jethro collected critical information regarding King Philip's plan to exterminate the English. Due to Jethro's ability to comprehend the Indian language, he was able to interpret their conversation and remember the plans and strategies set forth by the Indians

---

38. Bancroft, 1845, pp. 420–21.

39. Duane H. Hurd, *A History of Bristol County, Massachusetts, with Biographical Sketches of Many of Its Pioneers and Prominent Men*, part I, J.W. Lewis & Company, 1883, p. 5.

for killing the English. Jethro was not comfortable in the Indian village. Possibly, he was troubled to hear that the Indians planned to annihilate people he knew. After some time in captivity, Jethro escaped and revealed King Philip's plan to the English. After revealing this information, without delay, the English counter-attacked the Indians, and the planned massacre against the English in Taunton was prevented. In recompense for the many lives Jethro saved, in 1676, the General Court and the Courts of the Assistants in Plymouth ordered the liberation of Jethro from slavery after two years of service from the date of the revelation of the Indians' plan to attack New England. The account of Jethro's manumission is recorded in the Records of the Colony of New Plymouth in New England reads as follows:

"Jethro had to serve to the estate of his former master, Captain Willett, under the administration of John Saffin for two years. During the two years, Saffin was responsible for his accommodations. In addition, at the end of the two years, Jethro was deemed to be liberated from bondage."[40]

The impact made by the vital information Jethro revealed to English authorities is well-documented by Francis Baylies, author of *Historical Memoir of the Colony of New Plymouth*. According to Baylies, when the authorities learned about the Indians' plan to destroy Taunton, the English fortified the town militarily. When the Indians reached Taunton on July 11, 1676, they encountered a fierce opposition from the English. Because the attackers could not penetrate the defense of the English, the Indians were forced to flee after burning only a few houses.[41] After the defeat of the attack of the Indians, on August 1, 1676, the English took revenge on King Philip by arresting Wootonekanuse, Philip's

---

40. See *Records of the Colony of New Plymouth in New England: Court Orders [Being the Proceedings of the General Court and the Court of Assistants], 1633–1691*, New Plymouth Colony and Nathaniel Bradstreet Shurtleff, Press of W. White, 1859, p. 216. Also see Samuel Hopkins Emery, *History of Taunton, Massachusetts: From Its Settlement to the Present Time*. D. Mason & Company, 1893, p. 405. The account of Jethro was also recorded by Samuel Adam Drake and Major Church. Nathan Henry Chamberlain also discussed the death of Captain Hezekiah Willet, the master of Jethro. See Samuel Sewall and the world he lived in, 1897, p. 123.

41. See Frances Baylies, *Historical Memoire of the Colony of New Plymouth*, vol. 2, Boston: Wiggin & Lunt, 1866, p. 140.

wife, and his nine-year-old son. Also, several women and children were taken captive by the English, and on August 12, 1676, the English killed King Philip near Mount Hope in Pokanoket (the town of Bristol) by the English.[42]

In 1686, the English were at peace with the French in Europe. In colonial America, Chevalier de Troyes from Montreal ordered the occupation of the Hudson Bay Company forts. This expedition was done during the administration of Governor Jacques-René Brisay de Denonville of Quebec. The expedition was comprised of 30 regular soldiers and 68 Canadian soldiers. In the same expedition, d'Iberville, Saint Helene, and Maricourt, the sons of distinguished soldier, translator, and governor of Montreal, Canada, Charles le Moyne, were enlisted. In addition to the sons of Le Moyne, Antoine Silvy, a Jesuit, served as chaplain. They marched with the Canadian regulars to occupy the English forts. When the expedition was completed, the French captured from the English Fort Haynes, Fort Ruppert, and Fort Albany.[43] English forts were captured without resistance because King James II did not want to fight the French, who were subjects of King Louis XIV, his strong ally in Europe. During the attack of Ireland, King James II was militarily supported by the king of France. He was supplied with French troops.[44] According to C.L. Thomson, "King James II was in the pay of Louis XIV; he could not make any active resistance to the aggression of the Canadians."[45] Unlike Thomson, Francis Parkman notes that "the monarchs of England and France were closely united. Both hated Constitutional liberty and held the same principles of supremacy in church and state. While King James II was in conflict with his subjects, he was in constant need of his great ally, and dared not offend him."[46] While King James II was submissive to the King of France, Thomas Dongan, the governor of New York, stood firm to protect the English territories. Similarly, he bridged a good re-

---

42. Hurd, 1883, p. 7.

43. C.L. Thomson, *A Short History of Canada*. Punam Lnaccuk, 1911, p. 82.

44. See *A New Naval History ; or, Compleat View of the British Marine, etc.*, 1757, p. 549.

45. Ibid.

46. Francis Parkman, *France and England in North America: Count Frontenac and New France under Louis XIV, 1877*, Little Brown, 1891, p. 119.

lationship with the Iroquois, which he made subjects of the crown of England. He employed provocative methods to engage the Iroquois in his struggle against the French.[47] As the King of France was determined to occupy the colony of New York, Dongan gave his best possible effort to deny them the accomplishment of such design. He received weapons secretly from the King of England to resist the attack from the French.[48]

In the same year, King James II appointed commissioners with the power to negotiate with the King of France for the restitutions of the Hudson Bay English forts captured in 1686. Possibly, the occupation of the English forts by the French was the commencement of the conflicts between the two nations in North America. Even though King James did not react militarily, the colonists in Massachusetts marched against the French but were incapable of ousting the French from the forts.

In 1687, the conflict continued with a different approach. The Indians in Canada, supported by the French, began making complaints about the behavior of the English regarding their territorial interests. The French accused the English of violating their territorial internal integrity. Consequently, the French began making incursions against English properties and killed some of the colonists in the northern frontiers. Sir Edmund Andros, governor of the colony, was in New York when he heard about the murders. He returned to Boston to avenge the criminal acts committed by the French Indians. Upon Andros' arrival in Boston, he prepared for an expedition against the Indians that was launched in 1688. Governor Andros was accompanied by seven to eight hundred men whom he impressed for the march to the eastern country. During the march, many soldiers died due to hardship.[49] The expedition was fruitless because he did not encounter any Indians.

On March 24, 1687, a militia act was passed allowing for preparation of the war against the Indians, allies of the French in Canada. Blacks and Indians were among militiamen in New England during time of war. The Act was inclusive, for it did not restrict African Americans and friendly Indians from carrying arms. Additionally, the Scotch and

---

47. Ibid., p. 120.
48. Ibid., p. 136.
49. Joshua Coffin, *A Sketch of the History of Newbury, Newburyport, and West Newbury, from 1635 to 1845*, S.G. Drake, 1845, p. 151.

Irish were not prohibited from being enlisted in the militia. According to Moore, the Militia Act, established during the administration of Sir Edmund Andros, stipulated that "no person whatsoever above sixteen years of age remain unlisted by themselves, masters, mistress or employer."[50] Sir Edmund Andros, governor appointee of the New England colonies by King James II established the Militia Act before the first (King Williams' War) of the series of French and Indian wars. Sir Andros arrived in Boston in 1686, three years before the crowning of King William and Mary to the throne of England. Before the confrontation against the Indians, Andros attempted to resolve the dispute between the English and French by following diplomatic channels. He ordered the liberation of the Indians arrested for the murder of English colonists. However, the Indians did not reciprocate. They did not free the detained Englishmen in their custody. As a result, Sir Andros was driven to use force against the Indian nation.[51] When the Indian War began in 1687, the French were acting in secret. They furnished weapons and other military means to the Indians. Samuel Adams Drake contends that Jesuit missionaries provided powder and guns to the Indians. Additionally, the missionaries promised the arrival of two hundred Frenchmen to further support their allies.[52] Historically, French missionaries instigated Indians to work against the English. Moreover, they were against any English' settlements extensions in North America. The French had a plan to occupy New England and thereafter the province of New York.

In 1689, King James II was deposed from the English throne. He was considered an unworthy king due to his unjust governing policy. Thomas Mortimer, an English soldier, statesman, and judge noted that "English subjects were injured during his [James'] reign and the king was enthusiastic to acts of bigotry."[53] After James II was removed from the throne, on April 11th, King William III of Orange and Queen Mary

---

50. Ibid. The militia law of Sir Edmund Andros was enacted one year before King William's War (1688–1698).

51. Drake, 1897, p. 12.

52. Ibid.

53. Thomas Mortimer, *A New History of England from the Earlier Accounts of Britain to the Ratification of the Peace of Versailles, 1763*, Wilson, 1766, p. 1.

II, daughter to James II, were crowned co-regents-the king and queen of England, Scotland, and Ireland. The ceremony was conducted at Westminster Abby by the bishop of London, Henry Compton. After officially assuming the throne of England, King William III indicated his disapproval of the policy observed by King Louis XIV of France. William III leveled several charges against Louis XIV, charging the King of France as a disturber of peace and prejudice to the trade and prosperity of England.[54] Moreover, William III charged Louis XIV "with going to war against the allies of England, in violation of the treaties concluded under the guaranty of the English crown." Additionally, Louis XIV was accused of having encroached upon the fishery of Newfoundland, invading the Caribbean Islands, forcibly seizing the provinces of New York and Hudson Bay, and continuing to use privateers to seize English ships. Further, the King of France was condemned for prohibiting the import of English goods. He was charged with persecuting English subjects on pretense of religion, contrary to expressed treaties and the law of nations. To make his actions even more egregious, Louis XIV sent armament to Ireland, in support of the rebels in that kingdom."[55] Due to these multiple charges, King William III officially declared war against the king of France on May 7, 1689.[56]

In 1690, the French in Canada were directly involved in the war between the English colonies in North America and Indians fighting in the same territory. French involvement was no longer a secret military mission or secret collaboration with Native Americans. Count Frontenac, a strong, French military man, conducted an expedition against the English. The war waged in 1690 also was fought in Europe between the French and English. As in Europe, the colonies in North America were involved. When the war was officially declared in England, Sir Edmund Andros was under arrest in Boston, Massachusetts, and Sir William Phipps was appointed royal governor in New England. Unlike Sir Andros, Sir Phipps did not rest. He raised a body of 700 men and marched against the French. Thomas Mortimer notes that

---

54. Thomas Mortimer, 1766, Ibid., p. 7.
55. Ibid., pp. 1–7.
56. Ibid.

in 1690, Sir William Phipps, with a fleet and land forces from New England, took the fort and town of Port Royal (since called Annapolis Royal), in the bay of Fundy, from whence the French had so greatly distressed [English] trade in America.[57]

Governor Phipps' expedition was conducted according to the mandate of King William III. Before declaring war, the King stressed openly his disappointment concerning the threat of commerce by the king of France. Similarly, Phipps lamented about the French privateers who attacked the English ships. In addition to retaliating against France, Phipps planned the fall of Canada because the English believed Canada was the center of all the evils which threatened the existence of the New England colonies.

The governor of Quebec, the Marquis of Vandreuil, sent French soldiers and Indians to attack the frontier towns in colonial New England.[58] The war which started in 1688 was ended by signing the Ryswick Peace Treaty on September 20, 1697. In Boston, the treaty took effect December, 1697, and in Quebec, in the peace treaty was put into action September, 1698.[59] After the signature of peace, Acadia was restored to France. Heretofore, Acadia had been temporarily occupied by the English. The Treaty of Ryswick was the first of such consensus observed for some time by the concerned parties in Europe in regard to their interests in colonial America.

After one year following the establishment of the militia law of Sir Edmund Andros in 1687, records indicate that a black servant of Colonel Tyng was in the expedition of 1686 under Captain Brackett. It was in this expedition that Captain Brackett and Colonel Tyng's slave were killed.[60] In 1689, when Major Benjamin Church was sent to defend

---

57. Mortimer, 1766, p. 27.

58. King William's war was fought also in the New England. When the French and Indians attacked the frontier towns of the colony, colonial governors in New England ordered the enlistment of able men to defend the colonies.

59. Daniel White Wells and Reuben Field Wells note that the peace of Ryswick, signed in September 20, 1697, was proclaimed in Boston in December and in Quebec, September 22, 1698.

60. Austin Jacobs Coolidge and John Brainard Mansfield, *A History and Description of New England, General, and Vermont*, vol. 1, A.J. Coolidge, 1859, p. 269. The Negro men

the territory of Maine, black soldiers and friendly Indians accompanied him. The Collections of the Maine Historical Society notes that

> Major Church of Massachusetts in 1689 saved the town and fort from destruction by his timely arrival by sea from Boston with several companies of troops, consisting of whites and blacks and friendly Indians from Cape Good.[61]

The number of blacks who participated in the expedition are not stated in the historical record. In like manner, the locations from where these enlisted black soldiers sailed were not revealed in the Collections of the Maine Historical Society. The best possible speculation is that they were recruited from Boston and the surrounding towns because Major Church embarked from that city. When Major Church organized his first expedition to the territory of Maine, he raised a hundred men from the Massachusetts colony. His mission was to protect the borders from the enemies. According to Samuel Adams Drake, the march to save the Maine territory began on August 28, 1689, and militiamen arrived at Falmouth, Maine, on Friday, September 20, 1689.[62] It took Major Church almost 22 days before his arrival in Falmouth. During his expedition, 21 men were killed and the others were wounded. On the enemy's side, the number of dead and wounded was not measured because they took with them killed and wounded Indians.

From the minutes of the Council of Massachusetts, in 1697 Addington Davenport, clerk of the Assembly, ordered the payment of £20 for a black man impressed for the war who died on board a ship. The payment was paid to the owner as disbursement for farming.[63] Such payment to the owners of slaves who served in colonial war was common. Lorenzo

---

belonging to Colonel Tyng and Captain Brackett were killed in the expedition against the Indians in 1686.

61. Major Benjamin Church had Negro soldiers and friendly Indians with him during the expedition of 1689. See *Collections of the Maine Historical Society*, 1896, p. 5.

62. Drake, 1897, p. 36.

63. See *Minutes of Council of Massachusetts*. Calendar of State Papers, Colonial Series. Great Britain, Public Record Office, 1905, p. 19.

CHAPTER 6

Johnston Greene recorded that in 1690, the general court paid £20.10 to a slave owner when he served the military in the place of his servant who died on board a ship while serving the military.[64] This slave probably died during the expedition organized by Sir William Phipps in 1690. These are a few records revealing the participations of blacks in King William's War.

The Militia Act of 1693 excluded blacks and Indians from militia services.[65] They were exempted as were the ministers, justices of the peace, and teachers. In the Watch Law of 1699, blacks and Indians were not excluded from performing those services. The Watch Law of 1699, section 2 stipulated that

> by the authority aforesaid, that all male persons in each town respectively of the sixteen years or upwards, being able of body, or having estate sufficient to hire, shall be liable to watch and ward, either in their own persons or by some other sufficient person or persons in their room, when duly warned to attend the same, except the members of the council, justices of the peace, members of the assembly for time being, the president, fellows and students at college, ministers, grammar school masters, the sheriff of each military company and troop for time being, the officers of the governor's troop of guards, and persons living miles from the place where the guard is kept.[66]

From the language of this law, blacks and Indians were not mentioned among the people who were listed among the exceptions to the law. The law more than likely was established due to the pressure of Queen Anne's War. The watch and warding (patrol) were ordered to monitor the French and their allies' movements in towns. The communal policing approach was utilized to prevent massacres and other violent crimes often committed by Indians during the war.

In 1702, after the death of King William III, Princess Anne of Denmark was crowned Queen of England. She was the second daughter of

---

64. See Green, 1968, p. 187.
65. See *The Charter and General Laws of the Colony and Province of Massachusetts Bay*, Boston, T.B. Wait and Company, 1814, pp. 263.
66. Ibid., p. 340.

James, Duke of York, who later became King of England with the royal title King James II.[67] Upon Princess Anne's coronation, she declared, as had her predecessor, to reduce France's power. Therefore, she carried a preparation for that end. In general, she followed the policy of King William III. Additionally, she assured her allies that she would defend the interests of England by soliciting her allies' help. When Queen Anne was crowned, the succession of Spain's King was influenced by the King of France, who desired the crowning of a French subject. On the contrary, Queen Anne was against any interference from France. From the onset of her reign, Queen Anne worked to diminish the power of France in Europe. So in concurrence with the Commons, she declared war against France and Spain. The possession of Spain by the French King was a troubling matter to the Queen of England. Queen Anne expressed her fearful concern about the political behavior of the French King. She noted that "the king of France had taken, and still keeps possession of great part of the Spanish dominions, exercising an absolute authority over all that monarch, having seized Milan and Spanish low countries by his armies, and made himself master of Cadie."[68] As both countries France and England fought for political power and commerce in Europe, the American colonies became involved indirectly. Unlike during the reign of King William III, the Canadian French and their Indian allies attacked the New Hampshire and Massachusetts colonies.

Queen Anne's War, which started in Europe, had an effect on the New England colonies whose inhabitants were the most victimized. This war in Europe was called the War of the Spanish Succession. In colonial New England where the French and Indians were active, the town of Deerfield was badly affected. Many people were massacred by the Indians. Samuel Adams Drake notes that the Deerfield settlement suffered catastrophic destruction. Therefore, Governor Joseph Dudley, who arrived in Boston in 1702, was obligated to defend the colony from the massacres committed by the French and their Indian allies. At the start of the war, blacks were not employed in public services. As the war

---

67. Mortimer, 1766, p. 123.
68. Ibid., p. 128.

continued in 1708; however, the general court of Massachusetts passed an Act to include blacks in public service. According to the Act Free Negroes, article 2,

> [A]ll free male Negroes or mulattoes of the age of sixteen years and upwards, able of body, in case of alarm, shall make their appearance at the parade of the military camps of any of the precincts wherein they dwell, and attend such services as the first commission officer of such company shall direct, during the time the company continues in arms on pain of forfeiting the sum of twenty shillings to the use of the company, or performing eight days labor as aforesaid, without reasonable excuse made and accepted for not attending of alarm.[69]

This incident is a palpable example indicating that during war time or any time there was the threat of war, colonial officials always valued the military services of black people. This was the first time in the colony that blacks were fined for not appearing at the parade location when called upon by government officials. This may be perceived as enforcing black men for military duty, when needed. The eight days of required service was more than likely one of the punishments enforced to those men who did not answer the call to perform military duty, pay the fine, or did not have money to pay the fine. Queen Anne's War ended with a series of 23 signings and conventions, most of which occurred at the peace treaty of Utrecht in the Netherlands on March 30, 1713. According to the treaty, France ceded Nova Scotia and Newfoundland to England.[70] Mortimer notes that "after the Treaty of Utrecht, the island of St. Christopher, Hudson Bay and a strait of that name ceded to Great Britain. On the other hand, Acadia with Port Royal and the fort occupied by the English were restored to the King of France. Moreover, the Canadian French were restricted from abusing the Five Nations of

---

69. *The Charter and General Laws of the Colony and Province of Massachusetts Bay*, Boston, T.B. Wait and Company,1814, p. 340.

70. Thomas F. Waters, Sarah Goodhue, John Wise, and Ipswich Historical Society, *The Society*, 1917, p. 41.

the Indians—Cayuga, Mohawk, Oneida, Onondaga, and Seneca—who became subjects of Great Britain."[71]

African Americans as Soldiers in the French and Indian Wars in Colonial Massachusetts

From the beginning of 1700, England and France faced continuous military and political conflicts. The effects of the political and economic disputes between these two countries impacted the political and military conditions in colonial America. Successions disputes, commercial interests, and territorial dominance caused many wars in America. The inter-continental wars between the French and the English, which started in 1688 during the accession of King William and Mary to the throne, continued during the reign of King William III and during Queen Anne's reign. In like manner, during the reign of King George, the French, supported by their Indian allies, committed many depredations in the English-occupied territories. During this era, diplomatic channels between the French and English toward the Indians were always maintained. Each group dialogued with the Indians in support of French and English interests, respectively. This was palpable during Queen Anne's War. Governor Joseph Dudley of Massachusetts and Governor Pierre de Riguad, Marquis de Vaudreuil-Cavagnial of Canada called upon the Indians to execute Queen Anne's War. Governor Vaudreuil, due to his marital connection with the Indians, was able to receive much support from them.

In Europe, the conflict started when the King of France interfered with the succession of the English monarch during the reign of King William III. While the French admired King James, the English did not. As a result, King James escaped to France, where he died. King William III, after coming to the throne, formed many alliances against the French.[72] His rule was short, and he died March 8, 1702.[73] Queen

---

71. Mortimer, 1766, p. 258.
72. George Sheldon notes that King William of England formed an alliance with Austria and other power against France. See Sheldon, 1895, p. 283.
73. Ibid.

CHAPTER 6

Anne, his successor, continued the same volatile political approach toward the king of France.

Queen Anne's War (1702–1713), which started in Europe, also was fought in colonial New England for the control of territory and commercial interests. This war raised questions in this researcher's mind regarding colonial officials' stance on the role Africans and African Americans could, and eventually would, play in the colonies when there was the threat of war or when the colonies were engaged in war. Did colonial officials overlook exclusionary militia laws which barred black men from military duty? Did colonial officials call upon men of color for military support? Did black men fight for their masters? Did military officers take with them their black servants or slaves to theaters of war? Did slave owners lend their black servants and slaves for military hire? All these questions cannot be answered in a vacuum. Recorded war and military data reveal that free Africans and slaves did protect lives and properties and defended the internal integrity of the colonies. The collected data fills a great void in easily accessible historical knowledge concerning the role of free blacks and slaves in colonial America. In short, mining the truth concerning the full contributions men of color made to the welfare and safety of colonial New England more than satisfies this researcher's quest for answers to questions that have plagued him for years. The path of this research has led to the names of black men who, heretofore, have been shrouded in obscurity.

During Queen Anne's War, the slave of Samuel Lynde was among the defenders of peace. Lorenzo Johnston Greene says that Lynde's slave was a cook aboard a privateer on which his master served.[74] In the town of Deerfield, where the war caused great devastation, Primus, a Negro, was on the list of those who fought in the Deerfield Meadows, 1703–4.[75] In the same town, Frank Negro, the slave of Mr. William, was killed.[76] George Sheldon, who recorded the death of Frank Negro, did not clarify if he was killed on the battleground. It is noteworthy that the inclusive militia policy was observed in Deerfield. The city was al-

---

74. The slave of Samuel Lynde of Boston served in 1702 aboard a privateer according to Lorenzo Greene Johnston. See *The Negro in Colonial New England*, 1969, p. 121.
75. See Sheldon, 1895, p. 298.
76. Ibid, p. 306.

ways attacked by the Indians and the Canadian French. To illustrate, in 1704, Major Hertel de Rouville and his Indian militiamen burnt houses and took the people of Deerfield into captivity. During the attack of the town, Reverend John Williams was victimized horribly. His two children and his African American servant were murdered.[77] After the Indians killed Williams' children and servant, they took Williams into captivity.

In 1707, free blacks were required to respond to the alarm when called by the commanders of the militia of their precincts. Those who failed to respond were fined 25 shillings.[78] This Act was passed during Queen Anne's War, and it was under the obligations of the war that the officials made such a decision. Although it is difficult to collect names of African Americans who served during Queen Anne's War due to the recording system of the time, this Act remains concrete support indicating that African Americans were called upon to suppress the enemies. New laws and/or changes to old laws were established when social problems arose. Such laws were intended to remedy conditions that warranted jurisprudence or when there was a need to bring about changes. Laws during war times have the same effect as those enacted during peace time. As to the act of 1707 noted above, Article 2 of An Act for the Regulating of Free Negroes reveals explicitly that free Africans were accounted as defenders of the colony even though they were prohibited from attending military training.

During Queen Anne's War, African Americans were among soldiers who were stationed at the garrison at Castle William. From the acts and the resolves, public and private, of the province of Massachusetts Bay, Indians, Negroes, and mulattoes were not allowed to receive red coats reserved for the soldiers.[79] The reason why colonial officials denied Indi-

---

77. Henry White, *Indian Battles: With Incidents in the Early History of New England*. D.W. & Co. 1859, p. 88.

78. See *The Charters and General Laws of the Colony of Massachusetts Bay*, published by the order of the General Court, T.B. Wait and Company, 1814, p. 386. The first article of "An Act for the Regulating of Free Negroes" stipulated that they do work equivalent to training such as repairing highways and cleaning the streets. Article 2 allowed them to serve in the militia or military company in case of war or an attack from the enemies.

79. *The Acts and Resolves, Public and Private, of the Province of the Massachusetts Bay*, John Henry Clifford, Wright & Porter, Printers to the State, 1902, p. 364.

ans, Negroes, and mulattoes the red coats privilege is unknown. And yet, while colonial officials denied these groups the honor to receive the red coats, the servants of the captains were allowed to receive the coats. Apparently, the servants of captains had the same privilege as the English to wear red coats because they went to war at the request of the said captains.[80] It was common for high-ranking officers to receive payment for the military service performed by their servants. The number of servants each captain commissioned was not mentioned in the Act. In addition, the racial make-up of the servants is unknown.[81] Queen Anne's War ended by the Treaty of Utrecht signed March 30th, 1713, between Great Britain and France. After the signature of the treaty, the King of France ceded the Bay and Straits of Hudson, the Island of St. Christopher, Nova Scotia, and Newfoundland to the Queen of Great Britain.[82] On the other hand, the king of France was granted the liberty of fishing on the Island of Breton and on other islands in the Gulf of St. Lawrence. Dennis Ambrose O'Sullivan notes that "the English secured the fur trade of the Hudson Bay after the signing the Utrecht Treaty."[83] The same treaty gave the King of France the right to fortify French territory. The French built a fortress at Louisburg in Cape Breton or L'Isle Royale.[84]

During the Indian incursions in 1725, African Americans were active in the militia of the colony. Research reveals that Nero Benson, a black man, was enlisted that the same year. According to Duana Hamilton Hurd, Nero Benson was enlisted as a trumpeter in the company of Isaac Clark's troop in Framington, Massachusetts. Apparently, Benson was a member of a Colonial Era militia that comprised a marching band most likely made up of fifers, drummers, trumpeters, and pipers. Such bands acted as their European predecessors. The bands served to regulate daily

---

80. Ibid.

81. Duana H. Hurd notes that Nero Benson was a trumpeter in Captain Isaac Clark's troop in 1725.

82. Abiel Holmes, *The Annals of America: From the Discovery by Columbus in Year 1492, to Year 1826*, vol. 2, Hillard and Brown, 1829, p. 570.

83. Dennis A. O'Sullivan, *Government in Canada*, The Lawbook Exchange, Ltd., 1887, p. 253.

84. William Douglass, *A Summary, Historical and Political, of the First Planting, Progressive Improvement, and Present State of the British Settlement in North America*, printed, London, reprinted Boston, New England, 1755, for R. Baldin.

life in military camps, give signals or pass orders in battle, and boost the morale of soldiers during wartime. Benson was the servant to Reverend Mr. Swift. According to the narrative of William Barry, Nero Benson performed militia duties for three weeks. The muster roll of the company of troops under the command of Captain Isaac Clark shows sentinels and troop members were on duty from August 2 to September 18, 1725. Nero Benson was listed under the sentinels, a separate roster from the troops.[85] Another author who mentions the military service of Nero Benson is Josiah Howard Temple. In addition to Benson's military duties, Temple notes that Benson was a religious man. He was a member of Reverend Swift's Church. In 1735, he freely joined a different church in Hopkinton.[86] Just as previously cited authors have said, Lorenzo Johnston Greene mentions that a servant of Reverend Swift was a trumpeter in the company of Captain Isaac in 1725.[87] In Framingham, even though the town was not subjected to the attack of the French and Indians, men were sent to protect the frontier. It is unknown whether or not African Americans took part in the defense of the frontiers. Before the official announcement of King George's War in 1744, the King of England declared war against the King of Spain and France in the West Indies. After the declaration of war, the English Crown requested military contributions from the colonies in North America. Southern and Northern New England colonies were obligated to furnish men for military duty. Among the soldiers enlisted for the expeditions against the French and Spanish West Indies were African Americans.

African Americans in the Expedition of 1740 in West Indies

In 1739, the King of England declared war against the King of Spain's interest in the West Indies, a region in the North Atlantic Ocean in the Caribbean that includes island countries and three major archipelagos. England's call for military assistance was the first time in the history

---

85. William Barry, *A History of Framingham, Massachusetts*, J. Munroe and Company, 1847, p. 63.
86. Josiah H. Temple, *History of Framingham, Massachusetts: Early Known as Danforth's Farms, 1640—1880, with a Genealogical Register*, Town of Framingham, 1887, p. 235.
87. See Green, 1968, p. 187.

of America that men were engaged in war outside their own colonies. Before exploring the history of the inclusion of African Americans in this expedition, it is pertinent to investigate the reason the King of England declared war against the King of Spain and attacked the French colonies in the same region. France was an ally to Spain in the execution of wars against England's interests in colonial America.

With respect to the English expedition in the West Indies, the war of 1739 between the Kings of England and Spain was based on commercial interests. Charles Knight, an English author, wrote that Spain and England were commercial enemies for a century and a half. As commercial competitors, the two countries executed aggressive policies to undermine the progress of each other. Possibly, the Spanish did not allow the English to make profits from their domains. When the English attempted to evade the control of the Guarda Costa, conflict emerged between England and Spain.

Due to the harassment and unjust confiscations of English goods subject to the Spanish guards, England declared war against Spain. According to the Society of the Colonial Wars, the Spanish Guarda Costa committed many depredations against English ships in violation of the Law of Nations.[88] The Kings of England and Spain had signed a maritime treaty of friendship, but the treaty was not observed by the King of Spain. The Guarda Costas acted arbitrarily to the English. These Spanish guard ships were entrusted with the search of commercial ships entering the Spanish domain. But according to English writers, the Guarda Costa employed cruel and oppressive methods upon the English.

The Crown of England valued commercial superiority upon the water highway. Therefore, hoping to destroy his competitor, the King requested from his colonies in America the enlistment of men for the expedition against the Spanish West Indies. Among the volunteers were African Americans. Various documents verify that African Americans served on ships as well as in the field. In the publication, issue 5 of the *Society of the Colonial War*, names of African Americans who served on

---

88. See Walter K. Watkins, *Massachusetts in the Expedition under Admiral Vernon in 1740–41 to the West Indies. Year-Book of the Commonwealth of Massachusetts for 1899*, Publication No. 5, 1899, p. 66.

the ship are mentioned. Similarly, those enlisted on the muster rolls are recorded. According to the speech made by Governor Shirley of Massachusetts to the General Court on the Expedition of West Indies, 1,000 African Americans and 2,400 whites enlisted under Captain John Winslow.[89] These soldiers sailed to the Island of Cuba which ended in a failed expedition. According to New England historians, few people returned from the expedition due to tropical diseases. Justin Winsor, a local historian of the town of Duxbury, wrote that among 500 Massachusetts men sent to the expedition in West Indies, only 50 returned. The information collected from William Douglass, a Massachusetts historian, relates that multiple thousands of inhabitants in the colony were carried off to the Spanish West Indies during the war.

In 1740, when the war against the domains of the King of Spain started, African Americans were included. Among the men commanded by the Honorable Spencer Phipps from July to November 20, 1740, we found that Cuffe Negro was enlisted as a sentinel. Cuffe was the servant of His Honorable Jeffrey York.[90] The men under the command of Honorable Spencer Phipps enlisted for the defense of the coast. On the muster roll of His Majesty Snow's *Prince Orange* dated November 26, 1740 under the command of Captain Edward Tyng, Sylhax and Syphax, both African Americans, are listed foremost for that expedition. In addition, John, a Negro, is a foremost who served in the war. Sylhax Negro also served in the company of Edward Tyng in 1741. He was enlisted on November 12, and his service ended on February 10. His term of service was three months. For the military duties performed by this African American, he was paid £6 monthly. As he spent three months in the war, he was paid a total of £19.10.[91] On the other hand, Syphax Negro who served in 1742, in the company of Captain Edward Tyng, was paid

---

89. See Speech of Governor Shirley to the General Court. Publication, issue 5. Society of Colonial Wars in the Commonwealth of Massachusetts. Publisher not identified, 1899, pp. 120–121.

90. For the information of Cent'l Cuffe Negro, see *Muster Roll of Castle William, The Honorable Spencer Phips, Commander, July to Nov 20, 1740, Year-Book of the Society of Colonial Wars in the Commonwealth of Massachusetts for 1899*, Publication No. 5, 1899, p. 98.

91. Ibid. See *Muster Roll of His Majesties* Snow Prince of Orange *Commencing from 26 November 1740*, p. 98. See also the Proceedings of the American Antiquarian Society, 1902, p. 297.

£8 monthly. He spent three months in the war and was paid a total of £21.8.8.⁹² These Negroes received the same salary as the English. Scipio was enlisted in the same expedition as Syphax. Scipio was one of the common names given to the Africans by their masters in New England. As Scipio had only one name, he was likely an African American.⁹³ If he were an Englishman, he would have a first and last name. Scipio, a servant, was enlisted in the company of Captain Edward Tyng listed on the muster roll of the company of His Majesty's service. Captain Edward Tyng was commissioned by Governor Jonathan Belcher as captain of his Majesty's South and North Batteries and Fortifications in Boston on April 16, 1740. He was also the successor to Captain Cyptian Southack after he resigned as commander of the Province Snow's *Prince of Orange*, the first sloop purchased during the administration of Governor Belcher. The *Snow Prince of Orange* was used for the execution of the war against the Spanish and the French.

According to Waldo Lincoln, the *Snow Prince of Orange* was used to patrol the coast of the colonies. This sloop was built in the ship yard of Benjamin Hollowell, the owner. The governor by the order of the General Court of Massachusetts commissioned Hollowell to build the ship. It was purchased at the value of £6,500. It was armed with sixteen carriage guns with a ball of six pounds. It had also many sword guns. From 1740 to 1742, the sloop cruised from Boston to Virginia. Sometimes, Captain Tyng went for five to six weeks patrolling the water highway. African Americans enlisted under him went with him. In 1742, Governor William Shirley of Massachusetts traveled aboard the Snow *Prince of Orange* to the West Indies. In 1744, the sloop patrolled the water at Annapolis Royal.⁹⁴

In 1745, Governor Shirley organized the expedition for the capture of the French fort at Louisburg, which has been discussed during the discussion of the impact of African Americans in New Hampshire and Connecticut. As in other colonies, African Americans were also enlisted

---

92. For Syphax Negro, see *Muster roll of the company in His Majesty's service under the command of Edward Tyng on board the* Snow Prince of Orange, 1742. Proceedings of the American Antiquarian Society, American Antiquarian Society, 1902, p. 296.

93. Ibid., p. 295.

94. Waldo Lincoln, *The Province Snow* Prince of Orange, Press of C. Hamilton, 1901, pp. 3, 50–53.

in Massachusetts. From 1744 until the end of the war in 1763, African Americans defended the Massachusetts colony. They were enlisted as soldiers and sentinels. When the governor called upon volunteers, African Americans responded to the call. Some of them possibly served as substitutes for their masters. Others were servants to high-ranking military officers.

William Loren Katz notes that Abijah Prince served in His Majesty's service during King George's War.[95] Prince was one of the most noted African servants in New England. According to George Sheldon, Prince was born about 1706. Shelton did not record the town where Prince was born. Sheldon believed that Prince was brought to Northfield from Wallingford, Connecticut, by Reverend Benjamin Doolittle, a minister of the place. After the death of Reverend Doolittle, Sheldon believed that Prince was freed and received real estate from the reverend. In 1751, Prince was a land owner in three divisions of Northfield. He kept his share of land until in 1782 when he sold it. As a humble and honorable man, Prince also received land from Deacon Samuel Field, one of the grantees of Guilford, Vermont. Before his death, Deacon Field promised a hundred acres of land to Prince. Upon Field's death, his son David honored the promise made by his father by presenting the hundred acres to Prince. The former slave remained in Guilford with his family until 1764. After amassing much land, he became one of the grantees of Sunderland, Vermont. He was listed in the charter and drew an equal share as other grantees of the town.[96]

In 1743, the Massachusetts colony had a large number of Africans, as noted by Prince Hall, who died in 1795. It is possible that many of them served in the French and Indian War, which ravaged the colony during the mid-18th century. Hall did not record the exact number of Africans who lived in Massachusetts during the period in question. In Massachusetts, militiamen and soldiers protected the frontier towns, the forts, and harbors, and others were fighters. Additionally, a great

---

95. For military service of Abijah Prince, see William Loren Katz, *The Black West*, Harlem Moon/Broadway Books, 1971, p. 24.
96. Shelton, 1896, pp. 898–900.

number served as seamen and privateers. African Americans were assigned the same military duties as white men were assigned. Moreover, the repairs and the constructions of forts were parts of the duties entrusted to the military.

Names of African Americans continue to be mined from historical records to prove that men of color made outstanding contributions to the protection and safety of American colonies. On His Majesty's muster roll of the company under the command of Lieutenant Elisha Hawley dated from December 1747 to March 1748 at Fort Massachusetts, Negro Peter Attucks of Leicester was among those who defended liberty during the war. Attucks was the slave of John White.[97] According to local historians in Massachusetts, Fort Massachusetts was built for the defense and protection of the western part of the colony against Indians. Therefore, soldiers and militiamen garrisoned at the fort were entrusted with patrolling the area, all the while anticipating attacks from enemies. As a soldier at the fort, Attucks performed patrol duties as did other soldiers. Author Grace Greylock Niles (1912) writes that at the request of Colonel Stephen Stoddart, a hundred soldiers were stationed at the fort. Niles stipulates that the duties of the soldiers at Fort Massachusetts were to patrol the area leading to Lake Champlain, Portsooac, and Fort Dummer on the Connecticut River. A similar view was noted by Hamilton Child. According to him, Fort Massachusetts was built for the protection of the western frontiers of Massachusetts from Indians incursions. In the town of Woodstock, Ceasar Negro, the slave of Hezekiah Ward, was a soldier listed in the company of Lieutenant Elisha Hawley.[98] He, too, was garrisoned at Fort Massachusetts like Moses Roper Attucks.

In 1745, during the expedition for the capture of Louisbourg, Priamus, servant of Captain John Boyden was enlisted as a musician. Priamus Lew served under the township of Dracut, the town to which had immigrated from Groton. Members of the Lew family were

---

97. Grace G. Niles, *The Hoosac Valley: Its Legends and Its History*. G.P. Putnam's Sons, 1912, pp. 532–533.
98. Ibid.

reputed musicians in Dracut. Lew's son, Barzillai, was enlisted in the military during the Revolutionary War. He was at the battle of Bunker Hill.[99] Further information on Barzillai Lew will be discussed in the next chapter.

In 1749, Attucks and Ceasar were under the command of Captain Ephraim Williams, Jr. at Fort Massachusetts. Captain Williams established his headquarters at Fort Massachusetts where he was in charge from March 7, 1745 to 1755. Captain Williams had 56 men in his charge from September 11, 1748 to March 11, 1749. Two African Americans were numbered among the 56. Moses Peter Attucks and Ceasar Negro were re-enlisted in the 1749 expedition. Attucks was the slave of John White at the time of militia services.[100] Historian Arthur Latham Perry believed that Cesar Negro, the servant of Hezekiah Ward, did military service for the account of his master. He also noted that Moses Peter Attucks did military service on behalf of his master. His opinion was that the names of the masters of these two blacks were in the margin of the muster rolls over the names of the servants.[101] During the French and Indian War, slaves and servants frequently were enlisted as substitutes to their masters. In return, a bounty was paid to the owners of such men who served in the war.

In 1755, before the King of England issued a formal declaration of war that would become the Seven Years War, in the town of Holland, Massachusetts, Samuel Dearing enlisted in the company of Captain Ebenezer Moulton of Brimfield, Massachusetts. The slave and captain served during the expedition of Crown Point. Dearing was faithful to his master and served his master's family for many years. Dearing died when he was about 102 years old.[102] Possibly, Dearing accompanied his master in the Crown Point expedition, as was the case for many military officers of the time. They always brought with them their African servants to the war. In Ipswich, Massachusetts, in the same year, Scippio

---

99. Silas R. Coburn, *History of Dracut, Massachusetts*, Press of the Courier-Citizen Company, 1922, p. 334.
100. Ibid.
101. Arthur L. Perry, *Origins in Williamson*. C. Scribner's Sons, 1894, pp. 232–34.
102. Martin Lovering and Mrs. Ursula N. MacFarland Chase, *History of Holland, Massachusetts*. Tuttle Company, 1915, pp. 686–87.

Wood was enlisted in the company of John Whipple of Hamlet.[103] Due to his name, there is a reason to believe that he was an African slave. During the slave era, many slaves were named Scippio. It does not seem that the name Scippio was given to the English.

In 1756, during the Seven Years War, African Americans were called upon to defend liberty. The French were disliked in the Massachusetts colony. William J. Smith, who wrote *A Review of the Military Operation in North America*, says that the French were jealous of the growth of the English colonies in America and started extending their frontiers.[104] The French and Indian War, which started in Virginia, was fought in New England, as well. During the Seven Years War, a different approach was taken regarding the execution of conflict. The objective of the war was no longer just to fight the French and win the war. Now the war efforts were committed to terminate the domination of the French in colonial America. Hoping to terminate French domination, military officers observed inclusive militia policy. Indians and Africans (free and slaves) were recruited for this new aim. From 1756 to 1763, many towns in New England furnished men for the war effort. Likely, the defense of the colony had become everyone's duty.

During the Seven Years War, in the little town of Deerfield where Indians killed many people, the local militia was inclusive. African Americans were among the soldiers who suppressed the enemies. George Sheldon, author of *Negro Slavery in Old Deerfield*, recorded that Cesar, servant of Timothy Childs, was a soldier in the French and Indian War several times. He fought in two wars defending his master's country.[105] At the time of his enlistment, Cesar was still in bondage. But for the honor of freedom and the love of his master's land, he fought against enemies who were a constant threat to the Massachusetts colony. The researcher of this present work did not find any promises of freedom

---

103. Romans F. Waters, Sarah Goodhue, and John Wise, *Ipswich in the Massachusetts Bay Colony*, Ipswich Historical Society, 1917, p. 173.

104. William J. Smith, *A Review of the Military Operation in North America, &c.*, New England, New Haven, 1758, p. 7.

105. George Sheldon, "Negro Slavery in Old Deerfield," *The Bay State Monthly*, John N. McClintock and Company, 1893, p. 53.

which would motivate Cesar to enlist in the Deerfield militia. It appears that Ceasar enlisted because of his conscience.

In addition to Cesar, servant to Timothy Childs, another Cesar, servant to Lieutenant Jona Hoyt, was a soldier in the French and Indian War in 1755.[106] As his master was a local lieutenant of the militia, possibly this second man named Cesar enlisted by his master. Cesar was a common name for African bondsmen during this era. Samuel Childs had a servant named Cesar who, too, was a soldier in the said war.[107] Colonel Ebenezer Hinsdale of Deerfield made a contribution to the war by sending his servant to fight for the defense of his country.[108] Religious authorities also sent their servants to war. Reverend Jonathan Ashley of Deerfield enlisted his servant, Titus, in the Seven Years War. Titus served from 1754 to 1757.[109] While African Americans in Deerfield were baptized, research has yet to discover evidence that Titus was connected to the church, a matter that was significant in the lives of some servants. For example, Cesar, a servant to Lieutenant Jona Hoyt, was baptized on July 26, 1741, and there is evidence that Cesar, a servant of Timothy Childs, was also baptized. George Sheldon identified him as a Christian soldier.[110]

A similar African American resident of Deerfield who served in the French and Indian War was Cato. George Sheldon notes that Cato served in one of the expeditions of the French and Indian War.[111] Possibly, Cato served in the Seven Years War because that was the last war fought between the French and the English. Cato's mother, Jinny Cole, was kidnapped from Africa and brought to Boston by Minister Ashley. After spending time in Boston, she was sold to Deerfield. Even though Jinny was cared for, she never forgot her daily life in Africa. Due to the attention her master gave to his child, Cato, Jinny Cole was thankful and served her mistress accordingly. It was common during the colonial era for slaves to have loyal masters who treated them well.

---

106. Ibid.
107. Ibid.
108. Ibid.
109. Ibid., p. 54.
110. George Sheldon, *A History of Deerfield, Massachusetts: The Times when the People by Whom It Was Settled, Unsettled and Resettled*, vol. 2, Deerfield, MA: Press of E. A. Hall & Company, 1896, pp. 894, 896.
111. Sheldon, 1893, p. 55.

CHAPTER 6

In the little town of Hingham, Massachusetts, blacks fought the French and Indians. In the company of Captain Edward Ward, Primus Cobb and Flanders were the two African Americans enlisted as privates.[112] In the town of Crofton, George Gire, a Negro, was enlisted as a private in 1761 under the command of Captain William Paige. This African American was paid £30.00 for his pension by the order of the General Court of Massachusetts.[113] From the town of Canton, during the expedition of Nova Scotia in 1755, Mingo, the black servant of Hector Royall, was enlisted.[114] The servant of Hector Royall was enlisted in the company of Captain James Endicott. In the town of Malden, Jacob Lynde served with his servant Titus, Negro in 1760.[115] In Newton, Quartus, a Negro imported from Barbados, served in the service of the king of England in the war.[116]

In 1758, after many military defeats, the Massachusetts General Court raised a large number of men for the expedition against Ticonderoga, Crown Point, and all of Canada. According to Thomas Hutchinson, 7,000 men were raised in the colony of Massachusetts for the expeditions.[117] In the number of Massachusetts soldiers, African Americans were included in the military round-up. The enlisted included Thomas Ashley, Elihab Fish, and Eleazer Fuller, among others.[118] In 1759, during the expedition of Canada, Fortunatus Burnee, an

---

112. Edward T. Bouve, *History of the Town of Hingham, Massachusetts*, vol. 1, Published by the Town, 1893, p. 265. See also Benjamin Quarles, *Black Mosaic*, Univ. of Massachusetts Press, 1988, pp. 33–34.

113. He received the pension for two years. See *The Acts and Resolve, Public and Private, of the Province of the Massachusetts Bay*, 1922. See also Frederick Clifford Peirce, *History of Crofton, Worcester County, Massachusetts*, Press of C. Hamilton, 1878, p. 100.

114. Daniel T. V. Huntoon, *History of the Town of Canton, Norfolk County, Massachusetts*, J. Wilson and Son, 1893, pp. 613, 616.

115. Deloraine P. Corey, *The History of Malden, Massachusetts 1633–1785*, The author, 1898, p. 427.

116. Samuel F. Smith, *History of Newton, Massachusetts, Town and City*. American Logotype Company, 1880, p. 538.

117. Thomas Hutchinson, *The History of... Massachusetts Bay*. Crown in Cornhill, 1828, pp. 68–69.

118. See *Return of the Men Enlisted and Impressed for His Majesty's Service in the Intended Expedition against Canada, 28 April to May 2, 1758*, Massachusetts Historical Society. Other soldiers enlisted were: Samuel Gilbert, Obed Hatch, Peter Isac, Benjamin Mingo, Daniel Myrick, Samuel Perry, Jr. Joshua Nye, John Richards, John Swift and Jabez Tupper.

African American, was enlisted under the command of General Jeffrey Amherst and Colonel Abraham Williams. Burnee was a man of Grafton, Worcester County.[119]

Dan, a Negro, was in the King's service from 1760 to 1761.[120] John Rowe records in his diary that Cato, a Negro man, was on board a warship in 1769. In the city of Sudbury, Massachusetts, Richard Heard petitioned to the General Assembly for the service of his slave during the French and Indian War. The General Assembly granted Heard's request, so his slave was enlisted in the company of Captain John Nixon. Heard's servant was taken to Deerfield where he became sick. According to the petition of Heard, his black servant took a horse belonging to Heard to the war. His claim for the damage was 25 shillings. The money was to be paid to Colonel John Noyes on behalf of the petitioner.[121] In the town of Abington, Plymouth, David, a colored man and son of Anthony Dwight, served in the French and Indian War. David was killed during his military service. In 1758, the Massachusetts colony had a large number of militiamen. According to Hurd, 6,925 men were fighting against the French and Indians. The expenses for the war were £4,000,000. The colony received £3,000,000 as reimbursement from England.[122] During the French and Indian War, the governors of Massachusetts were the pioneers. They always planned the expeditions for other New England colonies. As to the status of David and his father Anthony Dwight, the author who mentioned their military services failed to indicate if they were free men or not. However, it is noteworthy that there is no indication that the men served on the account of a master. In addition, there are no indications that they belonged to any masters.

The enlistment of blacks in colonial wars was also noted by Jeremy Belknap, founder of the Massachusetts Historical Society. According to

---

119. Frederick Clifton, *History of Crofton, Worcester, Massachusetts: From Its Early Settlement by the Indians in 1647 to the Present Time, 1879, Including the Genealogies of Seventy-Nine of the Olden Families*, Part I, Press of C. Hamilton, 1879, p. 100.

120. Lucius R. Paige, *History of Hardwick, Massachusetts: with a Genealogical Register*, Houghton, Miffin, 1883, p. 267.

121. See Alfred Sereno Hudson, *The History of Sudbury, Massachusetts, 1638—1889*, R.H. Blodpett, 1889, p. 143.

122. Duane H. Hurd, *History of Plymouth County, Massachusetts*, J.W. Lewis & Company, 1884, p. 466.

him, before 1763, "there were many blacks in colonial Massachusetts, but many of them perished during the two preceding wars. Many of them enlisted either into the army or on board vessels of war."[123] Possibly, the two wars to which Belknap refers are King George's War (1744–1748) and the French and Indian War (1756–1763). The participation of blacks in the French and Indian War was also mentioned in the Collections of the Maine Historical Society. According to society record, Sir William Pepperrell, after the conquest of Louisbourg, maintained a splendid barge "with a black crew dressed in uniform in 1759."[124] The Seven Years' War ended with the surrender of Canada and the great West Basin to Great Britain in 1763.[125] In addition to soldiering, African Americans were appointed to minor offices in colonial Massachusetts.

African Americans as Civilian Officers in Colonial Boston

In colonial Massachusetts, there were many minor local officers such as the selectmen, fence viewers, deer-reeves, hog-reeves, and chimney sweepers. Among these civilian officers, the selectmen were the most noted in the local community and were empowered with legislative and executive power. As legislators of the towns, they made rules and regulations for the management of the local government. Construction of bridges, roads, and schools was under the jurisdiction of the selectmen of the towns. In addition, right to residency in the town was under the control of the selectmen. In their capacity as executive officers, the selectmen had the power to appoint other minor civil officers at the meeting of the freemen and other holders in the city.

There are at least two questions that warrant being asked, especially given the many roles that black people played in varying capacities in New England. During the early years in colonial Massachusetts, were there any blacks appointed as minor officers by the selectmen of the towns? If there were, in which capacity were they appointed? During

---

123. For the quote of Dr. Jeremy Belknap, see *The Collections of the Massachusetts Historical Society*, The Society, 1835, p. 190.

124. For the quote on the black crew of Sir William Pepperrell, see *Collections of the Maine Historical Society*, Vol. VIII, 1876, p. 214.

125. Perry, 1894, p. 75.

the Colonial Era, a large number of free Africans as well as slaves resided in Boston. Therefore, this discussion focuses more on the same town for the collection of data concerning the appointment of free Africans in public service.

The questions asked above will be answered through the consultation of the data from the records of Boston and other towns. Based upon the *Early Records of Boston*, the first recorded civilian functionaries of color were chimney sweepers. These employees were appointed by the selectmen of Boston at the meeting of the free holders and other inhabitants. The record shows that the first chimney sweepers of color were appointed in 1689. From 1690 to 1693, among the appointed chimney sweepers, there was an African American.

In 1686 and 1687, the selectmen of Boston were ordered to appoint chimney officers. In their vote, local officials prohibited the supervision of the chimneys by persons who were not appointed by the selectmen.[126] The chimney sweeper was an appointive officer or government functionary during the Colonial Era. In Connecticut, for example, Isaac William Stuart notes that the first chimney sweeper of Hartford appointed in 1639 was a town functionary. He also notes that the chimney sweeper's "duty over chimney was municipal." The first chimney sweeper in Hartford was John Gunnings. In Massachusetts, the control of the chimney more than likely was under the jurisdiction of the selectmen from 1653 to 1654, after the Great Fire that caused major damage in the town. Consequently, fire regulations were enacted the same year. According to Justin Winsor and Clarence F. Jewett, in 1653 and 1654, an order was passed requiring "every householder to provide a ladder of twelve foot long, with a good large swab at the end of it to reach the roof of a house to quench fire." This was the first time in the history of Boston that there is a regulation for the management of extinguishing fire. In addition, people were prevented from carrying fire from house to house in an uncovered pan.

From the Report of the Record Commissioners of the City of Boston, Jeremiah, a black man, was appointed to the office of chimney sweeper 1689.[127] Between 1689 and 1690, colonial officials did not exclude

---

126. Boston Records, *1660–1701, Rockwell and Churchill*, City printing, 1881, p. 191.
127. *Report of the Record Commissioners of the City of Boston*, vol. 7, 1881, p. 197.

African bondsmen from being appointed to or chosen for the position of chimney sweepers. It was in a public meeting of freeholders and other inhabitants of the city of Boston that the selectmen chose "Jeremy, Negro" as a chimney sweeper. He was the sweeper for the year 1690.[128] Jeremy was the first black appointee to a minor local office in colonial Massachusetts. In 1693, "Jeremie, Negro" appeared as chimney sweeper.[129] In the Report of the Record Commissioners of the City of Boston, Jeremie was recorded as "Jeremiah, Negro," the chimney sweeper. It is unknown if these two names pertain to one person, but with different spellings. Nonetheless, Jeremy is possibly a free Negro since he is not identified as being enslaved. Thus, as a free black man, he would have some of the same privileges as white men in the colony before and up to the 1690s. During the selection of Jeremie or Jeremiah, other officers were chosen; Joseph Payes, Richard Drew, and John Stride were Caucasian chimney sweepers. A black man named Will, who belonged to Mr. Andrew, was chosen at the meeting of the selectmen, the freeholders, and other inhabitants of the city as chimney sweeper.[130] Since Will did not possess his freedom, it is likely that the salary he earned would have been given to the man who owned him.

It is difficult to come up with the correct assertions as to why the selectmen chose these people of African descent as chimney sweepers. Similarly, it is unknown why these blacks joined the meeting of the selectmen, the freeholders, and other inhabitants of Boston. Were they considered citizens during this period? Were they allowed to hold minor positions in the local government? Was the meeting of the selectmen and freeholders open to blacks during the colonial period in Massachusetts?

These questions are best answered according to the form and character of the meeting. From the records of the meeting of the selectmen and freeholders, the assumption is that men of color could participate in meetings and hold minor local offices during this period. The selection of these blacks in the meetings, without noted objections from

---

128. Ibid., p. 200.
129. Ibid., p. 205.
130. Ibid., p. 214.

Caucasians, reveals they were treated with some consideration during the formative years of Boston. With respect to the employment in the city government, perhaps there were blacks who performed some other duties which were not recorded. It is possible that there was recorded information of the employment of people of African descent in minor local offices in colonial Massachusetts, but those records have been lost or destroyed.

A similar appointment of a black man as chimney sweeper happened in 1715 or earlier. From the *Records Relating to the Earlier History of Boston, Volume 11, Part 1884*, "Tobie, Negro" was permitted by the selectmen of the city to be employed as chimney sweeper. The approval reads as follows: "the selectmen do approve of Mr. Cookson's Negro man named Tobie to be employed under him for sweeping of chimneys in this town. Sweeping be limited to the grounds of the North Military Company as they are now grounded."[131] The approval of Tobie's employment shows that he was hired to perform public services in the account of his master. The involvement of the selectmen in the hiring of a chimney sweeper tells us that there were some requirements set before any person would be appointed to this position.

Before the employment of Tobie, Negro on September 26, 1704, historical facts reveal that the selectmen of Boston ordered Tim Wodsworth to employ many free Negroes for highway maintenance at his convenience. On July 16, 1707, the employment of Negroes for the maintenance of the highways became a law. The order enacted by the selectmen of Boston is as follows: "The selectmen do order & assign each free Negro & Mulatto man of this town forthwith to attend and perform four days labor, of repairing the streets and highways which is to be part of their services for this present year, (reserving their remaining service until further order) and that constable Samuel Salter do warn them to attend said service at such time and place as they shall appoint."[132] Highway services were considered by Boston officials to be the equivalence of

---

131. For the quote of the Selectmen of Boston, see *Records Relating to the Early History of Boston (Mass.) Registry Dept. A Report of the Record of the City of Boston, Containing the Records of Boston Selectmen, 1701 to 1715*, No. 39, 1884, p. 239.

132. Ibid., pp. 59–60, 73.

military duty. In 1708, the Act for the Regulation of Free Negroes passed by the General Court stipulated:

> whereas in the several towns and precincts within this province there are several free Negroes and mulattoes able of body, and fit for labour, who are not charged with trainings, watches, and other services required of her majesty's subjects, whereof they have shared in the benefit, Sect.1 required so many days work yearly of each free male Negro, or mulatto, able of body, dwelling within such town or precinct, in repairing of the highways, cleansing the streets, or other service for the common benefit of the place, as at the discretion of the selectmen may be judged on equivalent to the services performed by others.[133]

As to the employment of African Americans in the colonial government, references show that Mesheck, a mulatto servant to Mr. Hinsdale, was in the colonial pay when he worked at Fort Dummer for Mr. Hinsdale. The duties of Mesheck were not listed by George Sheldon, the local historian of Deerfield. In addition to Mesheck's employment by the colonial government, he was charged with the management of his master's affairs when his master was managing a different business. Apparently, Mr. Hinsdale had many business locations. In 1752, Mesheck owned his own business. It is unknown whether or not he still continued to receive pay from the colonial government for his service to his master when he became a business owner.[134]

In colonial New England, in 1652, government officials in Massachusetts enacted the first act for the inclusion of African Americans, Indians, and Scott in the militia. In 1656, Indians and African Americans were excluded from performing militia duties. However, during the French and Indian War, governors in this colony from time to time ordered the enlistment of able men in the militia without regard to race or national origin.

---

133. See *Charters and General Laws of the Colony and Province of Massachusetts Bay*, 1814, p. 386.
134. See Sheldon, 1893, p. 51.

Chapter 7

African American Militiamen and Soldiers
in the Revolutionary War: 1770–1783

The impact of African Americans concerning the maintenance of peace, security, and safety in colonial New England was seen at the battles of Concord, Lexington, Cambridge, Bunker Hill, and in other parts of the United States. During these conflicts, black militiamen performed excellent work protecting their masters' territories. The African American militiamen were loyal, resilient, and determined to defend freedom. According to historian Duane Hamilton Hurd, "colored people were patriots."[1] A similar observation was made by Josiah Howard Temple. He noted that African Americans in Framingham, Massachusetts, were loyal to the Americans.[2] Hurd and Temple's accounts are ample proof of the attachment African Americans had with their masters. It is noteworthy that free African Americans and slaves were patriotic.

In Massachusetts, New Hampshire, Rhode Island, Connecticut, and Maine, African Americans filled the ranks of the American army. As slaves and free men, they did not care about the conditions in which they lived in the country. Instead, they volunteered to defend the land of their masters. Among newly enlisted African Americans were veterans of the colonial wars. Others enlisted by the authorization of their masters. Patriotic Americans did not hesitate to permit their slaves to serve in the local militia. Slave owners who were against the English were more than likely to include their slaves in the military or militia.

---

1. Duane H. Hurd, *History of Middlesex County, Massachusetts*, J. W. Lewis & Company, 1890, p. 624.
2. Josiah H. Temple, *History of Framingham, Massachusetts: Early Known as Danforth's Farms, 1640–1880, With a Genealogical Register*, Town of Framingham, 1887, p. 275.

Furthermore, high-ranking officials called upon their slaves to serve among the Americans. It does not appear any laws were enacted for the exclusion of African Americans in the militia, and due to the urgency and the intensity of the war; it does not appear that a selective method was enforced to enlist men in the militia. Massachusetts men joined the force in large numbers to protect their land against the British.

Inhabitants of the New England colonies exhibited vigorous patriotism from the beginning of the conflict with the British in the Revolutionary War. When the British attacked Lexington City, the onslaught was alarming to both white Americans and African Americans (free and slaves). Defense of the Massachusetts province was everyone's duty, and African Americans were among the rank of American soldiers who challenged militarily the army of the crown of England. The patriotic spirit of New England's inhabitants is articulated by Charles Hudson, author of *The History of the Town of Lexington*. Hudson wrote that the inhabitants of New England resisted the unjust attacks of the British due to firm principles of patriotic values. Though the New Englanders resisted the invading British, the colonists were unaided by military skill. They were poorly armed in the defense of their valued rights.[3] Similarly, Elias Phinney believed that firmness and decisiveness helped the inhabitants of Lexington to face the almighty military power of the British.[4] African Americans, who detested injustice and slavery, were prone to join their white brethren to incapacitate the British from implementing unjust measures against the Americans.

The many regulations enacted by the British Crown against the Americans regarding trade and taxes were felt by everyone, including African Americans. Additionally, African Americans did not have any connections with the British. However, the plights of their masters directly affected the lives of African slaves and servants. Similarly, free

---

3. Charles Hudson says that the inhabitants of New England fought brilliantly during the alarm of Lexington and others due to their patriotic endeavor, and they were not militarily trained. See *History of the Town of Lexington, Middlesex County, Massachusetts: History*, Houghton Mifflin, 1913, p. 123.

4. Elias Phinney says that "the inhabitants of Lexington took a firm stand in favor of the rights and liberties of the province." See *History of the Battle of Lexington*, Phelps and Farnham, 1825, p. 11.

African Americans were affected economically when the British implemented unfair measures against the Americans. In addition to economic legislation, the arbitrary justice system enforced by the British was alarming. Americans believed that they were enslaved by the British king. Therefore, the involvement of all able-bodied men during the Lexington, Concord, and Cambridge attacks was imperative. The inclusive militia policy observed by captains of the local militias was a decision made in the best interest of the Americans.

The deeds and courage exhibited by African Americans during the Revolutionary War were recorded by many writers of the American Revolution and by local historians. Authors such as Emory Washburn, William Barry, James Thatcher, George Livermore, and Sarah Loring Bailey, among others, have documented the impact made by Peter Salem and Salem Poor during the war (their deeds will be detailed later in this chapter). Similarly, some authors recorded the patriotic nature of African American soldiers when defending their masters during the war. For example, Herbert Baxter Adams and John Martin Vincent describe an incident at Fort Griswold. As the British killed Colonel William Ledyard, a member of the Connecticut militia, Ledyard's African American soldier avenged the colonel's death. Immediately, without fear, the African slave took his bayonet and killed the soldier. Ultimately, the avenging slave was then killed by another British soldier in retaliation. The soldier pierced the slave with thirty-three bayonet wounds.[5] Another high-ranking officer received support from African Americans. Major William Lawrence of Rhode Island was secured by African American soldiers when the British tried to capture Lawrence as a prisoner. Reverend S. K. Lathrop recounts that Major Lawrence never forgot how black men rushed to his rescue when they discovered he was in danger of being captured by the enemy. For the rest of his life, the major exhibited kindness and hospitality toward any African American whom he encountered near his house.[6]

At the start of the Revolutionary War, blacks were enlisted in the militias of many towns in Massachusetts and other New England colonies.

---

5. Herbert Baxter Adams and John Martin Vincent, *Slaves in the Revolution*, in the Johns Hopkins Studies in Historical and Political Science. Johns Hopkins University Press, 1893, p. 397.

6. Rev. Samuel K. Lathrop, *Memoir of William Lawrence*, Priv. Print., 1856, p. 9.

From Cambridge, Lexington, Malden, Boston, Dracut, Framingham, Worcester, Arlington, Natick, Needham, Stoneham, Plymouth, Chelmsford, Oxford, Boston, and Braintree, African Americans voluntarily enlisted to help suppress the British attacks at Lexington, Concord, and Cambridge. The participation of African Americans in the beginning of the war was signaled by General Thomas in a letter to John Adams. In this letter, General John Thomas wrote to Adams that "we have some Negroes: but I look on them, in general, equally serviceable with other men for the fatigue; and in action among them have proved themselves brave."[7] Even though high-ranking officers such as General Thomas advocated the enlistment of blacks in the army, government officials in the Southern states would not allow blacks to carry weapons, fearing a revolt from them against their masters. Samuel Swett, author of *History of Bunker Hill Battles: With a Plan*, says that "many Northern blacks were excellent soldiers, but Southern troops could not brook [tolerate] equality with Negroes. On November 15, 1775, Washington prohibited their enlistment."[8]

The policy of the Americans regarding the enlistment of blacks was inconsistent like their forefathers during the colonial wars. There was no settled policy for the recruitment of blacks in the Revolutionary War. The policy changed from time to time in accordance with the pressures of war and public opinion. To illustrate, while General George Washington rejected any recruitment of blacks at first, on December 31, 1775, he changed his stance on this issue. The following quote indicates Washington's change of policy:

"It has been represented to me, that the free Negroes, who have served in this army, are very much dissatisfied at being discarded. As it is to be apprehended, that they may seek employ in the ministerial army, I have presumed to depart from the resolution respecting them, and have given license for them being enlisted. If this is disapproved of by Congress, I will put a stop to it."[9] Washington was familiar with the en-

---

7. Henry Carey Baird, *George Washington and General Jackson, on Negro Soldiers...* H.C. Baird, 1868, p. 5.

8. Samuel Swett, *History of Bunker Hill Battles: With a Plan*, Munroe and Francis, 1827, p. 25.

9. Jared Sparks, *The Writings of George Washington*, vol. 3, American Stationary Company, J.B. Russell, 1834, p. 218.

listment of African Americans in the militia of the Virginia colony. He understood they were dependable war companions to the Americans. Furthermore, he was an eyewitness of the loyalty of African Americans during military conflicts. He knew that they would not desert the war.

Before Washington changed his policy concerning the enlistment of African Americans into the Army, Massachusetts Bay had been sent a detailed mandate describing who to reject from the military. Dated July 31, 1775, from New York, Massachusetts Bay military officers received the mandate saying, "You are not to enlist any deserter from the ministerial army, nor any stroller, Negro, or vagabond, or person suspected of being an enemy to [the] liberty of America nor any under eighteen years of age."[10] These orders were possibly political maneuverings to avoid infuriating Southern leaders in the beginning of the Revolutionary War. But when the idea to recruit African Americans was presented to Congress, the general policy was in favor of including those men who had served during the battles of Lexington and Bunker Hill. The decision on the question of blacks in the army decided by Congress reads as follows: "that the free Negroes, who have served faithful in the army at ... Cambridge, may be re-enlisted therein, but not others."[11]

When Washington had a conference with Benjamin Franklin, Benjamin Harrison, Thomas Lynch, and the Committee of the Provincial Government of Massachusetts, he changed his policy regarding the enlistment of blacks. On October 23, 1775 when the subject of the recruitment of blacks came into discussion, Washington noted, "Ought not Negroes to be excluded from the new enlistment, especially such as slaves? All were thought improper by the council of officers."[12] These illustrations show that the inclusion of blacks for the executions of the

---

10. See Aoration Gates, *Principles and Acts of the Revolution in America: Or An Attempt to collect and preserve some of the speeches, orations, & proceedings, with sketches and remarks on men and things, and other suggestive or neglected pieces, ...* Printed and pub. for the author, by W.O. Niles, 1822, p. 423.

11. See *Proceedings of the Massachusetts Historical Society*, vol. 6, The Society, 1863, pp. 175–78. The journal notes that "on the memorable 17th of June, 1775, Negro soldiers stood side by side, and fought bravely, with their white brethren." The deeds of Peter Salem and Salem Poor were also mentioned.

12. George Livermore, *An Historical Research Respecting the Opinion of the Founders of the Republic on Negroes as Slaves, as Citizens, and as Soldiers.* J. Wilson, 1862, p. 130.

Revolutionary War was inconsistent. It seems that Washington understood the importance of including African Americans in the rank of the United States' army. This political maneuvering was employed as a diplomatic strategy to soften the tone of those who refused the inclusion of African Americans in the Continental Army. Additionally, General Washington was a leader prone to principle. He always made his decision by conscience, not by inducement.[13] Furthermore, he believed in democratic norms. Therefore, he charged the American Congress to accept the resolution to employ African Americans among the military rank. He understood that the decision of members of the American Congress on this matter was acceptable by all.

As the war continued, New England colony legislatures adjusted their policies regarding the enlistment of African Americans in the defense of liberty. As illustration, in 1777, African Americans (slaves, servants, and free) were permitted to enlist in the Continental Army. Likely, in Rhode Island and in Massachusetts, in 1778, African Americans were allowed to enlist in the Continental Army. But before these dates, they were part of the men who defended the city of Cambridge, Bunker Hill, and Concord.

In colonial Connecticut and New Hampshire, blacks also responded during the first alarm of the Revolutionary War. They did not enlist as trumpeters or servants for carrying the belongings of their masters, but as soldiers, ready to fight and defend their masters' land as well as the land of their masters' birth. Under fire of the British army, black soldiers did not give in like their white brethren. They continued to defend liberty until military officials requested them to return home. There were black soldiers who died during the battle of Bunker Hill and Lexington in 1775. To illustrate, the black servant of Nathan Abbot was killed on June 17, 1775, in battle.[14] Another Connecticut black man who enlisted in the local militia was Lemuel Haynes.

---

13. James H. Stark, *The Loyalists of Massachusetts and the Other Side of the American Revolution*, J.H. Stark, 1907, p. 36. Stark says that "America had found in Washington a leader who could be induced by no earthly motive to tell a falsehood or to break an engagement or to commit a dishonorable act."

14. See the *Essex Antiquarian: An Illustrated Magazine*. The Essex Antiquarian, 1897, p. 31.

Lemuel Haynes

In Connecticut, he was among the minutemen who could be ready to defend the colony at a minute's notice. He marched in the alarms of Lexington, Concord, and Bunker Hill. He continued to serve in other expeditions as the war continued.[15] According to his biographer, Timothy Mather Cooley, Haynes enlisted as a minuteman in 1774. Before joining the war, he spent one day of the week in manual exercises to hold himself in readiness for the actual service. His first military action was at the Battle of Lexington. After this battle, Cooley notes that Haynes joined the American army at Roxbury. At this time, he was no longer a minuteman but a volunteer soldier. In such capacity, he marched with his fellow Americans in the expedition to Ticonderoga.[16]

Haynes was born in 1753 in West Hartford from the union of an African man who was a slave and a white woman who was an indentured servant of Scottish descent. According to Cooley, his mother was from a respected ancestry in New England. For unspecified reasons, Haynes was rejected by his mother. It appears that he met her only once at the house of a relative. Haynes did not know his father. At the age of five, the child was taken to Granville, Massachusetts, to serve Deacon David Rose as a bondsman until Haynes reached twenty-one years old. At the house of Deacon Rose, the child was cared for as if he were the natural-born son of the Roses. Consequently, Haynes became attached to Deacon Rose and to Mistress Rose.[17] It was in the house of the deacon that Haynes began his religious training. Eventually, he became licensed to preach. Haynes accepted the preaching post at the Congregational Church of Middle Granville, making him the first African American minister of an all-white congregation.

Timon, a Negro, marched from Wethersfield, Connecticut, to Lexington on April 19, 1775, in the largest company of that city under the

---

15. Philip S. Foner, *Blacks in the American Revolution*, Westport, CT, London, England: Greenwood Press, 1910, p. 42.

16. Timothy M. Cooley, *Sketches of the Life and Character of the Rev. Lemuel Haynes, A.M.: From Many Years Paster of a Church in Rutland, VT and Late in Granville, New York*, Harper, 1837, pp. 28, 45–46.

17. Ibid.

CHAPTER 7

command of Captain John Chester.[18] Timon was the only person of the African race enlisted with Wethersfield as a private. There is no indication whether Timon marched in other alarms. It appears that he was a free man because the name of a master was not mentioned by James Hammond Trumbull, the local Connecticut historian. In a like manner, Trumbull did not state the status of Timon. According to Trumbull, the company commanded by Captain Chester was filled with volunteers from Wethersfield who were not attached to any regiment.[19] As other Wethersfield men, Timon was a volunteer from that city. Another African American who served in the alarm of 1775 was identified as Negro Ceasar. He was listed with the Connecticut men recruited from Voluntown.[20]

The number of black militiamen from Massachusetts who responded to the attacks on Lexington, Concord, Cambridge, and Bunker Hill is not small, as some writers have documented. It appears that African Americans were among the field soldiers in relatively large numbers even though there is recording inconsistency regarding their militia services in the battles of 1775. From the contemporaneous *Records of the Massachusetts Soldiers and Sailors* and the work of modern historians, many names of blacks have been recovered who responded to the alarms of Lexington, Concord, Cambridge, and Bunker Hill. There were black servants who accompanied their masters during the battles. Patriotic African Americans participated in the Charleston battle and other battles fought in New England. In the Battle of Charleston, Massachusetts, Salem Poor was a black man credited for being a brave soldier, a discussion that is forthcoming in this chapter.

History reveals that the Massachusetts Colony established an act to exclude blacks in the militia during the Revolutionary War. The instructions given to recruiting officers in Massachusetts spelled out clearly that Negroes were exempted from serving in the military.[21] However,

---

18. James H. Trumbull, *The Memorial History of Harford County, Connecticut, 1633–1793, Town Histories*. E. L. Osgood, 1886, p. 472.

19. Ibid.

20. See Connecticut Historical Society, *Lists and Return of Connecticut Men in the Revolution, 1775–1783*, Connecticut Historical Society, 1909, p. 12.

21. Ezekiah Niles, Horatio Gates, Adj. Gen. Centennial offering Republication of the *Principles and Acts of the Revolution in America*, ... New York, Chicago [etc.] A.S. Barnes 7 co.1876, p. 423.

did the recruiting officers follow the mandates of the act? If not, were black soldiers registered on the muster rolls of the towns?

Searching for the answers to the aforementioned questions has led to revelations about the military service performed by blacks upon responding to the alarms of 1775. Moreover, the sacrifices made by African Americans during risky missions will be noted. Additionally, the responses to these questions unveiled pertinent information on the exceptional deeds black soldiers accomplished during military confrontation against the British Army.

Throughout the country, historians have recorded many facts regarding military duties performed by African Americans during the Revolutionary War. The aims of this discussion are to highlight the patriotic endeavors demonstrated by black soldiers and to spotlight outstanding contributions made by African Americans which changed the magnitude of the war. Slaves felt they had a vested interest in participating in the Revolutionary War. Colonists wanted to divest themselves and their territories from the grip of Great Britain. Slaves felt if they helped colonists to free themselves from their British stronghold, then the New Englanders would reciprocate and free the enslaved men, women, and children living in the colonies. Crispus Attucks' patriotic fervor was demonstrated when he and other colonists confronted a British soldier who chastised a boy who had complained because he had been cheated by one of the soldiers. It was a risky mission undertaken by Attucks and the other colonists to confront armed British soldiers about this matter. When the confrontation took place, someone hit a soldier which resulted in gunfire. Rapid, responsive gunfire ended with Attucks being the first person and the first African American to lose his life for liberty in the American Revolutionary War. A total of five American colonists were killed and six wounded. It was also during this Boston Massacre that the inclusive war effort was advocated by the inhabitants of Massachusetts.

During the occupation of Boston, African Americans were among those who marched against the malfeasance of the British soldiers. They joined their Caucasian counterparts to rebel against the British soldiers' brutal methods in dealing with the Americans. African Americans did not care about the status they held at the time. It appears that there was no discrimination against African descendants during that day. From various documents consulted, there are no records indicating that free Africans and/or slaves were excluded from the mob. Even though some of the enlisted men were slaves, it seems that they believed that the occupation of Boston by British soldiers was a violation of the rights of the inhabitants of the city. The British soldiers were such an affront to people of color that they made extraordinary sacrifices that went beyond risking their lives in battle. As previously mentioned, Crispus Attucks was one such person. As a runaway slave, he was not afraid of being discovered by his former master, who advertised Attuck's escape in the newspaper. Attucks still appeared in public without taking into consideration that he was a fugitive who could be captured and returned to his slave master.

Crispus Attucks

When it came to the defense of American freedom, Crispus Attucks, a mulatto, was among the martyrs of the 1770 American Revolution.[22] It is unknown if Attucks had any military training. Additionally, there is no data indicating why he took leadership of the decision to confront British soldiers who had Boston under siege. The information written by many writers indicates that he was the ringleader, but their commentary does not specify how this slave became the ringleader of a multitude of people in Boston. Moreover, if he were not a resident of Boston as records indicate, why was he accepted as a Bostonian? Such a question is difficult to explain or answer. But the reality is that Attucks has been accredited with being the ringleader among people who challenged the British the day the massacre happened. During this period, African Americans did not hold positions of power. It is amazing to see an African American organizing a mob against the global superpower of the time. By reading the contributions of Attucks, there are many questions that come to mind. Was Attucks selected by a group of people, or was he a self-appointed ringleader? How did he end up being part of the group?

The answers to these questions are matters of speculation. But the most important part of the account is that a mulatto stood firmly against

---

22. Crispus Attucks, the first person to die for the American Revolution, was a ring leader. He died on March 5, 1770.

the unjust acts committed by the British soldiers. Moreover, it seems that Attucks, who believed in justice and freedom, could not stay calm when witnessing the intimidation of British soldiers. He had to make his voice heard at any cost. From the account of John Adams as collected by Josiah Howard Temple, Attucks was a large man whose looks scared people.[23] On the day of the Boston Massacre, it is reported that he ordered his followers to stand against the British. As John Adams noted, people heard him saying, "Don't be afraid of them! They dare not fire! Kill them! Kill them! Knock them over!"[24] In addition to the record of Temple, James Henry Stark notes that Attucks, acting as the leader of the Boston incident, knocked down one of the soldiers and got possession of his musket.[25] Based upon the testimony of John Adams and James Henry Stark, Attucks truly was a person who believed in freedom, as well as free expression. John Adams conducted the defense of the British soldiers, but it is unknown if his account was a legal strategy to protect his clients. Contrary to Adams, Frederick Kidder notes that when a resident of Boston accused a sentinel of beating him the day before the massacre, the crowd yelled, "Kill him! Knock him down!" He went on to relate that as the people yelled to kill him, the sentinel moved back to the Custom House and loaded his gun. When Bostonians threw missiles at him, he took his musket and warned the rioters to keep off. It was at this time that sentinels started discharging their muskets upon the citizens. As a result, Crispus Attucks was killed. During the same incident, several others were wounded and killed, some who included Samuel Gray who was shot, Patrick Carr who was mortally wounded, and James Caldwell who was also killed.[26]

---

23. Josiah H. Temple, *History of Framingham, Massachusetts: Early Known as Danforth's Farms*, Town of Framingham, 1867, p. 255. John Adams who defended the soldiers noted that "Crispus Attucks was a stout fellow, whose very looks were enough to terrify any person.... When he came down upon the soldiers, by the sentry-box, pushed him."

24. Ibid.

25. James H. Stark, *The Loyalists of the Massachusetts and the Other Side of the American Revolution*, J.H. Stark, 1907, p. 44. Stark says that "had the soldier did not killed Attucks, there was no doubt as Attucks took the musket, he would killed the soldier."

26. Frederick Kidder, *History of the Boston Massachusetts*, March 5, 1770. J. Munsell, 1870, pp. 4–6.

According to many records, Attucks was killed by Hugh Montgomery, a soldier of Captain Thomas Preston.[27] Attucks was a fugitive slave from Framingham, Massachusetts. When he escaped from his master, the slave owner made an advertisement on October 2, 1750, for Attucks' recovery.[28] It was common for slave masters to advertise for runaway slaves or to advertise for those which were subject to be sold. While a fugitive, Attucks did not go into hiding from his master; instead, he joined the public mob for the common cause. The spirit of Attucks during the Boston massacre shows how blacks in Massachusetts were loyal and patriotic to the land where they lived. The death of Attucks is noted by many writers for the cause of liberty in the United States.

Historically, in colonial New England during war, the color of skin was not taken into consideration. The inclusion of blacks for the defense of the colony was common. Unlike in the former wars, during the occupations of Boston, African Americans and their white brethren stood firm against the threat of the British government and their soldiers. In 1775, during the battles of Lexington, Concord, Cambridge, and Bunker Hill, African Americans joined forces with their white counterparts to deny the British the occupations of those cities. When the news of the British attack upon Lexington spread throughout the Massachusetts province, African Americans from Arlington, Lexington, Cambridge, Needham, Stoneham, Oxford, Chelmsford, Plymouth, Andover, Framingham, Braintree, Concord, Worcester, Malden, and Leicester responded to the alarms. In other colonies such as Connecticut, Rhode Island, New Hampshire, and Maine, African Americans enlisted from various cities to defend liberty.

Black Soldiers during the Battles of Lexington, Concord, Cambridge and Bunker Hill

In Needham, when local officials were informed that Lexington, Massachusetts was under British attack, Abel Benson sounded the trumpet

---

27. See William Cooper Nell, *The Colored Patriots of the American Revolution*. R.F. Wallcut, 1855, pp. 14–16.

28. For the advertisement of Crispus Attucks, see Duana Hamilton Hurd, *History of Middlesex County, Massachusetts*, J.W. Lewis & Co., 1890, p. 623.

to alert the people about the start of the war. Although it was a sudden attack, inhabitants of many cities responded without delay. Like their white brethren, African Americans carried arms for the defense of liberty. The battles of Lexington and Concord were fought on April 19, 1775, and the Bunker Hill or Breed's Hill battle was fought on June 17, 1775 between British and American troops.

At the start of the Battle of Lexington, local historians in Massachusetts agree that Prince Estabrook, a Negro, fought with his American brethren against the British. From the work of Frank Warren Coburn comes the acknowledgement that Estabrook was wounded during the battle.[29] In the Acts and Resolves passed by the General Court of Massachusetts, the legislatures wrote that a Negro man participated on Lexington Common."[30] This vivid data shows the inclusive military duties observed at the beginning of the war. Estabrook was in the company of Captain Jonathan Parker the day of the Lexington Battle and continued to serve in other battles during the war.[31] It is plausible to believe that when the alarm of the war sounded, local government did not prevent local men as well as slave soldiers from engaging in the war. In Worcester, Charles Nutt wrote, "in the early days free Negroes were present in that town. One of them was in the company of Captain Timothy Bigelow who responded to the Lexington alarm."[32] Nutt did not mention the name of the African American.

Another African American enlisted during the alarm of Lexington for a few days was from Braintree, Massachusetts. Pompy, a black man, was among the minutemen who marched on the Lexington alarm. He marched from South Precinct in Braintree for four days under the company of Captain Seth Turner.[33] It is unknown whether or not after his

---

29. Frank W. Coburn, *The Battle of Lexington Common, April 19, 1775*, The Author, 1821, p. 39.

30. See *Acts and Resolves Passed by the General Court of Massachusetts*, Secretary of the Commonwealth, 1861, p. 609.

31. See William Estabrook, *Genealogy of the Estabrook Family, including the Esterbrook and Easterbrooks in the United States*, William Andrusa Church, 1891, p. 26. Prince was the slave of Benjamin Estabrook.

32. Charles Nutt, *History of Worcester and Its People*, Vol. 1, Lewis Historical Publishing Co., 1919, p. 373.

33. See *Massachusetts Soldiers and Sailors*, vol. 12, Wright and Potter Printing Co., 1904, p. 520.

four days Pompy continued to serve in the local militia. There is no record revealing that his term of enlistment was extended. In the town of Stoneham, Job Potamea, a Negro, and Isaiah Barjonah, a mulatto, served the province during the alarm at Cambridge. These two African Americans were enlisted in Captain Benjamin Locke's company in West Cambridge. In the same company, Cato Wood, a black man, from Charleston was enlisted. Similarly, Cuff Whittemore, an African American from Cambridge, was a minuteman in the same company as the other African Americans listed above. Captain Benjamin Locke's company numbered fifty non-commissioned officers and privates. Henry Hill, a Negro, was a soldier who fought in the battle of Lexington for the defense of freedom and liberty.[34] In Brookline, Prince was enlisted in the company of Captain Thomas White, in Colonel William Heath's regiment, which marched on the alarm of Lexington. His term of service was 23 days. He was reported as Joh' a Boylston's Prince.[35] These black men showed bravery and loyalty to the cause of the Americans and for their own freedom, because British soldiers were not selective of their enemies.

During the alarm of Cambridge, many African Americans proved their loyalty to the American colonies. At the start of the war, black men exhibited a degree of courage and bravery unexpected of them by their military generals and the government officials who initially denied men of color the opportunity to serve in the military. Among those who performed military duties during the alarms of Cambridge were: Titus Burn, Alexander Ames, Brazillai Lew, and Cato Howe of Plymouth.[36] In addition, patriotic African American men in Framingham, Massachusetts, were on active military duty during the Lexington, Concord, and Cambridge alarms.

Barzillai Lew was listed June 15, 1775, in the militia. At 30 years old, he served in the company of John Ford. Before his enlistment in the militia, Barzillai was a cooper and a resident of Chelmsford. On May 6, 1775, he was enlisted as a fifer and drummer. On the muster roll of August 1, 1775, he was in the company of Colonel Ebenezer Bridge.

---

34. Nell, 1855, p. 21.
35. *Massachusetts Soldiers and Sailors of the Revolutionary War*, vol. 12, 1904, p. 788.
36. Neil, *The Colored Patriots of the American Revolution*, R.F. Wollcut, 1855, p. 21.

Barzillai also was enlisted on May 6, 1775, to serve for three months and three days. On September 25, 1775, he was on the list of men coming home from the war.[37] Barzillai Lew was from a prominent black family. According to Silas Roger Coburn, author of *The History of Dracut, Massachusetts*, Lew was the son of Primus Lew, a colored man who lived on Totman Road, previously named Zeal Road in the town of Pawtucketville. Later, the road was named after Barzillai.[38] Primus Lew was a well known African because of his musical expertise. In 1760, Primus was in Farrington's Company of Croton during the reduction of Canada. Historian Wilson Waters believes that Primus Lew was born in Croton, Massachusetts.[39]

In the company of Captain Peleg Wadsworth was Quam, a Negro who served in the Revolutionary War in 1775. Quam was from Plymouth, where he enlisted first on May 26, 1775, for a month-and-eight days of military service. He was also on the muster roll dated Aug. 1, 1775.[40] Captain Wadsworth was a resident of Kingston. In Malden, Massachusetts, Hill (or Hills) Prince was another African American who served in 1775 for the defense of the province against the British. Prince served for eight months with Captain Nathan Hatch. In addition, Prince served in the company of Lieutenant-Colonel Bond in 1775. Deloraine Pendre Corey, author of *The History of Malden*, believes that Prince was a black servant of Thomas Hills. Similarly, Aaron Oliver, a mulatto from Malden, was enlisted on April 23, 1775, in the company of Captain Ezra Towne.[41] In the company of Captain Aaron, Cato Underwood was an African American who reported to the alarm of August 1775 as a private. His service was for seven days during his enlistment from Natick.[42] In

---

37. Wilson Waters, *History of Chelmsford, Massachusetts*, Town, 1917, p. 327.
38. Silas R. Coburn, *History of Dracut, Massachusetts*, Press of the Courier-Citizen Company, 1922, p. 324.
39. Waters, 1917, p. 275.
40. *Massachusetts Soldiers and Sailors of the Revolution*, Massachusetts Office of the Secretary of State, Wright and Potter Printing Co., State Printers, 1904, p. 885.
41. Deloraine P. Corey, *The History of Malden, Massachusetts, 1633–1785*, The author, 1898, p. 427.
42. *Massachusetts Soldiers and Sailors of the Revolutionary War: A Compilation from the Archives*, vol. 6, Massachusetts, Office of the Secretary of State. Wright and Potter Printing Company, State Printers, 1907, p. 251.

1778, at the age of 24, Underwood was among the Massachusetts men enlisted for the enforcement of the Northern Army.[43]

In the town of Andover, African Americans were active during the alarm of 1775. According to historical records, Cato was listed as a private in the company of Benjamin Farman under the regiment of Colonel James Frye. The date of Cato's return from Cambridge was mentioned as October 6, 1775. During his enlistment, he was identified and reported as a Negro. After the military execution of Cambridge, Cato re-enlisted in the Continental Army. On February 17, 1778, he was in the company of Captain Samuel Johnson of Essex. His term of service expired in January, 1780.[44] In the same town, Philipp Abbot, servant of Nathan Abbot, fought in the Battle of Cambridge. According to the record of the Massachusetts Office of the Secretary of State, Abbot was killed on June 17, 1775.[45] He was among other Americans who lost their lives for freedom. In Charleston, Massachusetts, Cato Wood, an African American, was among those who fought during the battle of Cambridge.[46]

In Massachusetts, African Americans in the town of Framingham were involved in the struggle for liberty as were their white brethren. They served as minutemen as well as soldiers during the Revolutionary War. Additionally, others acted as trumpeters. At the alarm of Lexington, when the Framingham militia marched for the defense of liberty, few of them were part of that force. They marched from Framingham to Lexington. African Americans who reported to the alarm of Lexington remained with their troop for a while. According to Josiah Howard Temple, of the 153 Framingham men who answered the Lexington alarm, only eight returned home the following day. As for the African Americans, Peter Salem served four days. In addition to the Lexington

---

43. George Kuhn Clarke, *History of Needham, Massachusetts, 1711–1911*, privately printed at the University Press, 1912, p. 478.

44. See *Massachusetts Soldiers and Sailors of the Revolutionary War: A Compilation from the Archives*, vol. 3. Massachusetts Office of the Secretary of State. Wright and Potter Printing Company, 1897, p. 211.

45. See *Massachusetts Soldiers and Sailors of the Revolutionary War*, vol. 1. Massachusetts Office of the Secretary of State. Wright and Potter Company, State Printers, 1896, p. 14.

46. William Richard Cutter, *History of the Town of Arlington, Massachusetts*, D. Clapp & Son, 1880, p. 18.

alarm, Framingham's African Americans served in the alarm of Cambridge and during the continuation of the war. Among those who enlisted in 1775 during the war were black soldiers Brin (commonly called Blaney) Grusha, Jim Riggs, Peter Salem, and Cato Hart.

Blaney Grusha was formerly the servant of Colonel Micah Stone. This African American was a self-sufficient man. In 1757, according to Temple, he was listed as a tax payer in Framingham. Regarding his military services, he fought at the Battle of Bunker Hill and in other battles. After the alarm of Lexington when Captain Thomas Drury formed a company of men for eight months of service, Blaney Grusha was listed. Records show that he was enlisted on May 4, 1775. According to Temple, Grusha was at the Battle of Bunker Hill. He was in the company of Captain Thomas Drury, as were Peter Salem and Cato Hart.[47] From the account of William Barry, Grusha was a private.[48] As did Grusha, Cato Hart, an African American, enlisted on May 4, 1775, in the company of Captain Thomas Drury for the same amount of time. Also, Hart was among the men who enlisted for the march for Ticonderoga by Captain Simon Edgell. In 1777, Cato Hart served in the Continental regiment as a Framingham man before the regiment was disbanded. Hart was honorably discharged and received 200 acres of land according to the act the Massachusetts legislature passed in 1801. The act ordered 200 acres of land to be given to officers and soldiers enlisted in the state of Massachusetts who served in the war.

Another African American who received 200 acres of land for serving three years in the Continental Army was John Harvey of Southborough, who later moved to Framingham. His deed of land was dated August 6, 1805. Likewise, there was Isaac How, an African American, who obtained 200 acres of land for his military service by the order of the Massachusetts legislatures. However, he sold his land for $100 to Lawson Buckminster.

Jim Riggs was among the Framingham enlistees who served in the Revolutionary War. The time of his enlistment was not recorded

---

47. Josiah H. Temple, *History of Framingham, Massachusetts: Early Known as Danforth's Farms, 1640–1880; with a Genealogical Register*, Town of Framingham, 1887, p. 280.

48. William Barry, *A History of Framingham, Massachusetts*, J. Munroe and Company, 1847, p. 159.

by Temple or other Framingham local historians. Riggs was born in St. Domingo and was a mulatto. He was once a slave in the South, but he escaped from his bondage. After venturing for some time, he arrived in Framingham. According to his own account, in 1755 he served as hostler to Colonel George Washington in the campaign against the French in 1755. Riggs was an industrious man. He made baskets for the families of Buckminster. In the same city, Cato Hanker was another industrious worker. He was listed as a shoemaker by the local historians. Charles Nutt writes that Jeffrey Heminway, a mulatto, served in the Revolutionary War in the quota military of Framingham, Massachusetts, from 1775 to 1777. In 1778, Heminway was listed in the town of Worcester until 1780. Similarly, the son of Jeffrey Heminway, Adam, served as a soldier in the company of Captain John Bigelow in 1775.[49] The African American community in Framingham contributed largely during the struggle for the War of Independence as they did in other towns in Massachusetts.

From 1777 and thereafter, African Americans enlisted in the Continental Army. From the work of Temple, researchers discover that Cato Freemen was in the Continental Army. He was included in the army in January 1777. Likewise, Abel Benson, Peter Davis, and John Burk—all; identified as colored—were in the army in 1781. Abel Benson and Peter Davis received a pension from the government for their military service. Obviously, these African Americans were loyal to America. Not one of them deserted, nor was either of them ever suspected or accused of duplicitous military activities. In regard to their military service, Temple noted that African Americans were patriots. With such qualifications as these, clearly black men were not in the field just as drummers, trumpeters, guides, and scouts, but as soldiers.

In Massachusetts, the Act of July 2, 1775, exempted African Americans from being recruited in the army. However, after passing this law, military officials permitted men of color to serve in the alarms. It is difficult to know why officials disregarded that Act by enlisting Negroes in the militia. This enlistment by towns under the pressure of war was

---

49. See Charles Nutt, *History of Worcester and Its People*, vol. 1, Lewis Historical Publishing Company, 1919, pp. 148–49.

consistent with the colonial policy and continued during the provincial government. After the exemption of the African Americans from the militia, Will, an African American resident of Oxford, Massachusetts, was enlisted in the company of Captain William Campbell in August 1775. He was first enlisted in May 1775 for three months service. He was discharged on October 5, 1775. On October 7, 1775, his name was listed among soldiers who returned from the alarm.[50]

Also, African Americans acted as spies during the Revolutionary War, an extension of their military service. The services black men offered to their masters went beyond expectations. As slaves, they did not turn against their masters; instead, they performed exceptional services, which were recorded by historians. From the beginning of the war until its end, African Americans were deeply involved in the fight against injustice and the fight to gain and preserve freedom. There are many African Americans who served in the war but are not mentioned in the history books and various military records. But the names of those who excelled in their deeds were always recorded by historians. Slaves such as Peter Salem were among those who exhibited exceptional courage during the war.

Peter Salem

The various written histories of wars in New England confirm convincingly that African Americans in Framingham, Massachusetts, defended the colony. Moreover, men of color defended the interests of their masters time-after-time without concern for themselves. From the earlier wars to the Revolutionary War, African Americans were in the field fighting all enemies who jeopardized the peace and safety of the colonists. During the Revolutionary War, African Americans in Framingham proved that they were reliable partner for the security and the safety of the entire colony, as well as for their own town. It is difficult to estimate how many

---

50. See *Massachusetts Soldiers and Sailors of the Revolutionary War*, Vol. 7. Massachusetts Office of the Secretary of State. Wright and Potter Printing Company, State Printers, 1908, p. 377. Also Will was listed in the Book of George Fisher titled *History of the Town of Oxford, Massachusetts*. Published by the author with the co-operation of the Town, 1892, p. 125.

of Framingham's African slaves were enlisted in the Revolutionary War. However, those who have been recorded in this chapter acted heroically. From the account of Nathan Hurd, Framingham men who responded to the alarm against the British to Cambridge totaled 153. Among this number, only eight of them returned the following day. Hurd also noted that for an eight-month service in 1775, 85 soldiers from Framingham were enlisted.[51] In the two companies of Captain Luke Drury and Captain [Jason] Gleason, 65 and 50 men, respectively, from Framingham were enlisted. It was in Captain Drury's company that Peter Salem was enlisted.[52]

When the British went to Lexington and Concord to disarm the Americans, African Americans responded voluntarily as readily as their white brethren. In Framingham, one of the slave owners—for the love of his country—liberated his slave to fight for liberty. That slave was Peter Salem. The contributions made by Salem during the Revolutionary War have been noted by many historians. In regard to his life in slavery, Salem was owned by several masters. He was first the slave of Major Lawson Buckminster, but the major later sold Salem to Captain Jeremiah Belknap.[53] Peter Salem sometimes was called Salem Middlesex.[54] During the early stage of the conflict, Salem served as a minuteman in the company of Captain Simon Edgell on April 19, 1775.[55] It was not unusual for slaves to be sold from master to master. But at the start of the war, many patriotic masters liberated their slaves to fight for America. Peter Salem followed the example of his forefathers who fought during the colonial wars. Emory Washburn, historian and former governor of Massachusetts, says that Salem was enlisted in the regiment of John Nixon. The courageous black man employed all his fighting skills, loyalty, and devotion for the cause of liberty.

Opposing Salem was Major John Pitcairn, a Scottish Marine officer who was stationed in Boston at the start of the War of Independence.

---

51. Hurd, 1890, p. 625.
52. Ibid., p. 626.
53. Barry, 1847, p. 64.
54. Ibid.
55. Hurd, 1890, p. 628.

Pitcairn was just as determined to fight for the British Crown as Salem was to defend America. When opposing sides are fighting to the death, war becomes a battle royal, both between armies and between individuals. So when Peter Salem found an opportunity to kill Major Pitcairn he did not hesitate to shoot. Major Pitcairn was a significant target to kill. His death inflicted psychological and morale pain to the British Army and to the political elites in England. With the death of Major Pitcairn, the British soldiers were demoralized. Emory Washburn describes the scenario that ended Pitcairn's life: "He [Pitcairn] was shot down as he mounted the redoubt, crying out exulting[ly], 'The day is ours!' and fell into the arms of his son, who tenderly bore him off the field to a boat, and thence to a house in Prince Street, Boston, where he died."[56] Emory also noted that "the death of Major Pitcairn, with its accompanying circumstances, formed one of the most touching incidents of that eventual day."[57] While the British troops grieved their loss, Pitcairn's death was a comfort and boost to the Americans because the military conflict at Lexington had commenced when Pitcairn gave the order. Additionally, the Americans recognized that Pitcairn was a brave and courageous soldier, his death simultaneously weakened the British military.

The death of Major Pitcairn has been well-documented. The morale shock to the British soldiers and to Major Pitcairn's son were recorded by Samuel Swett, author of the first published account of the battle. In his account, he says that, "when slain, his [Pitcairn's] son in agony exclaimed, 'I've lost my father.' His soldiers ceased firing, and responded with that most eloquent eulogy, 'We've all of us lost a father.'"[58] Arthur Gilman notes that Pitcairn was just and impartial to his men.[59] Similarly, Samuel Adams Drake wrote that Major Pitcairn was warmly attached to his soldiers.[60] Therefore, it is sound to note that with declarations of the Major being thought of as a father to his men, the British

---

56. Emory Washburn, *Historical Sketches of the Town of Lester, Massachusetts: During the First Century from Its Settlement*, J. Wilson, 1860, p. 309.
57. Ibid.
58. Swett, 1827, p. 25.
59. Arthur Gilman, *Theotrum mojorum*, Lockwood Brooks, 1876, p. 66.
60. Samuel A. Drake, *Old Landmarks and Historic Personages of Boston*, 1873, p. 217.

marines were not as productive a military unit the day Pitcairn died as they had been when he was alive.

Authoritative information has not been revealed concerning how British soldiers maintained their war spirit after the death of Major Pitcairn. However, it is likely that the soldiers followed one of two extremes. Either they were so disheartened by Pitcairn's death that some time had to pass before they could return to their usual robust fighting, or they turned their leader's death into a combustible fuel that made them fight more vigorously to honor him.

Nonetheless, Peter Salem served with loyalty and courage throughout the war. On April 24, 1775, he was enrolled in the company of Captain Thomas Drury for eight months of service. Further, Salem served as bodyguard to Colonel Thomas Nixon and was among the soldiers who fought in the battle of Bunker Hill on June 17, 1775. Having proved himself an outstanding soldier, Salem was sent by Captain Drury as a support to Colonel William Prescott in the redoubt.[61] In 1777, Peter Salem re-enlisted to continue his fight in the Revolutionary War. He was enlisted in the company of General Thomas Nixon and served as a servant to the general.[62] In 1782, he re-enlisted in the army at Framingham to serve for three years, as noted by Temple.[63] The enlistment of Peter Salem was conducted with the permission of his master because Salem was a slave at the time. During his lifetime, he was a religious man. He was admitted to the Congregational Church in colonial New England on August 16, 1750, under the auspices of the Half-Way Covenant, a limited church membership established in 1662 that put certain restrictions on baptism, taking communion, and voting as these related to the church. After Salem's military service, Major Lawson Buckminster, Captain Jeremiah Belknap, and Samuel Hemenway agreed to take care of Salem by giving a bond to the town. These American patriots valued the service of Salem for the service he furnished to their country. Possibly, after his years of military service, Officer Salem did not have sufficient money to support himself, for he died at the house of William Walkup, Sr., on

---

61. Hurd, 1890, p. 628.

62. Washburn, 1826, p. 51.

63. Temple, 1887, p. 320. Temple also listed that Peter Salem was re-enlisted in 1777. See page 305.

August 16, 1816. However, due to Salem's valiant contributions to the town and the country, he was buried in the north central part of the Old Cemetery where, later, a monument was built in his memory.[64]

Salem Poor

In Hanover, Massachusetts, an African American exhibited exceptional courage during the battles of Lexington and Cambridge. Local historians in Hanover and national historians have noted that Salem Poor made a major contribution during the Battle of Cambridge. According to Sarah Loring Bailey, Colonel James Abercrombie, a British army officer, was shot by Salem Poor while he sprang on the redoubt. For his military skills during the Battle of Charlestown, Massachusetts, historians have noted that Poor fought bravely, not like an ordinary soldier, but like a man who was in command. Unlike in the Battle of Bunker Hill, during the Battle of Charlestown, Poor was complimented by government officials for his courage, soldiery, and tenacity during the fight. When the British soldiers violently attacked Charlestown, Salem Poor and the other Americans did not give up the fight. Private Poor exhibited high military skill while fighting. According to John Davis, Poor "was more than an ordinary soldier, and he was a commanding officer during the battle of Bunker Hill."[65] During the war, the British destroyed the city of Charlestown without mercy. Even though there were many Americans killed, Poor and other American soldiers continued to defend the town against the British. Under the pressure of the war, the Americans retreated. While retreating, Poor stood as a soldier and fired at Lieutenant-Colonel James Abercrombie.[66] The colonel was instantly killed.

Due to his heroic deed, the Massachusetts General Assembly valued Poor's contributions. In addition, a recommendation was written to recognize his military accomplishments during that event during the battle of Charlestown, which reads as follows:

---

64. Hurd, 1890, p. 628.
65. John Davis, *An Oration pronounced at Worcester (Mass.) on the Fortieth Anniversary of American Independence*, William Manning, 1816, p. 56.
66. Sara L. Bailey, *Historical Sketches of Andover (Comprising Andover), Massachusetts*, Boston: Houghton, Mifflin, 1880, p. 323.

> "to your Honl. House (which we do on justice to the character of so Brave a man) that, under our own observation, we declare that a Negro man called Salem Poor, of Col. Frye's Regiment, Capt. Ames' Company, in the late battle at Charlestown, behaved like an Experienced officer as well as an Excellent soldier. To set forth particulars of his conduct would be tedious: we would only leave to say, in person of the said Negro centers a brave and gallant soldier. The reward due to so great & distinguished a character we submit to the Congress."[67]
>
> Cambridge, Dec. 5th, 1775

It is worth noting the declaration of Poor's deeds because the British aggressively fought the battle. They burnt many buildings in the city. Moreover, many American soldiers were killed. It was really one of the harshest fights during the Revolutionary War at its beginning. The British did not spare any space during the Battle of Charlestown, punishing the Americans dearly.

With respect to Poor's early life, little is known. As other Africans in the colony, he was a slave. According to some authors, he was freed in 1767 after paying his master for his manumission. Records show that Salem Poor was a free man before the Revolutionary War. According to the 1771 Vital Records of Andover, Salem Poor is mentioned as a free Negro. Likely, Nancy, the woman he intended to marry, was listed as a free woman (mulatto). The intention of his marriage was recorded on November 4, 1771.[68] It appears that Private Poor was not a slave, as Sarah Loring Bailey has noted. In 1747, when he was baptized, he was mentioned as "Salem, Boy," servant to John and Rebecca Poor.[69] If the account mentioned in the Vital Record is correct, it is plausible Poor was held as a servant for many years preceding his liberation. As noted, in Massachusetts, Africans and Europeans were identified as servants in most cases.

---

67. Ibid.

68. See *Vital Records of Andover, Massachusetts, to the End of the Year 1849* ... Andover (Mass.) Topsfield Historical Society, 1912, p. 59.

69. Ibid., p. 391.

Prince and the Secret Mission for the Arrest of Major General Prescott

In Cambridge, Peter Salem shot Major Pitcairn. Likely, in the same battle, Salem Poor shot Lieutenant-Colonel James Abercrombie. In Charlestown Rhode Island, it was Prince, a black man, who risked his life on a secret mission for the arrest of Major-General William Prescott.[70] Historically, Anglo-Americans do not believe in being humiliated. When General Charles Lee was arrested and humiliated by Colonel William Harcourt of the English army, the Americans were disappointed. Moreover, the Americans were deceived about the manner in which General Lee was treated. George Henry Moore and the New York Historical Society wrote that "Lee surrendered his sword to Colonel Harcourt, begging to spare his life."[71] This humiliation was detested by the Americans. As revenge, they planned a secret mission for the seizure of Major-General Prescott, the commanding British officer at Newport. Sarah S. Cahoone wrote that the purpose of the capture of Prescott was to retaliate for the arrest of General Charles Lee, officer of the Continental Army.[72]

For the secret mission, Lieutenant-Colonel William Barton selected 40 trusted men. As always, the general included African Americans, the general's military companions. James Kingsley Thatcher, surgeon for the Massachusetts 16th Regiment and military journalist, noted that Prince, an African American, was selected for the mission. After Barton selected his men, he managed five boats sailing to the area where Prescott resided. To avoid any detection of the oncoming army, the ships traveled at night. Samuel Greene Arnold recorded that it took the fleet of ships four days to reach the location due to a storm.[73]

---

70. See Benjamin F. Riley, *The White Man's Burden: A Discussion of the Interracial Question, with Special Reference to the Responsibility of the White Race to the Negro Problem*, B.F. Riley, 1910, p. 75.

71. George H. Moore and New York Historical Society, *Mr. Lee's Plan—March 29, 1777: The Treason of Charles Lee, Major General, Second of the Revolution*, C. Scribner, 1860, p. 63.

72. Sarah S. Cahoone, *Sketches of Newport and Its Vicinity: With Notice Respecting the History, Settlement and Geography of Rhode Island. Illustrated with Engraving*, J.S. Taylor & Company, 1842, p. 212.

73. See Samuel G. Arnold, *History of Rhode Island and Providence Plantation: 1701–1790*. A. Appleton & Company, 1889, p. 402.

Upon arriving at the site where Major-General Prescott lodged, the secret army entered his residence before the general was aware of his arrest. Prince suddenly burst inside the room and seized Prescott where the general was in bed utterly surprising him.[74] His Aide-de-camp who attempted to escape was arrested. He was surprised how the Americans avoided any detection. As he was being taken to safety, he questioned Lieutenant Colonel Barton, "Sir, I did not think it possible you could escape the vigilance of the water guards."[75] The arrest of Major-General Prescott was a success for the Rhode Island militia. It is unknown why Barton selected Prince for such a delicate mission. Regardless, Americans joyfully embraced this successful mission, and Barton was awarded a sword for his excellent endeavor. The arrest of Prescott resulted in the liberation of Major-General Charles Lee in an exchange of prisoners. Even though the name of Prince was listed as a member of the mission, little was recorded about his status and family history. His identity as a free man or slave is unknown. Similarly, his place of residence was not mentioned.

The Arrest of a British Soldier by Ceasar, a Connecticut African American

William Chauncey Fowler recorded pertinent information about the arrest of a British soldier by Ceasar. Fowler believed Ceasar, a resident of Lebanon, Connecticut, seized the soldier possibly while Ceasar was on guard. When he brought the prisoner to the camp, some of his fellow soldiers were ecstatic for his bravery. However, other young officers among them were displeased about the seizure of the British soldier by Prince. As a result, a Court Martial was organized against Caesar. Without delay, Ceasar was brought before a judge. According to Fowler, the trial was conducted with scrupulous regard to form and ceremony. During his court appearance for the defense of his case, Ceasar started

---

74. James Thatcher, *A Military Journal During the American Revolutionary from 1775 to 1783*, Silas Andrus & Son, 1854, pp. 86–87.

75. Ibid.

joking. When he was questioned about his action, he replied, "If I remember, 'I took him,' this makes success the measure of merit, though not secundum artem [according to standard procedure]."[76] During the adjudication of the case, General Lafayette, French aristocrat and military officer, was one of the judges or judge advocates. For some reason unknown, he illustrated the importance of obeying military orders. He noted that in his country, disobeying military orders deserved death. He went on to note that success in the execution of war depended on a firm obedience to given orders.[77]

Even though General Marie-Joseph Paul Yves Roch Gilbert du Motier, Marquis de Lafayette, a French aristocrat and military officer, lamented about the offense committed by Ceasar, after the hero was condemned, he was not punished. Although Ceasar was pardoned, he was displeased with General Lafayette's comment advocating death for men who disobey military orders. Hoping to relieve his anger, Ceasar said, "Old Fayette carried the joke too far."[78] Surely, Lafayette did not believe that arresting a war prisoner was a crime. Fowler's account does not detail much about Ceasar. It is unknown whether he was a slave. Similarly, there is no description of the area where Ceasar captured the British soldier. Moreover, the fate of the British soldier detained at the American camp was not recorded. Possibly, during the Revolutionary War, many British soldiers were taken as prisoners-of-war by Americans, but there are no records to indicate whether they faced martial court.

The alarms of Lexington, Concord, and Cambridge were responded to by the inhabitants of New Hampshire. Throughout the history of New England, the colonies observed inclusive military policy against any threat to their existence. Unlike the former wars, during the alarms of Lexington, Concord, and Cambridge, African Americans were included in the militia. New Hampshire men shared the burden of defending the colonies with their brethren from Massachusetts, Rhode

---

76. William C. Fowler, *The Historical Status of the Negro in Connecticut: A Paper Read Before the New Haven Colony Historical Society*, Walker, Evans & Cogswell Company, 1901, p. 22.
77. Ibid.
78. Ibid., p. 23.

Island, and Connecticut. Just like New Hampshire's white inhabitants, African bondsmen were enlisted to defend freedom and liberty. On the list of Captain Stephen Clark's military company, two blacks were enrolled. Jubil Martin and Sidon Martin were listed on the Bureau of Pension in Washington, D.C., as men who served in 1775.[79] Similarly, on the list of Captain Robert Follett, artillery man at Kittery Point, two other blacks were enlisted. William Negro and Cicero Negro were soldiers in that company.[80]

The enlistment of people of color during the battles of Lexington, Concord, and Bunker Hill was conducted from several perspectives. Blacks enlisted voluntarily and others by the consent of their masters. Slave owners in colonial New Hampshire overlooked local or provincial laws regulating the enlistment of people of African descent in local militia during the battles of Lexington, Concord, Cambridge, and others. From the *Provincial and States Papers, Vol. 17*, the record shows that in New Hampshire, on June 12, 1775, blacks were enlisted by consent of their masters in the company of Captain Arthur Gilman. The *Provincial and States Papers* documents give such an account. The document tells of Sippio, Archelus, and Robin as being enlisted by the consent of their master. In the same paper, Robin is referred to as Reuben Roberts, Negro. At the start of the war, Sippio was 27 years old, Archelus was 22 years old, and Robin or Reuben was 23 years old. In addition to these men, Jubil Martin and Sidon Martin were African Americans listed in 1775 under the direction and care of Hall Jackson.[81]

Unlike other black soldiers in New Hampshire, Tony, or Anthony Clark, was a fiddler in the Revolutionary War. He was at the Bunker Hill battle as a waiter, where he served General George Washington. According to the *New Hampshire State Magazine* of 1895, Anthony Clark fiddled for officers during the war. He also distributed cartridges at Bunker Hill. The same *State Magazine* notes that he witnessed many battles and was present at the surrender of Charles Cornwallis. "Old Tony," as Clark was called, was possibly permitted to carry a weapon while distributing

---

79. See *New Hampshire Provincial and State Papers*, vol. 17, 1889, p. 24.
80. See *New Hampshire Provincial and State Papers*, vol. 14, 1885, p. 237.
81. See *New Hampshire Provincial and State Papers*, vol. 17, 1889, pp. 7–8, 23–24.

cartridges to soldiers. Due to his military services, upon his death at approximately 102 years of age, Old Tony was given a military funeral.[82] Anthony Clark is also credited with instructing people on being polite.[83] This docile appearance may have been Clark's ruse to gain the approval of his community so he could be integrated into it.

Another African American who served to defend the colony against the British in New Hampshire was Judge Hall, also known as "Old Rock." Hall was born in Exeter, New Hampshire. He was among the soldiers who fought at Bunker Hill and continued his service for eight years.[84] From the account of George Waldo Browne, Hall was listed from Hillsborough in the company of Colonel Moses Nichols.[85]

It is not likely to comprise an exact number of militia men who served in New Hampshire in 1775. According to the *New Hampshire Provincial Papers*, the number of men who went from the state to Cambridge is unknown because many of the men who engaged in battle were not organized in companies, and some returned home after being absent for one to two weeks. Others were enlisted for the specified time of eight months. Although black men served for these short periods during the beginning of the alarm, their names were not recorded.

African American Seamen and the Beginning of the Navy in America

Before exploring the presence of African Americans in the navy from respective colonies or as members of the Continental Navy, it is significant to give a brief narrative about the emergence of the American Navy. The employment of African Americans as seamen and privateers dates in retrospect to the Colonial Era. In Rhode Island, many men of color served as seamen and privateers during King George's War and during the French and Indian War.

---

82. See *The Granite Monthly: A New Hampshire Magazine*, vol. 19. Granite Monthly Company, 1895, pp. 415–16. The same information can be found in the *History of Merrimack and Belknap Counties, New Hampshire*, Part 2, 1885, p. 672.
83. See *History of Merrimack and Belknap Counties, New Hampshire*, 1885, p. 672.
84. Nell, *The Colored Patriots of the American Revolution*, R.F. Wallcut, 1855, p. 119.
85. George Waldo B., *The History of Hillsborough, New Hampshire, 1735–1921*, vol. 1, John B. Clark Company Printers, 1921, p. 142.

CHAPTER 7

Like during colonial wars, the Revolutionary War was conducted on land and sea. History reveals that each province in New England purchased a sloop, a small, square-rigged warship with two or three masts, to defend commerce. Additionally, sloops of war were utilized as an arm for the destruction of the British economy and naval military equipment. Officials of the Continental Congress fitted warships for the execution of war on the water highway. From the records of the Massachusetts Historical Society, the hostility carried by the Americans toward the British at sea was carried out by continental vessels, state navies, and privateers.[86] The men enlisted to sail these sloops of war were ordered to destroy the military and economic power of England on the water highway.

Throughout the history of the American colonies, the sea force was always executed to inflict commercial pain to enemies. To illustrate, during colonial wars the private citizens of Rhode Island as well as colonial officials advocated the use of privateers for the destruction of French and Spanish ships. The practice of giving prize money to pay crew members who participated in privateer activities was observed. Colonial governors and the King of England legalized attacks on enemy ships. It was a tradition in colonial New England for each colony to commission the inhabitants to engage in privateer assignments during military conflicts.

In 1775, when the British unjustly attacked Americans in Lexington, Concord, and afterward Cambridge, colonial officials in Rhode Island chartered two sloops to protect their sea towns. Edward Field wrote that the *Sloop Washington* and *Sloop Kathy* were used to protect trade.[87] The *Sloop Washington* was both larger and designed to carry 80 men. It was equipped with 10 four pounders and 14 swivel guns, as recorded by Field. On the other hand, the smaller of the two ships, *Sloop Katy*, was made to carry 30 crewmen.[88] These were the first sloops purchased to protect sea towns. *Sloops Washington* and *Katy* were under the command of Captain

---

86. See *State Navies and Privateers, Proceeding of the Massachusetts Historical Society*, The Society, 1913, p. 179.

87. Edward Field, *Esek Hopkins, Commodore in Chief*, Preston & Rounds Company, 1898, p. 63.

88. Ibid.

Abraham Whipple with the title of Commodore.[89] Captain Whipple was a reputed privateer man in Providence, Rhode Island. During the French and Indian War, he was very active as a privateer. He captured approximately 23 ships. During the Revolutionary War, the value of goods captured by him amounted to $1,000,000.[90] He commanded the *Providence*, the Continental naval vessel built in that state. In the *Journal of the Continental Congress*, Whipple is mentioned as commander of the ship *Columbus*.[91] Local historians believe the beginning of the American Navy as a branch of the military occurred in Rhode Island. This account has been noted, too, by the Massachusetts Historical Society. According to the historical society journal, "the first American armed vessels commissioned by any public authority were two sloops fitted out by Rhode Island on June 15, 1775."[92]

At the start of the Revolutionary War, inhabitants of Rhode Island feared an attack from the British. As precautions, militiamen were put on readiness, anticipating British military assault. Regarding sea force, Rhode Island men were familiar with sea life. Many private citizens within the colony owned sloops for commercial purposes. But during war times, these commercial sloops were transformed into military. This was the case when Captain Abraham Whipple captured the British frigate *Rose* in the Narragansett Bay on June 15, 1775.[93] Throughout the year, the British army cruised continuously in Narragansett Bay, where military guards blocked free circulation of ships. They denied ships from Rhode Island to leave or enter the bay. As a result, the Rhode Island legislature appointed Captain Whipple as commander of the newly purchased sloops with the mandate of patrolling the water highway along the bay. As an experienced captain, Whipple chased the *Rose*, and captured it.[94] Historically, the capture of the British frigate

---

89. Samuel G. Arnold, *History of the State of Rhode Island and Providence Plantations: 1701–1790*. D. Appleton & Company, 1889, p. 351.

90. See *Ships and Shipmasters of Old Providence*, 1920, p. 10.

91. See *Journals of the Continental Congress*, Printed and Published by Way and Gideon, 1823, p. 511. Also *Proceedings of the Rhode Island Historical Society*, 1877, p. 21.

92. *Proceeding of the Massachusetts Historical Society*, The Society, 1913, p. 180.

93. Ibid.

94. See Report of the Commodore, Abraham Whipple Society, of Pawtucket, Rhode Island. *The American Monthly Magazine National Society*, vol. 11, 1897, p. 654.

by Whipple was the first British defeat during the Revolutionary War. The Daughters of the American Revolution contend that "Captain Whipple deserved credit for being the first American to have fired the first gun under the authority of the colonial government at the beginning of the war."[95] About the capture of the British *Sloop Rose*, Samuel Greene Arnold wrote, "this was the beginning of a glorious era in the naval enterprise of Rhode Island."[96] The incident was possibly glorified by the Americans. The British sloop *Rose* was commanded by Captain James Wallace.

In 1772, Captain Whipple was a major player in the destruction of His Majesty's vessel of war, the *Gaspee*. After the Providence men set fire to sloop *Gaspee*, Captain Wallace, His Majesty's commander in Rhode Island, wrote to Whipple saying, "I will hang him [Whipple] at the yard-arm."[97] According to the *Records of the Colony of Rhode Island and Providence Plantations*, John Brown, a prominent merchant of Providence and Joseph Brown of the same town were the principal actors who destroyed the *Gaspee*. They were assisted by Simeon Potter of Bristol, Doctor Weeks of Warwick, and Richmond of Providence.[98] The *Gaspee* was commanded by Lieutenant Thomas Duddingston, who was charged with the prevention of illicit trade in Rhode Island.[99]

The response to the letter written by Captain James Wallace to Captain Abraham Whipple reads, "To Sir Wallace James, Sir: Always catch a man before you hang him. Abraham Whipple."[100] Whipple has been credited for his courage and for the missions he carried out as a commanding officer in the navy. Due to his familiarity with risky priva-

---

95. Ibid.

96. Arnold, 1889, p. 350.

97. Richard Mather B., *History of Newport County, Rhode Island, From the Year 1638 to the Year 1887, Including the Settlement of Its Towns, and Their Subsequent Progress*, L.E. Preston Company, 1888, p. 314.

98. *Records of the Colony of Rhode Island and Providence Plantations, in New England: Printed by order of the General Assembly*, vol. 7, A.C. Greene and Brothers, State Printers, 1862, p. 94. See also William Reed Staples, *The Documentary History of the Destruction of the Gaspee*. Knowles, Vose and Anthony, 1845, p. 17.

99. See *Ships and Shipmasters of Old Providence*, Providence, R.I.: Printed for the Providence Institution for savings, 1920, p. 11.

100. Thomas Williams Bicknell, *The History of the State of Rhode Island and Providence Plantations*, vol. 2, American Historical Society, 1920, p. 742.

teer missions, Whipple did not believe that it would be an easy task for him to be captured by Wallace.

In Massachusetts, the inhabitants of Machias under the leadership of John and Jeremiah O'Brien and Captain Benjamin Foster captured the British war sloop *Margaretta*. John O'Brien stood against the intimidation of the British men of war. An armed British sloop, commanded by Captain James Moore, was stationed at Machias River in the little town of Machias. The inhabitants refused to take down the liberty pole, a wooden pole planted to symbolize the colonists' displeasure with British authority. During this event, John O'Brien rejected firmly the order of Captain Moore. The presence of the British captain was a nuisance to the inhabitants of Machias. As a result, a plan was put into place to seize the captain when he went to church. But after being warned, the captain escaped without delay.

The escape of the British captain did not discourage the Machias patriots. Instead, they formed a group of almost 30 persons and sailed to the Machias River in the lumber sloop *Unity*. At the river, Jeremiah O'Brien was chosen as the commander of the *Unity*. The colonists began chasing the *Margaretta*. After many challenges, the *Margaretta* was captured from the British and brought to Machias. This tug-of-war was the first seizure of the British armed sloop by individual people in the Massachusetts colony. After the capture of the *Margaretta*, the armaments from the ship were transferred to the *Unity*, and Captain O'Brien was appointed commander of the sloop. In July 1775, O'Brien captured the *Deligence* and *Tapnoquism* near Buck's Harbor, is what is now eastern Maine. O'Brien became the commander of the *Margaretta* after it became a sloop of war and his younger brother, William, was his lieutenant.[101] The newly captured *Deligence* was commanded by John Lambert, and John O'Brien was his lieutenant. According to Andrew M. Sherman, the *Deligence* had the capacity to carry 40 men, and the ship carried eight guns and 20 swivels.[102]

---

101. Thomas Clark, *Naval History of the United States, from the Commencement of the Revolutionary War*, 1814, p. 18. See Andrew M. Sherman, "Capt. John O'Brien," *The American Historical Magazine*, vol.4, nos. 1–3. American Historical Company. National American Society. Publishing Society of New York, 1909, pp. 443–48.
102. Ibid.

CHAPTER 7

In 1775, the Massachusetts colony chartered a vessel for General George Washington from private citizens of the state. On October 16, 1775, Daniel Adams, mariner, and Colonel Ephraim Bowen agreed on the use of the schooner *Harrison* for General Washington. The settled agreement was that the schooner must cruise the waterway from Cape Cod to Cape Anne. In the same year, the Massachusetts vessel, the *Brigantine*, was chartered from John Torrey, Benjamin Wormwell of Plymouth, and Ephraim Bowen. This vessel was fitted for cruising from Cape Cod to Cape Ann and elsewhere. It seems that Wormwell and Bowen were open for the discharge date of the ship. Moreover, General Washington was given permission to use the vessel, as needed.[103] With the execution of sea forces, the Continental Congress established laws governing captured warships and privateering.

Laws Governing the Capture of Enemy War Ships and Privateering

Historically, Anglo-Americans and Anglo-Saxons have believed in solving problems through legal mechanisms. It is the folkways of their forefathers. During the Revolutionary War, the same tradition was observed. Hoping to avoid arbitrary captures of British ships on the sea, the Continental Congress set forth laws which every American had to obey during war. On November 25, 1775, the Continental Congress authorized the capture of any armed vessels belonging to Great Britain used for the operation of war. And vessels carrying war equipment such as munitions were subjected to the same treatment. The trial methods for such cases were also documented. Moreover, the share of seized merchandise from enemy warships was determined.[104] Consequently, regulations regarding the prizes were set forth to avoid conflicts between the concerned parties.

---

103. Charles Henry L., *Naval Records of the American Revolution: 1775–1788*, Library of Congress. Manuscript Division. Gov. Print. Off, 1906, p. 9.

104. *The Case of Great Britain: As Laid Before the Tribunal of Arbitration, Convened at Geneva Under the Provisions of the Treaty Between the United States of America and Her Majesty the Queen of Great Britain, Concluded at Washington, May, 1871*. U.S. Government Printing Office, 1872, p. 711.

On March 23, 1776, the Continental Congress officially elaborated a resolution authorizing the use of pirate-armed vessels during the Revolutionary War. The mandates of officers navigating the waters on the pirate-armed vessels were to inflict commercial or military pain to the enemies of the United Colonies. Simultaneously, Americans were encouraged to fit privateer-armed vessels for the execution of war against enemies of the United Colonies. The methods of applying for the commission of privateer were adopted, as well.[105] After setting rules governing pirates' missions, Americans became heavily involved in privateering during the Revolutionary war. The British were surprised about the manner in which the Americans challenged the superiority of the British Navy. With the aim of excelling in the naval war, the Americans were obligated to form a naval force.

The American Navy

By July 1775, the American colonies were no longer separated from each other as they were under the rule of the British Crown. The concept of the United Colonies was no longer a regional design. The United Colonies comprised all the thirteen English colonies in America. As they became a unit, the military force, and the navy, were treated the same. Therefore, when the Thirteen United Colonies formed an army, General George Washington was appointed the commander of that army. Washington was from the colony of Virginia and a war veteran of the French and Indian War. His appointment was not based on public sentiment, but on his individual merit.

On October 13, 1775, the Continental Congress passed a resolution authorizing the establishment of the American naval forces. At first, two armed vessels were ordered. Then 17 days later, two more vessels were added.[106] Because four armed vessels were not enough for a war of such magnitude, Congress approved the building of more vessels for the same purpose.

Two months after that, 13 vessels were ordered for the American Navy by members of the Naval Committee. This six-man committee

---
105. Ibid.
106. Ibid.

included Silas Deane, John Adams, Stephen Hopkins, John Langdon, Joseph Hewes, and Richard Henry Lee. Members of the Committee were entrusted with purchasing war vessels upon the authorization of Congress. Additionally, the Committee suggested the types of vessels to be constructed and the areas where the vessels would be constructed. Accordingly, five ships of 32 guns each, five ships of 28 guns, and three ships of 24 guns were the vessels recommended by the Naval Committee. According to historian Edgar Stanton Maclay, the expenses for the construction of the 13 vessels amounted to $866,666.66.[107] The Committee recommended the construction of the vessels in various colonies: two were to be built in Massachusetts, Rhode Island and New York; one was to be built in New Hampshire and Maryland; and the remaining six vessels were to be built in colonies the Committee selected.[108] The names of the vessels built by the recommendation of the committee were: *Hancock, Randolph, Raleigh, Warren, Washington, Congress, Effingham, Providence, Trumbull, Virginia, Boston, Delaware,* and *Montgomery*.[109]

Esek Hopkins of Rhode Island was appointed commander-in-chief of the Continental Navy. Commonly called "Commodore," he was entrusted to formally organize the naval branch of the military.[110] Commodore Hopkins was born in providence, Rhode Island on April 26, 1718. His sea life was not a matter of coincidence. His brothers were deeply involved in the sea life. During the Revolutionary war, his brother, Stephen Hopkins was one of the naval committees, and he was an experienced captain.[111] Commodore Hopkins was an experienced military man. Before his appointment as commander-in-chief of the Continental Naval Force, he was a sea captain. He was among the most noted privateers in the history of Rhode Island. The Commodore was appointed

---

107. Robert Grieve, "Esek Hopkins, First Admiral of the American Navy," *The New England Magazine*, vol. 17. New England Magazine Company, p. 351.

108. Ibid.

109. Edgar S. Maclay, *A History of the United States Navy, From 1775 to 1793*, vol. 1, D. Appleton, 1894, p. 36.

110. Ibid.

111. Edward Field , Esek Hopkins, Commander-in-chief of the Continental Navy During the American Revolution, 1775 to 1778: Master Mariner, Politician, Brigadier General, Naval Officer, and Philanthropist, Preston & Rounds Company, 1898, pp. 6–14, 41, 48–50.

brigadier general of the Rhode Island colony militia. His appointment as navy commander-in-chief is possibly due to his handling of heavy guns during his previous years as a privateer. He was active during the old French and Indian War, a war that amassed him a fortune.

Active African Americans in the Continental and State Naval Forces

In 1775, men with maritime experience qualified for enlistment in the Continental Navy, the state naval forces, and on privateer vessels of war. African Americans with the same maritime experience as other seamen were also included. There were no restrictions on the employment of African Americans in the Continental Navy. Many of them were already seamen aboard privateers that preyed upon commercial vessels. Being accustomed to sea life, their selection in the colonies and Continental naval forces was not a matter of question. They were enlisted to serve aboard the vessels and galleys built in the colonies at the recommendation of the Naval Committee. Records attest to the fact that men of color were listed as members on the Board of Continental Frigates in Boston and Providence. In addition to the Continental naval forces, African Americans were enlisted in the state naval forces. In Massachusetts, Connecticut, and Rhode Island, names of African Americans who served on many state sloops are included on historical records. In New Hampshire and in Maine, African Americans were probably enlisted in the navy.

In Continental Naval Forces

On the Continental Navy frigate *USS Boston*, African Americans were included. In the company of Captain Hector McNeil of Boston, African Americans served under him. Among those who enlisted under McNeil were: Cato Austin and Nero Freeman. Austin was mentioned as gunner number one, and Freeman was gunner number eleven. In addition to the above names, Cuff Freeman and Wood Cato were part of the servicemen aboard the *USS Boston*. From the collection made by the Office of the Massachusetts Secretary of State, Sunday White was listed as seaman on the *USS Boston*. At the time when White served on the frigate, Captain Samuel Tucker was the commander. On March 15,

1779, White was engaged on the frigate where he served for a month. Tucker transferred to frigate protector on March 1, 1780. After serving for five months and sixteen days, he was discharged on August 17, 1780. He was identified as "Negro" during his enlistment.[112] Frigate *USS Boston* was built in the city of Boston at the request of the Naval Committee assigned by the Continental Congress on December 13, 1775. It was one of the largest ships built in Massachusetts. The frigate was built to accommodate 20 guns.[113]

In 1780, Cato Pembleton served on the Continental frigate *USS Dean*. Pembleton was under the command of Captain Elisha Hinman. At the time when Pembleton was enlisted, he was 30 years old. He was a mariner before joining the navy. Pembleton was a volunteer on board of the armed ship *Dean*.[114] It is possible that Pembleton was accepted to serve in the navy due to his sailing experience. He was a native of Massachusetts. His status is not mentioned, so researchers do not know if he was a free man or a slave. A similar African American man who served on the frigate *Dean* was Cato Lindal, a resident of Rhode Island. He served at the same time as Cato Pembleton. Lindal was 18 years old at the time when he enlisted in the navy. He was a mariner before his induction Into the navy.[115] The frigate *Dean* was built in Nante, France in 1777 under the supervision of Jonathan William, the grand-nephew of Benjamin Franklin of Philadelphia. In 1782, the frigate was later called the *Hague* instead of *Dean*.

In 1777, an African American served on board the frigate *Hancock*. John Brick was enlisted in the navy as a seaman. According to the certificate of service dated February 20, 1778, an African American named

---

112. *The New Hampshire Genealogical Record: Official Organ of the New Hampshire Genealogical Society*, Vol. 3–6. George W. Tibbetts, 1906, p. 31–37. In addition to the named black crewmen, Scipio Brown, Caesar Fairwell, Ceasar Lee, and Pomp Petters were other African Americans enlisted on board frigate *Boston*.

113. Ibid., p. 26.

114. See *Massachusetts Soldiers and Sailors of the American Revolutionary War: A Compilation from the Archives, Prepared and Published by the Secretary of the Commonwealth in Accordance with Chapter 100. Resolves of 1891*, vol. 12. Wright and Potter Printing Co. State Printer, 1904, p. 110.

115. See *Massachusetts Soldiers and Sailors of the Revolutionary War*, vol.9, Wright and Potter Co. State Printers, 1902, p. 825.

Brick lost his left leg during a battle against the British frigate *Fox*. For his disability, the General Court allowed him half-pay from his discharge August 7, 1777.[116] The Service history of Brick is incomplete. The initial date of his enlistment and the number of years he spent in the Continental Navy was not mentioned. The *Hancock* was built in Newburyport, Massachusetts, at the request of the Naval Committee. African Americans served in the state navy such as in Massachusetts and Connecticut.

African Americans in the Naval Forces in Massachusetts
In 1776, Massachusetts built many sloops and frigates to aid in fighting the war against the British. In Massachusetts, African Americans served aboard the sloop *Protector*. In 1781, Plato William, a Negro, was enlisted on the *Protector*, commanded by Captain John Foster William. Plato served on the ship for two months and six days. On May 5, 1781, he was captured by the British. Prince Quam, another African American, under the same Captain William was enlisted on March 13, 1780. Quam was discharged the same year on August 17. He served for five-months-and-four days aboard the *Protector*.[117] In Connecticut, African Americans were enlisted in the state navy. In Dracut, Massachusetts, Silas Royal served on the sloop *Franklin*, a privateer. Before joining the navy, he was enlisted in the company of Captain John Reed and the regiment of Colonel James Varnum. According to Silas Roger Coburn, an African American named Royal was the servant of General J. B. Varnum. It was in January 1776 that Royal joined the army.[118]

African Americans in the State Navy in Connecticut
Here, many ships and sloops were fitted out for the war. The Connecticut men were heavily involved as privateers. Many war sloops and frigates were built for the fight against the enemy. Privateers preyed on

---

116. See *Massachusetts Soldiers and Sailors of the Revolutionary War*, vol. 2, Wright and Potter Printing Company, State Printers, 1896, p. 480.

117. *Massachusetts Soldiers and Sailors of the American Revolutionary War*, vol. 19, Wright and Potter Printing Company, 1908, p. 471.

118. Silas Coburn, *History of Dracut, Massachusetts*, Press of the Courier-Citizen Company, 1922, p. 336.

enemy commercial ships without mercy. The primary purpose of the privateers was to disrupt commerce. Of note, fighters of the American Revolution introduced another type of warship. The brigantine was exceptionally useful because this vessel could travel faster, could maneuver easily, and could serve for many purposes. Additionally, the ship could be scaled up at various sizes to accommodate a variety of needs. Among the brigantines and sloops built in Connecticut were: the brigantines *Minerva, Defense, America,* and the sloops *Spy, Oliver Cromwell,* and others. African Americans were enlisted on board brigantines *Minerva* and *Defense.*

In 1776, Peter, an African American, was enlisted on the brigantine *Minerva.* He started his service on August 25 of the same year and was discharged on December 23, 1776. Another African American named Gift served on the *Minerva.* He was enlisted on August 25, 1776 and he was discharged on December 19, 1776.[119] The *Collection of the Connecticut Historical Society* does not mention the occupation of the one-name-only black men who were on board the ship. This trend continued even during the early days of the American Republic. Likely, African Americans were enlisted on the brigantine *Defense.* George, Negro, served on board the ship as seaman. He was enlisted on April 10, 1776, and discharged on November 15, 1776.[120] Peter, the Negro, previously mentioned, had a second commission to serve under Captain Seth Warner in the same year. He was enlisted as a seaman and served for a few months only. He started his service on August 29 and was discharged on November 25, 1776.[121]

African Americans in the State Navy in Rhode Island

In 1775, in Newport, Rhode Island, an inclusive policy was observed for the recruitment of Revolutionary War sailors. According to historians, in this year, whites and blacks were encouraged to enlist to work on the naval war vessels in the interest of the colony. Possibly, patriotic African Americans responded to the demand of the officials. In the same

---

119. See *Collection of the Connecticut Historical Society*, vol. 8, 1901, p. 229.
120. Ibid., p. 232.
121. Ibid., p. 237.

town, when Captain John Paul, an American privateer, was charged with the command of the frigate, *Providence*, he took with him two African Americans. Cato and Scipio were under Captain Paul during the Revolutionary War.[122]

At the beginning of the Revolution, the plight of the New England colonies against the British were defended by everyone able men including African descendants. However, with the formation of the Continental army, the inclusion of African Americans was rejected by members of the Continental Congress including General Washington. But this policy was reversed when their miltary contributions were valued by some Continental government officials. As a result, African Americans who served during the Battles of Lexington and Cambridge were authorized to enlist in the Continental Army. In the American Navy, there were no restrictions as to the inclusion of African Americans from the beginning to the end of the Revolutionary.

---

122. Charles Haven, *Ladd Johnston, Famous Privateersmen and Adventures of the Sea*, L.C. Page, 1911, pp. 241–44. John Paul Jones was a Scotch man who immigrated to America. He lived with his brother in Virginia and later he owned a plantation. During his life, he spent many years in seafaring. For a time, one of his crew members was Mungo Maxwell, a mulatto. It appears that he killed the black man because he felt threatened by him.

Chapter 8

Black Government-by-Proxy in Colonial New England

While on a visit in the colonies of New England, if you were told that blacks held a government-by-proxy for the control of people of their own color, the statement would sound absurd. But as a fact, in colonial Connecticut, Rhode Island, and New Hampshire, a black government was organized for the administration of their affairs among black people, as well as to manage the conflicts which happened between black slaves and their owners. Orville Platt, who discussed the existence of black governors in New England, agrees that conflicts between slaves and masters were solved in the black court.[1] Similarly, in Narragansett, Alice Morse Earle noted that Cuddymonk, a black governor, assisted with the resolution of the conflicts between blacks and white people.[2] In this case, the black governor did not serve only people of his color, but everyone who sought his legal assistance. In general, the services of the black governors benefited the New England colonies in terms of peace and security.

As to the existence of the black government, the *Federal Writer's Project* narrates that African Americans in Newport, Rhode Island, "establish[ed] their government in imitation of the whites."[3] The occurrence of a black government in Rhode Island, Connecticut, and New Hampshire was emphasized by many authors. In New Hampshire, Charles War-

---

1. See Orville H. Platt, *"Negro Governor"*, New Haven Colony Historical Society Papers, vol. 6, 1900, pp. 315–35.
2. Alice Morse Earle, *In Old Narragansett: Romances and Realities*, C. Scribner's Sons, 1898, p. 81.
3. See *Rhode Island, a Guide to the Smallest State*, Federal Writers' Project, 1937, p. 205.

ren Brewster notes that "blacks were authorized to form a mock government."[4] In Connecticut, Thomas Bailey Aldrich writes that "blacks were permitted to have a kind of government of their own, indeed, were encouraged to do so, and no unreasonable restrictions were placed on their social enjoyment."[5] A similar notation on the government of the black population was made by Orville Platt during his presentation before the New Haven Colony Historical Society on the subject in question. For him, the agents such as the governor, lieutenant-governor, the sheriffs, and justice of the peace who administered the services to black members of the community constituted an entire government. From the account of these aforementioned writers, the proxy government of the blacks was not a constitutional government, but a sort of customary or tribal government. The inscription written on the grave stone located in the public burial ground regarding Governor Boston Trowtrow supports the theory that the black government in Connecticut was tribal or customary oriented. The stone in the public burial of Governor Boston Trowtrow reads, "in the memory of Boston Trowtrow, Governor of the African tribe in this town who died 1772, age 66."[6]

It is possible that Africans in New England colonies observed the traditions of their forefathers in Africa. Though living in New England, these transplanted Africans organized an acceptable mechanism for the regulations of social norms and mores in accordance with the ancestors' folkways. To illustrate, in the forest alongside the Saugus River in Lynn, Massachusetts, where King Pompey resided, Africans celebrated the coronation of their king in accordance with the African royal norms. Flowers were given to him, and a musical ceremony was observed. Similarly, in Durham, where King Ceasar was crowned, a celebration was accompanied with music. The art of music is a way of life in Africa. Olaudah Equiano affirms that music was well introduced in his society. Music was played during celebrations such as retuning from triumphal war.[7] More

---

4. Charles Warren Brewster, *Rambling about Portsmouth*, Brewster, 1873, pp. 210, 212.
5. Ibid.
6. Frances M. Caulkins, *History of Norwich, Connecticut*, H.P. Haven, 1874, p. 330.
7. Olaudah Equiano, *The Interesting Narrative of the Life of Olaudah Equiano, Or Gustavus Vassa, The African. Sold*, 1790, p. 7. Musical instruments played during the ceremony included the trumpets.

details on the coronation will be discussed in the section covering the ceremony of the black governors and kings.

Edgar J. McManus also recognized the existence of a sub-government of black governors in the New England colonies, but he does not elaborate about the said government. In addition to his recognition of a black government, he does stipulate the judiciary duties of the black governors, judges, and magistrates in Connecticut.[8] It is especially noteworthy that government of colonial New England black citizenry was not discussed by modern American historians. It is well-documented that a de facto government of blacks existed in colonial New England. The administration of justice as well as regulations of norms, including the election processes, are tangible proof indicating the institutionalization of a visible black government. In reality, African Americans were aware that they had a government. The black governor was respected by the black population, and his decision was the law. His major role was to bring harmony within his constituents.

While the establishment of a black government during the colonial era is overlooked, many scholars discuss the election procedures of black governors in Massachusetts, Rhode Island, Connecticut, and New Hampshire. In addition, scholars have noted the elections of black kings in the same colonies. The reserved day for the election of a black governor in New England was called "Nigger' Lection Day." In colonial Massachusetts, an election day for the black governor was also observed, but at the time of this writing, researchers have not discovered any process noting the existing of a black government. For example, in Lynn, King Pompey apparently did not organize a group of government officials.[9] In Saugus, there is no record of any organized government or minor officers acting under King Pompey. It is unknown whether or not the King had minor officers administering the affairs black people in the local court in his name. Possibly, Africans who resided in Saugus consulted King Pompey to solve conflicts between African slaves and servants.

---

8. Edgar J. McManus, *Black Bondage in the North*, Syracuse University Press, 1973, p. 96.

9. Horace H. Atherton, *History of Saugus, Massachusetts*, Citizens Committee of the Saugus Board of Trade, 1916, p. 101. See also Alonzo Lewis, *The History of Lynn: Including Nahant*, S.N. Dickinson, 1844, p. 218.

Similarly, in the case of servants' disobedience, more than likely owners sought King Pompey's legal assistance for reprimanding the offenders. In Salem, Massachusetts, on a Wednesday in 1741, a holiday for African Americans was recorded by Benjamin Lynde of Salem.[10] The organization of African Americans' elections on the last Wednesday morning before the end of the week was also noted by Joseph Barlow Felt, the author of *The Annals of Salem*. From the records of these authors, the election of African governors started in Salem, Massachusetts. Felt says that during the Election Day, African Americans chose a governor for one year.[11]

In Connecticut, it appears that the governors served for a long period before being succeeded. The succession of a governor occurred in case of his death or if he developed health problems. This was the case of how John Anderson, the black servant of Governor Philip Wharton Skene in Hartford, was appointed to the governorship. An African slave known by only as Cuff, was elected after the death of London another black governor of Hartford. London died in 1770. It seems that when London was the governor of blacks in Hartford, he governed all the Africans in the colony. Governor Cuff served for ten years before resigning from his office on May 11, 1776. As a reminder, Governor Skene governed the territory of Crown Point and Ticonderoga. He was arrested by the Americans when the territory of Ticonderoga was captured and delivered to the Continental Congress in Philadelphia.[12] After being incarcerated in Philadelphia, Governor Skene was sentenced to parole in Hartford, Connecticut by the request of the Continental Congress. For his safety and the safety his family, he was transferred to West Hartford.[13] Major French and the son of Governor Skene were also on parole in West Hartford, Connecticut.

---

10. Fitch Edward Oliver, *The Diary of Benjamin Lynde and of Benjamin Lynde Jr*, Priv. Print [Cambridge, Reverside Press], 1880, p. 109.

11. Joseph Barlow Felt, *Annals of Salem*, vol. 2, W.& S.B. Ives, 1849, p. 419.

12. Frank Moore, *Diary of the American Revolution: From Newspapers and Original Documents*, Vol. 1, C. Scribner, 1860, p. 92. On his parole, Colonel Skene was ordered to remain within eight miles of the city between the Delaware and Schuylkill Rivers and not corresponding with any person on public subject during his parole time.

13. Royla Ralph Hinman, *A Historical Collection from Official Records, Files, &..., of the Part Substained by Connecticut, During the War of the Revolution: With an Appendix, Containing Important Letters, Depositions, &., Written During the War*. E. Gleason, 1842, p. 31.

In 1760, when Quaw, another slave known by a single name, was elected governor at Hartford in the town of Wethersfield, London Chester was also elected as the black governor. The elections of two black governors during the same year in Connecticut were due to the population increase. It is possible that Governor London Chester governed African Americans in Simsbury as well as Wethersfield. Similarly, African Americans who resided in Negrotown were also under his jurisdiction. Genealogist Abiel Brown notes that "many blacks lived on the east shore of New Hartford and on the North East part of Old Simsbury, which was called Negrotown."[14] It is possible that in Negrotown, a sort of local black government was organized for the administration of town affairs. If the town was formed of black people only, a sort of regulated mechanism was observed for the administration of justice.

With the black population increase, in Connecticut and Rhode Island for example, black governors were elected in various towns. Author Wilkins Updike agrees that in Rhode Island, the elections of black governors expanded in many towns due to the increase of their populations.[15] This was true in colonial Connecticut. In the earlier American republic, there were many elected black governors throughout many cities in Connecticut, more than in any other colonies. In addition to the governors, there were also more black kings elected in Connecticut than in New Hampshire. In Connecticut, in Durham and New Haven black kings were elected. In New Hampshire, records indicate that a black king was elected in Portsmouth only. Ceasar was the black king elected in Durham, and Lawson was the black king elected in New Haven. In Portsmouth, New Hampshire, another African by the name of Ceasar was elected king.

Black Governors in Connecticut in the Colonial and Earlier Republic Era

In Connecticut, where the colonial government had a liberal policy toward the blacks who populated the colony and the state, African

---

14. Abiel Brown, *Genealogical History: With Short Sketches and Family Records of the Early Settlers of West Simsbury, New Canton, Connecticut*, 1899, p. 141.

15. Wilkins Updike notes that when the slaves were numerous, each town held its election. See Wilkins Updike, *History of the Episcopal Church in Narragansett, Rhode Island*, H.M. Onderdonk, 1847, p. 178.

bondsmen elected their own governors in New London, Hartford, and Norwich. In these three towns, there were many African bondsmen during the colonial era. Frances Manwaring Caulkins, a local Norwich historian, noted that there were many black slaves in Norwich, and they were well-treated by their masters. There were also many blacks in Hartford. In fact, the population of African Americans was so large that they were able to elect a person of their own race as their governor. It appears that in New London, a black governor was elected earlier than in any other towns in Connecticut. To date, there is no conclusive evidence as to when an inclusive black government of black officials emerged in New England in general nor in Connecticut in particular.

Accordingly, historians believe that the system of electing a black governor in Connecticut emerged in 1749 due to the data collected from a gravestone in a burial ground in New London, Connecticut. Susan Campbell writes that on the burial site of Florio, a female African American, the name of her husband was mentioned. The stone on the graveyard reads, "Florio Hercules Wife of Hercules, governor of the Negroes."[16] The account of Campbell corroborates with that of James M. Rose and Barbara W. Brown. These two writers in their work titled *Tapestry, a Living History of the Blacks in Southern Connecticut* mentioned that Hercules was a black governor in New London, Connecticut.[17] Even though the name of Hercules appears on the gravestone as governor of the blacks, there is no conclusive evidence indicating that Hercules was elected in 1749. This date is only a tangible illustration indicating the existence of a black governor in New London. In 1756, according to Samuel Orcutt, 829 Africans lived in that city. Surely, a large number of Africans resided in New London County.[18] In his diary, Joshua Hempstead recorded a quite large number of Africans residing

---

16. See Susan Campbell, *Hartford Courant, Abolition & Slavery in New London. Travel into the Past at City's Well Preserved Historic Sites.* August 29, 2006.
17. James M. Rose and Barbara W. Brown, *Tapestry, a Living History of the Black Family in Southern Connecticut*, Genealogical Publishing Co., 1979, p. 37.
18. Samuel Orcutt, *History of the Towns of New Milford and Bridgewater, Connecticut, 1703—1882.* Press of the Case. Lockwood and Brainard Company, 1882, p. 136. The census was collected from various cities. In Groton there were 179 Africans. Lyme had 100. Killingsworth had 16. There were 233 Africans in Norwich. Preston had 78 Africans; 33 Africans resided in Saybrook at this period of time. 200 Africans lived in Stonington.

in that city. To illustrate, in 1745, he noted that Will Wright, a mulatto, and his family resided in New London. Adam, the servant of Hempstead, was also an African American, who lived in New London.

The account on the election of black governors in Hartford, Connecticut has been written by many authors such as Lorenzo Johnston Greene and Isaac William Stuart, the author of *Hartford in the Olden Times: Its First Thirty Years*. Additionally, the Hartford Black History Project lists names of black governors in the colony and the state of Connecticut. In the data collected from the Museum of Connecticut History, London, the black servant of Captain Seymour, was mentioned as the first elected black governor in Hartford, Connecticut elected in 1755.[19] It seems that he served for five years only. In 1760, he was succeeded by Governor Quaw, the servant of Col. George Wyllys. According to the informant of Isaac William Stuart, Governor Quaw was very dark, stiff, and proud. It seems that he was African-born.[20] He served almost for six years before he died. After his death, he was succeeded by Governor Cuff.

In 1766, Cuff was elected black governor in Harford, Connecticut. After serving for many years, he resigned his post and chose John Anderson as his successor. It was in 1776 that John Anderson became a black governor for African Americans in Connecticut. The appointment of John Anderson was suspicious to colonial officials in Connecticut. The account on the appointment of John Anderson by Governor Cuff will be discussed later in this chapter. As in Hartford, Connecticut, an African American was elected governor in the town of Wethersfield during the colonial era.

In 1760, as noted in the Hartford Black Heritage History Project, London Chester was elected governor of the black community in Wethersfield. While the project gave little detail on Governor London, Abiel Brown listed Chester as well as the name of his former master. According to Brown, London Chester was a black governor in Wethersfield, Connecticut. He was African-born and imported to the colony while he was young. Accordingly, he spoke the English language fluently. Before his liberation, he was a servant of Colonel John Chester,

---

19. William D. Piersen, *Black Yankees: The Development of Afro-American Subculture in Eighteenth-Century New England*. Univ. of Massachusetts Press, 1988, p. 129.

20. Isaac W. Stuart, *Hartford in the Olden Time: Its First Thirty Years*. F.A. Brown, 1853, pp. 39–39.

the elder. London Chester was married to a woman named Betty with whom he had a family. Brown did not list the names of Governor Chester's children. As to his wife, she died in 1787. In Wethersfield, where Governor Chester resided, African Americans were quite numerous. Brown writes that from 1750 to 1776, about four-or-five hundred Africans were held as servants in Wethersfield. Among the Africans who lived in Wethersfield were: Charles Prince, servant of Captain Dudley Case; Simon Fletcher, sometimes called Lieutenant Simon; and Caesar Willcox, whom Brown believed was African-born and owned by Joseph Willcox, who died in 1759.[21]

In 1770, in Norwich, Connecticut, Boston Trowtrow of Norwich was elected a black governor.[22] He died in 1772 at the age of 66, and his gravestone reads: "Boston Trowtrow Governor of the African Tribes in this town, who died 1772, age 66." The inscription shows that possibly each town had its own black governor. Trowtrow was a servant of Nichols of Hartford, who bequeathed him a beautiful estate. The house was located on Cole Street, where many colonial governors resided.[23] Cole Street was later named Governors Street because of its history of governors as residents. In 1772, Trowtrow was succeeded by Sam Huntington, the African servant of Governor Samuel Huntington of Connecticut. According to the Hartford Black History Project, he served in the position for almost 18 years. Frances Manwaring Caulkins writes that Sam Huntington served as governor longer than his master when he was the governor of Connecticut.[24]

Under the early American republic, African Americans elected black governors in cities such as Farmington, Durham, Derby, New Haven, Seymour, and Woodbridge.[25] Author Isaac William Stuart says also

---

21. See Abiel Brown, *Genealogical History: With Short Sketches and Family Records, of the Early Settlers of West Simsbury, Now Canton, Connecticut*, 1899, pp. 140–41. Also The Hartford Black History Project, *Emerging from the Shadows, 1775–1819; The Black Governors*.

22. See the lists of Negro governors in the Connecticut Public Library.

23. Stuart, *Hartford in the Olden Time*. F.A. Brown, 1853, pp. 33, 40

24. Caulkins, *History of Norwich, Connecticut: From Its Possession by the Indians to the Year 1866*. H.P. Haven, 1874. The Hartford Black History Project, *Emerging from the Shadows, 1775–1819: The Black Governors*.

25. See *The Lists of Negro Governors* in the Connecticut Public Library website.

that black governors were elected in Middletown and Wallingford.[26] In Windsor, Connecticut, "Nigger' Lection" was held till 1820.[27] On November 23, 1786, in Litchfield, Connecticut, Cesar Will, a free man, was recorded as governor of blacks. He was a former slave of Major Seymour.[28] There were many black governors elected in 1800 in Connecticut. Some of them even made military contributions during the Revolutionary War. Eben Tobias, the father of Honorable Eben D. Bassett, a grandson of an African prince, was a black governor in Derby. Tobias grew up in the family of Captain Wooster of Derby. The African American governor and slave was a man of tact, courage, and unusual intelligence.[29] Governor Eben Tobias's legacy continued with his son, who was educated at Yale College. Hon. Eben D. Bassett was the first African American appointed to an American diplomatic post. He was appointed consul general in Haiti and served as a soldier during the Civil War.[30]

Quosh Freeman, a black governor in Derby was a bodyguard for Isaac Smith when he was stationed at Danbury.[31] Roswell (Quosh) Freeman, the only son of Quosh Freeman, was an elected black governor in Derby. Governor Roswell Freeman was thin with a dark complexion. He was a fox hunter by profession. In Derby, he was credited as a man of principle who lived a quiet life. He lived on good terms with other people.[32] Samuel Orcutt writes that Governor Freeman was elected three times as governor. However, he was not popular among the black people because he did not give gifts to his constituents.[33] In addition to the towns listed above in

---

26. Ibid., p. 44.

27. For "Nigger 'Lection" in Windsor, Connecticut, see Alfred Emanuel Smith and Francis Walton, *New Outlook*, vol. 49. Outlook Publishing Company, Incorporated, 1894, p. 744.

28. *History of Litchfield County, Connecticut*, With illustrations and biographical sketches of Its prominent men and pioneers. Philadelphia, J.W. Lewis & Company, 1881, p. 142.

29. Orville H. Platt, *Negro Governors*, See *Papers of the New Haven Colony Historical Society*, Vol. 6, New Haven Colony Historical Society, 1900, p. 333.

30. Jane De Forest Shelton, "Making of America Project, The New England Negro: A Remnant." *Harpers Magazine*, vol. 8, Harper's Magazine Co., 1893, p. 536.

31. Samuel Orcutt, *History of the Old Derby, Connecticut*, Press of Springfield Printing Company, 1880, p. 182.

32. George Shelton, Negro slavery in old Deerfield [Boston.: Mass.: s.n.], 1893, p. 537.

33. Orcutt, *History of the Old Derby, Connecticut*, Press of Springfield Printing Company, 1830, p. 549.

Connecticut, the election of a black governor was also held in the city of Oxford, according to Samuel Orcutt.[34] In 1811, in Norwich, Connecticut, Mary Elizabeth Perkins notes that Ira Tossett was the last black governor in that town. Perkins, the author of the *Old Houses of the Ancient Town of Norwich*, did not record much information on him.[35]

Black Governors in Rhode Island during the Colonial and Earlier Republic

In Rhode Island, black governors during the colonial era were elected in Newport, Narragansett, and in South and North Kingston, where African slaves were numerous. Caroline Hazard notes that there were more slaves in South Kingston than in any other part of Rhode Island.[36] The account of Hazard correlates with the data recorded in the Rhode Island census of 1730, which recorded 333 black inhabitants in that year in Narragansett. On the other hand, in North Kingston, there were 165 blacks. These two towns were divided in 1722, and a separate charter was given to them. While South Kingston had many blacks, the town of Newport had 649 blacks in 1730. In North Kingston, there were 165 blacks. In South Kingston, 333 Africans resided in that town in 1730.[37]

The first black governor in Newport was elected in 1756.[38] The data of the first elected African American in Newport, Rhode Island was not recorded by earlier or modern researchers who explored this topic. There are records regarding the first black governor in South and North Kingston. Wilkins Updike, Thomas Robinson Hazard, Edgar Mayhew Bacon, Caroline Hazard, Orville H. Platt, Irving Berdine Richman,

---

34. Ibid.

35. Mary E. Perkins, *Old Houses of the Ancient Town of Norwich [Conn.] 1600–1800*, Bulletin Company, 1895, p. 83.

36. Caroline Hazard, *The Narrangansett Friend's Meeting in the XVII Century: With a Chapter on Quaker beginnings in Rhode Island*, Houghton Mifflin, 1899.

37. Elisha R. Potter, *The Early History of Narragansett: With an Appendix of Original Documents, Many of Which are Now for the First Time Published*, vol. 3, Marshall, Brown, 1835, pp. 113–14.

38. Federal Writer's Project, *Rhode Island, A Guide to the Smallest State*, Best Books On, 1937, p. 205.

CHAPTER 8

and William Johnston, among others who wrote on the black governors in Rhode Island, did not mention the names of black governors in South Kingston and North Kingston during the colonial era. In Little Compton, Primus Collins, a free African American, was elected as governor of the blacks. He was always identified as governor by his constituents.[39]

During the Early Republic, in 1795, black governors were elected in North and South Kingston.[40] In the 1800s, elections for black governors were held in Newport and Narragansett. In the 1800s, Will, the slave of Elisha R. Potter, and Cuddymonk, an African American, were elected governors in the Narragansett. Cuddymonk was elected in 1811.[41] John, the servant of Elisha R. Potter, was also elected in 1800. Aaron Potter was also another African American who was elected in 1800. He belonged to the family of Elisha. R. Potter. Updike believed that the election of black governors in Rhode Island ended after the War of 1812. The celebration of the black governor elected after 1812 happened at the woods on Rose Hill when possibly Aaron Potter was elected. In addition to the names listed above, Earle notes that Prince Robinson and Guy Watson were elected to governors in Rhode Island. Even though the names of these individual people were mentioned as black governors, Earle failed to detail the towns where they were elected. Additionally, she did not record how long Governor Robinson and Watson served in the office. In addition to the governors, a chief marshal and his assistants administered the election process. The count of number of votes was entrusted to the marshal. He was a sort of an election commissioner. The result of the election was also pronounced by him.[42] It is unknown whether or the chief marshal was elected by the blacks or appointed by the governor. In Newport, only franchised African Americans were allowed to vote.

---

39. Wilson R. Buxton and Roswell Beebe Burchard, *The Two-Hundred Anniversary of the Organization of the United States Congregational Church, Little Compton, Rhode Island, September 7, 1904*, United Congressional Society, 1906, p. 88.

40. Wilkins Updike, A History of the Episcopal Church in Narragansett, Rhode Island, H.M. Onderdonk, 1847, p. 178.

41. For the election of the slave of Hon. Elisha R. Potter, see Updike, 1847, p. 178, and for the election of Cuddymonk, see Alice Morse Earle, *The Old Narragansett: Romances and Realities*, C. Scribner's Sons, 1898, p. 89.

42. Updike, 1847, p. 178.

According to the African American rules, an African American who had a pig and sty was permitted to vote.[43] The manner on how this rule was enforced was not recorded. It is possible that the chief marshal and his assistant checked each constituent before voting.

The Black King in New Hampshire

Historically, in New England, during the colonial era and early American republic, kings were elected among African Americans. In the colony of New Hampshire, historical evidence shows that a black king was elected in Portsmouth.[44] To date, the title of governor has not been found in New Hampshire. Historians such as Charles Warren Brewster, Valerie Cunningham, and others list Nero Brewster, the servant of Colonel William Brewster, as the king of Africans in Portsmouth, New Hampshire. Brewster, the author of *Rambles About Portsmouth*, describes how King Nero dressed during the coronation. In regard to the election of a king among the Africans in New Hampshire, Brewster notes that "for many years they [Africans] held their annual election in June, usually on Portsmouth plains. They elected a king, who was also a judge."[45] The revelation of Brewster shows that the system of electing African kings in New Hampshire among the blacks did not start with the reign of King Nero Brewster. To date, the reign of King Nero remains the emblem of the king of Africans in Portsmouth, New Hampshire. Even though he is listed as king, his reign has not been explored.

---

43. Federal Writers Project, *Rhode Island: A Guide to the Smallest State*, Somerset Publishers, Inc., Jan 1, 1938, p. 205.

44. Charles W. Brewster, *Rambles about Portsmouth*, C.W. Brewster & Son, Portsmouth, Journal Office, 1859, p. 210; Valerie Cunningham, *Black Portsmouth: The Century of African-American Heritage*, UPN, 2004.

45. Brewster,1873, pp. 212–13. Mr. Brewster writes that "his full dress in small clothes required some filling in the back of the silk stockings, to give a proper contour to the person of the king." As Brewster, Sarah Haven Foster notes that " [African] slaves had every year a mock election at the plains, choosing a king, amid great festivities." The plain according to Foster was the first settlement of the province and it was quite a village. In 1725, the population of this village increased and numerous people resided there. See Sara Haven Foster, The Portsmouth Guide Book: Comprising a Survey of the City and Neighborhood, with Notices of the Principal Buildings, Sites of Historical Interest, and Public Institutions. Joseph H. Foster, 1876, p. 129.

In addition to the king, a viceroy named Willie Clarkson, a slave of Peirse Long, was elected. Jock Odiorne was elected sheriff, and Pharaoh Shores was his deputy.[46] These black leaders were among those who signed a petition in New Hampshire declaring the emancipation of the people of African descent from slavery. His majesty King Nero was a colonial soldier who fought in many wars. He endured pain during his captivity in Canada when he was seized at Fort William Henry.

Officers of the Black Government

During the colonial era, in Connecticut and Rhode Island, as well as New Hampshire, the Negro government was composed of among other officials a governor, a deputy-governor, a sheriff and deputy sheriff, counselors, marshals, constables, and other military officials.[47] The governor was the only elected political official. The title of black governor was sometimes referred to as town leader of the blacks, executive officer of the blacks, and head officer of the blacks.[48] Irving Berdine Richman termed the Negro governor in Connecticut as "Negro Town Leader."[49] In addition to civil officers, military officers were also appointed by the governor.[50]

Historically, during slavery, the elected governors were the servants or slaves of high-ranking colonial officials. In Connecticut, for example, London Chester, the first recorded Negro governor at Hartford, was the Negro servant of Col. John Chester of Wethersfield, Connecticut.[51] Colonel Chester was a government official who was born from a prestigious and influential family in Connecticut. He was a member of the council and a county court judge.[52] By being part of the family of Colonel Chester, researchers can speculate that Governor London received good training of every kind due to his master's educational

---

46. Cunningham, 2004, p. 13.
47. See Brewster, 1859, p. 210; Robert, 1906, p. 218; Stuart, 1853, p. 37.
48. Stuart, 1853, p. 37.
49. Irving B. Richman, *Rhode Island: A Study in Separatism*, Houghton, Mifflin, 1905, p. 157.
50. Stuart, *Hartford in the Olden Time: Its First Thirty Years*, F.A. Brown, 1853, p. 38.
51. Piersen, 1988.
52. James Trumbull, *The Memorial History of Hartford, Connecticut, 1633–1884*, vol. 1, E. L. Osgood, 1886, p. 271.

background. In addition to the training black servants received from their masters, elected Negro governors were well-equipped with the Africans' norms. To illustrate, Governor Boston Trowtrow was proud to note that stealing was not honorable to a Guinea man. From his statement, we can assume that the African tribal norms were enforced upon the Negroes in the colonies.

Peleg Nott, a Negro governor, who belonged to Col. Jeremiah Wadsworth.[53] Nott appears to be a knowledgeable Negro servant. He was a superintendent of his master's farm in West Hartford.[54] With the skills he acquired in managing the farm of his master, he was able to govern his fellow Africans. Historian Isaac Stuart notes that an informant whom he did not identify credited Nott as being the most independent and responsible man in the west division. Therefore, Nott's master did not oppose his election as Negro governor. Nott died after the inauguration of his governorship while mounting a horse. The history of Peleg Nott is very interesting. It appears that he was not happy about his status. He did not value the position which he held in his master's farm and in the black community. He believed only in his freedom. Anticipating his freedom, he requested that his master liberate him from bondage not by paying him a sum of money, but through a dialogue between both. The liberation dialogue between Peleg Nott and Col. Jeremiah Wadsworth was as follows:

"Massa, me want to be free," said Peleg.

"What do you want to be free for?" asked Wadsworth.

"Oh Massa, freedom's sweet," replied Peleg.

"Well then," said his master, "I'll make you free."

"When will you make me so?" inquired Peleg.

"Now," answered Col. Wadsworth, "you are free from this day." And he became so.[55]

This illustration indicates that even though black people had a government and handled their own problems to some extent, they disliked being under bondage.

---

53. Stuart, 1853, p. 39.
54. Ibid.
55. Ibid., p. 40.

CHAPTER 8

Before his death, Nott, like other Negro servants who were high-ranking military officers, participated with Col. Wadsworth during the American Revolutionary War. He drove a provision cart when his master was in charge of the commissary. In Hartford, those who knew Nott described him as "a first-rate feller," who looked remarkable when attired in his military dress.[56] The military uniform had been given to him by his master. In colonial days, slaves and servants were given arms by their masters in anticipation of possible Indian attacks. Possibly, weapons were also given to slaves and servants while they worked on farms. Pieces of military equipment were also offered to the slaves and servants by the owners when the territory was pressed for war. In Connecticut, as noted in the chapter dealing with the contributions of the Negroes in the French and Indian wars, there were many Negro slaves and servants who fought for the security of the colonies.

Quaw, the second Negro governor, who succeeded Governor London in Hartford, was a slave of Col. George Wyllys, the secretary of the colony of Connecticut and clerk of the town of Hartford, Connecticut. An old man living in Hartford told Isaac William Stuart that "Quaw was the stiffest and proudest 'Darkie' he ever saw."[57] Quaw was an African who was imported to colonial Connecticut as a slave. Sam Huntington, a Negro slave who took the name of his master, Samuel Huntington, the colonial governor of Connecticut, was elected governor of the Negroes. During the slavery era, it was not unusual for slaves in New England to take the names of their masters.

In the town of Seymour, Connecticut, Juba Weston, a slave belonging to General Humphrey, was elected Negro governor.[58] The first Negro governor in Derby was Quosh, who was enslaved as a boy after being sold to slave traders. According to Jane De Forest Shelton, Quosh was well-built and strong, and he belonged to Agar Tomlinson, who resided at Derby Neck. Tomlinson owned a large estate in Derby which was divided into quarters. In each quarter, small houses were built for the accommodations of his slaves. The entire estate was under the im-

---

56. Ibid., p. 39.
57. Ibid.
58. See George Shelton, "*The New England Negro: A Remnant on the Harper's magazine, vol. 88*", Harper's Magazine Company, 1893, p. 536.

mediate supervision of Quosh, his Negro servant.⁵⁹ Governor Quosh assumed dual duties. He superintended his master's employees and his African brethren. By handling multiple employments, Governor Quosh proved to be a very capable manager and leader. The responsibilities he had were not minimal. He was charged with managing servants, as well as safely keeping the account of his master.

The African bondsmen in Connecticut were educated in the houses of their masters. The process of educating the bondsmen began when they were young. Unlike Southern slaves, some bondsmen in the North were literate and able to read and write the English language. The education and skills they acquired from their masters and the training gained from managing farms and states were sufficient to allow slaves to govern their fellow black people when they were elected governors. In Connecticut, slave owners prepared their Negro servants from youth to be productive citizens. From the work history of Quosh and Peleg Nott, it can be stipulated that Negro governors in Connecticut were from honorable and dignified families. Their owners were among the powerful and most educated people in Connecticut. To illustrate, Colonel Wyllys was the son of Governor Wyllys, and he also held prestigious and powerful positions in the colony. He was also a college graduate.⁶⁰ The slave owners supported the candidacy of their servants to serve as leaders among their own because they were well-prepared to handle multiple tasks such as being a servant and managing the black community.

In Rhode Island, John was the slave of Elisha. R. Potter, a state legislator, when the former was elected a governor of the Negroes. John had been educated in the house of his master. He received political instructions when he was young. Just as John has been educated in the house of his master, Aaron Potter, another slave had a similar experience. Before he was elected governor around 1800, he had received lessons in the science of government when he was younger. When he was a teenager, Potter resided in the home of Elisha R. Potter.⁶¹ Similarly,

---

59. Ibid.
60. Trumbull, 1886, p. 271.
61. Thomas R. Hazard, *Recollection of Olden Times: Rowland Robinson of Narragansett and His Unfortunate Daughter: With Genealogies of the Robinson, Hazard, and Sweet families of Rhode Island*, J.P. Sanborne, 1879, pp. 121–22.

Prince Robinson, a Negro governor, received his early skills in the house of his master, Hazard Robinson. In Rhode Island, like in other colonies of New England, slaves received their industrial and social training in the house of their first master. This is the reason why many Negro governors in Connecticut had mastered literacy.

While there is no historical recorded data in regard to the selections and the appointments of Negro minor officers, researchers who have written about black governors and the election day process have emphasized how the black governors were selected. Frederick Calvin Norton and George Simon Roberts noted that the election of black governors was conducted by proxy, because all the Negroes could not attend the event.[62] George Simon Roberts went on to say that "the whites required that the black governor should be notable for his honesty."[63] From the statement of George Simon Roberts, it is worthy to note that white inhabitants in the colonies paid attention to the candidacy of the black governors. Black people also had their own expectations on the candidacy of a Negro governor. According to Isaac William Stuart, "The Negroes selected for the office was a person of much note among themselves, of imposing presence, strength, firmness, and volubility, who was quick to decide, ready to command, and able to flog." Stuart went on to note that it was necessary he should be an honest Negro, and be, or appear to be, "wise above his fellow."[64] Just as white observers, the Negroes' expectations about a candidate for a black governor were high. They believed in a person of exceptional quality to lead them.

Contrary to Connecticut, where the elected governor appointed his minor officers, in New Hampshire, the officials who formed the Negro government were elected by members of the black community. Charles W. Brewster, a native and the local historian of Portsmouth, New Hampshire, reveals that, "Negroes annually in June elected a king, (who was also a judge) a sheriff, and deputy, besides other officers."[65]

---

62. Frederick C. Norton, "Negro Slavery in Connecticut," *Connecticut Magazines*, vol. 1, The Connecticut Magazine Co., 1899, p. 322.

63. George S. Robert, *Historic Towns of the Connecticut River Valley*, Robson & Adee, 1906, p. 218.

64. Stuart, 1853, p. 38.

65. Brewster, 1859, p. 210.

It seems that the black governor in New Hampshire did not have the same executive power as the black governor in Connecticut. Due to his executive power, the governor in Connecticut was able to appoint or dismiss his appointed officials. On the contrary, in New Hampshire it does not seem that the king was able to that. William Chauncey Fowler recorded the election of King Caesar in Durham, Connecticut. According to Fowler, King Caesar was elected in the remembrance of the kings in Guinea.[66] The election of Kings in these two provinces was discussed by William Dillon Piersen. According to him, in the royal provinces, the Negroes elected a king.[67] But through the analysis of the records of Alonzo Lewis regarding King Pompey in Salem, Massachusetts, and the record of William Chauncey Fowler on King Caesar of Durham, Connecticut, including King Nero in Portsmouth, New Hampshire, it appears that the African royal blood lineage had an influence in regard to the election of kings in colonial New England. In the case of Massachusetts, King Pompey was not elected. He was considered as a king because of his African royal lineage. Similarly, there is no evidence indicating that King Ring in Bridgewater was elected. King Ring, the slave of Colonel Simeon in Bridgewater, believed in the African traditions. It is said that he "whipped the apple–trees, to make them grow."[68] This king, who might be African-born, followed his forefather's planting traditions. According to the African tradition, African forefathers sometimes conducted ceremonies in the garden while planting their harvests. As King Ring, Cuddymonk in Narragansett, who was not a king, believed in the African traditions. Alice Morse Earle says, "Cuddymonk was deeply and consistently superstitious, and knew a thousand tales of ghosts and spirits and witches and manitous, old African Voodooism and Indian Pow–wows. He was profoundly learned in the meaning of dreams and predictions. He did not hesitate to practice–or attempt to

---

66. William C. Fowler, *The Historical Status of the Negro in Connecticut: A Paper Read before the New Haven Colony Historical Society*, Walker, Evans & Cogswell Company, 1901, p. 21.

67. Piersen, 1988, p. 118.

68. Bradford Kingman, *History of North Bridgewater County, Massachusetts: From Its First Settlement to the Present Time, with Registers*, The author, 1866, p. 317.

practice–all kinds of witch–charms and able [sort] of witch–charms and conjures."[69]

Another king who was not elected by the Negroes was King Mumford in Salem. King Mumford who was identified as a big, burly, and powerful fellow lived in the vicinity of Nonantum Hall in the colony of Negroes. He was identified by his people as King Mumford.[70] A similar African king was Dick. Benjamin Waterhouse notes that there were about one-hundred-and-fifty prisoners. Among the Negroes, Dick was very large and Herculean. He was six-foot-five-inches in height and was called King Dick. He made rounds every day in the prison, inspecting the beds of his Negro subjects. When he made his round, he dressed in his large–skin cap and carried in his hand a huge club.[71] It appears that due to his title, he threatened Negroes who misbehaved in prison. He punished Negro prisoners who were dirty, drunk, or those who were negligent.[72] The assumption of Professor William Dillon Piersen stipulating that in the royal colonies Negroes were elected kings because their governors were appointed by the English king is questionable because it does not look like there were not any African kings elected in Massachusetts. In New York, a Negro organizer of the black Pinkster's ceremony, was called King Charles.[73] Pinkster Day was a day which everyone observed, and many activities were held by blacks and their white counterparts. The name Pinkster derived from the Dutch word for Pentecost and has been celebrated in New Amsterdam.[74] From all these illustrations, it appears Negro kings in colonial Massachusetts were identified by the Negroes due either to possessing certain physical attributes or to having some connections to a royal lineage in Africa.

---

69. Earle, 1898, pp. 79–80.

70. Carl Webber and Wirrifield S. Nevins, *Old Naumkeog: An Historical Sketch of the City of Salem, and the towns of Marblehead, Peabody, Beverly, Danvers, Winham, Manchester, Toufield, and Middleton*, A.A. Smith, 1877, p. 134.

71. Benjamin Waterhouse, *A Journal of a Young Man of Massachusetts* (Reprinted), William Abbatt, 1911, p. 193.

72. Ibid.

73. Alice Morse Earle, *Colonial Days in Old New York*, C. Scribner's Sons, 1896, pp. 195–97.

74. Ibid.

Power of the Black Functionaries and Their Jurisprudence

The power of the functionaries of the black government was sometimes misunderstood by earlier writers of the Negro governors. Isaac William Stuart said that "he could not find out for certain the precise sphere of the power of the Negro governor. However it is probable that the power of the Negro governor covered general matters, and ceremonies." Stuart goes on to say that the black governor "settled all grave disputes in the last resort, questioned conduct, and imposed penalties and punishments sometimes for vice or misconduct."[75]

The power of the black governor was complex, and it was difficult for Stuart to define accurately. His power covered many spheres of life such as the enforcement of norms, arbitration, punishments, and the administration of social events such as ceremonies. Possibly, the black governor, and his minor officers as well as counselors, enacted the norms which the black constituents had to observe. The norms were enacted by the officers for the black government even though they were unwritten, and every African American was requested to observe them. The governors had control over all the blacks living in the colonies where such government existed. In the *Connecticut Magazine*, Frederick Calvin Norton recorded that "black governors displayed every evidences of regal authority over his people."[76] In the same document, it was noted that some of them claimed descent from the African kings. It is plausible to note that the African jurisprudence as well as the power of the governors was similar to that of their forefathers in Africa. They were highly respected and honored. To illustrate, in Connecticut, Isaac William Stuart writes that "the black governor was respected as 'Gubernor' as noted many old gentlemen. Negroes through the state obeyed him implicitly."[77] The governor was like a father to the Africans in Hartford. Any act of disobedience toward him was possibly condemned by African Americans. Similarly, he was not permitted to disrespect his fellows. Mutual respect was surely observed and valued.

---

75. Stuart, 1853, p. 38.
76. Frederick Calvin Norton, "Negro Slavery in Connecticut," *Connecticut Magazine: An Illustrated Monthly*, vol.5, The Connecticut Magazine Co., 1899, p. 322.
77. Stuart, 1853, p. 38.

In Connecticut, white subjects expected the officers of the black government to keep the Negroes in order. In Hartford, Isaac William Stuart writes that "the black governor settled grave disputes in the last resort, questioned conduct, and imposed penalties and punished sometimes for vice or misconduct."[78] The statement of Stuart implicitly clarifies some of the duties performed by the black governor. Appeal cases were adjudicated by him as well as violation of grave social norms. Possibly, adultery was part of grave social norms. In the African tradition, adultery was a felony and punished with death. Perhaps, in New England, black governors or kings had the power to settle adultery, but not minor officers.

The judiciary power of the black governors and king was also mentioned by Thomas Bailey Aldrich, the author of *An Old Town by Sea*. He notes that in Portsmouth, New Hampshire, "in case of misdemeanor, African Americans were permitted to be judge and jury. Their administration of justice was often characteristically naïve."[79] From his account, we can conclude that power of the black king and his minor officers in New Hampshire was legalized by the colonial government. The process was legitimate and legal. As to the procedural law, it is sound to stipulate that the rule of evidence and the manner of adjudicating the case were African in nature. The object of the customary African jurisprudence was keeping harmony in the community. Therefore, arbitration and mediation were the preferred methods employed in the judiciary system. Possibly, due to insufficient knowledge on the African jurisprudence, Mr. Aldrich mistakenly labeled the African administration of justice as being naïve.

In Narragansett, Cuddymonk settled disputes between his African American brethren. According to Alice Morse Earle, his office had some power and commanded some respect among the white people.[80] She also noted that he handled cases brought to him by white people.[81] Cuddymonk had the power to regulate the relationship between black and white people without major problems because he was respected

---

78. Stuart, 1853, p. 38.
79. Thomas B. Aldrich, *An Old Town by the Sea*, Houghton Mifflin,1894, p. 78.
80. Earle, 1898, p. 81.
81. Ibid.

by both races. Through the black governors, political and economic mandates of the slave owners as well as other business people were more than likely fulfilled. Cuddymonk was elected twice as black governor due to his political skills, not because he belonged to a wealthy slave master.[82] He was not paid for his duties, but received small favors.[83] Possibly, his white friends as well as his black subjects offered him few emoluments for his service.

Through the components of the criminal justice which they administered, we can stipulate that the black government was well-structured. They also established a jurisprudence which was similar to the African tribal government. To illustrate, in the jurisprudence of the Negroes, the court proceeding was short. The councilors and the governor decided the verdict of the case and appeal cases. Immoral conduct of the black people was also punished. Sometimes, the punishments were administered in a public place as general deterrence to others. In Hartford, the punishment administered by Esquire Nep deterred many Negroes from misbehaving. An informant told Isaac William Stuart that "Old Nep always operated as a terror to the blacks, and kept them orderly. We have got a well-behaved set of them now, taken as a whole—it is certain. Many of them are 'prime' in a better than a mercantile sense. Our city in this respect is favored."[84] The perception of the inhabitants of Hartford indicates that the Negroes at Hartford were as well-mannered as their white counterparts in general. In addition to corporal punishment, restitution and fines were the types of punishments enforced by Esquire Nep in his court. Stuart says that one informant told him that "inhabitants of Hartford were satisfied from all they heard about the black governors. Their influences were useful because it kept the blacks in good order."[85]

The judiciary jurisdiction of the black government was given the same weight as the colonial administration in regard to minor crimes among blacks. The jurisdiction of the court was observed by both administrations colonial and the black-run government. This was shown

---

82. Ibid.
83. Ibid.
84. Stuart, 1853, p. 44.
85. Ibid., p. 43.

in Hartford when a Negro man was guilty of a crime; he was brought before Justice of the Peace, Jonathan Bull, Esq., for his trial. As the suspect was brought before the colonial judge, the case was transferred to the Negro Court by the order of Esq. Jonathan Bull.[86] The court case was finally adjudicated by Esquire Nep, a black justice of the peace. Accordingly, Esquire Nep ordered the criminal to give up all his tobacco and his gun as restitution. Additionally, the African slave received thirty lashes on his bare back. According to Stuart, the sentence was carried into effect on the South Green by candlelight. Nep was sometimes called Neptune and was a barber by profession. Esquire Nep was a man of principles and integrity. He was known for his sternness and firmness. He was an influential man among his colored people.[87] In Hartford, Nep was respected by the blacks and white people.[88]

In the Narrangasett Bay, Edgar Mayhew Bacon noted that the "Negro governors enjoyed much influence over their black constituents, and were the arbiter of their private differences."[89] By arbiter or referee, Bacon meant that they were judges who settled cases involving black people.

In New Hampshire, Charles Warren Brewster narrates the court case of King Nero; Prince Jackson, a Negro man, was seized by a Negro sheriff, Jock Odiorne, for stealing an axe. When Jackson was before his Majesty King Nero, the evidence was presented and examined. After this deliberation, Jackson was found guilty. As a custom, when a person was found guilty in the Negro court, he was sentenced to receive some amount of lashes administered by the sheriff or his deputy. In this case, Jackson's penalty was to receive twenty lashes on the bare back at the town pump.[90] According to Brewster, during the administration of the punishment in King Nero's court, there was a general gathering of the slaves who witnessed how the offender was lashed.[91] In regard to the case of Prince Jackson, Sheriff Jock Odiorne took off his coat before

---

86. Ibid., p. 44.
87. Ibid.
88. Ibid.
89. Edgar M. Bacon, Narragansett Bay: its Historic and Romantic Associations and Picturesque, Putnam, 1904, p. 242.
90. Brewster, 1859, p. 210.
91. Ibid.

the administration of the punishment, tied up the convict to the pump, and ordered his deputy to punish the criminal. Deputy Pharaoh Shores announced before the execution of the punishment, "Gemmen[gentelment], this way we s'port[support] our government."[92] After the address, Jackson received his twenty lashes and was advised to avoid any presence on the side of Christian Shore, where he stole an axe. But the punishment and the warning did not have any effects on his behavior. He ended up being caught for a major crime which Brewster did not specify. For the major crime, possibly a felony, Jackson faced the colonial justice.[93] In his second arrest, as it was a major crime, he was taken to the county court. From these illustrations, it is plausible to stipulate that minor (misdemeanor) cases among the blacks were settled in the black court, and major crimes (felony) committed by the Negroes were under the jurisdiction of the county court. As there was no data regarding the classification of crimes in the African American jurisdiction during the period under examination, it is difficult to argue with exactitude how court officers in the black government determined which crimes were classified as a misdemeanor or a felony.

Sociological Aspects of the Blacks' Election Day

Before the discussion of Nigger Lection Day [Black's Election Day] as a political event, it is instrumental to relate the sociological aspect of the said event. Through the writing of many local historians in colonial New England, Nigger Lection Day has been portrayed as a social event and a holiday for African bondsmen. In Rhode Island, the author of the *Rhode Island Historical Society* called the Negro Election Day the most interesting social custom of the Negroes in that colony.[94] Joseph Barlow Felt, a the local historian of Salem, Massachusetts and Alonzo Lewis, and James R. Newhall, local historians of Lynn, Massachusetts, related the activities of the Negro's holiday. Alonzo Lewis and James R. Newhall reported that in the house of King Pompey, one of the slaves of

---

92. Ibid., p. 211.
93. Ibid.
94. See the *Publications of the Rhode Island Historical Society*, vol. 2, Rhode Historical Society, 1894, p. 139.

Thomas Mansfield of Lynn, Negroes gathered yearly celebrating their holiday. According to these authors, Pompey was a prince in Africa, but was brought to Lynn as slave.[95] In Lynn, his royal blood was observed by those who knew about his heritage and gave him his royal respect he deserved as if they were in Africa. According to the historical records, slaves in Lynn and the surrounding towns, including Boston, went to Pompey's house for the celebrations of the Negro Holiday.[96] During this event, the Negroes danced and talked about their past histories in Gambia in Africa, while those who were born in colonial America listened. Some of the Negroes brought with them gifts for King Pompey.[97] This was a delightful day for the people of African descent, because they expressed their feeling freely and enjoyed the day as if they were free from bondage. Music, dancing, and sporting were healthy for their well being. The events more than likely were celebrated the same way as they were in Africa.

At the house of King Pompey close to the Saugus River, Alonzo Lewis says that "maidens gathered flowers to crown their old king, and men talked of the happy hours they had known on the banks of the Gambia."[98] This day was dear to the Africans. Whether from Gambia or not, many African slaves imported from colonial America lived near the Ocean or big rivers, where Europeans had access. It is unknown whether or not all the slaves who visited King Pompey were from Gambia. The celebration of the Negro Holiday was mentioned by Benjamin Lynde in 1741. This is the first record and compelling evidence of the Negro Holiday in the provincial government of Massachusetts. There are many accounts on the Negro Holiday, but Benjamin Lynde recorded the exact date when the event happened. Based on the record in the Diaries of Benjamin Lynde and Benjamin Lynde Jr., the holiday for African Americans was very important. In those diaries, Benjamin Lynde gave his servant Scipio five pounds and William two pounds and six

---

95. Alonzo Lewis and James Robinson Newhall, *History of Lynn, Essex County, Massachusetts, including Lynnfield, Saugus, Swampscott, and Nahant, 1629—[1893]*, G.C. Herbert, 1890, p. 344.

96. Ibid.

97. Ibid.

98. Ibid.

cents for the celebration of the Negro Holiday held in May, Wednesday the 27th, 1741, in Salem, Massachusetts.[99] The General Election of the Provincial Government of Massachusetts according to the charter of 1691 was scheduled on the last Wednesday in May. During the provincial government, the General Election of Massachusetts was scheduled on a Wednesday in May and continued the same from 1693, to the adoption of the Constitution of Massachusetts.[100] The holiday Lynde talked about happened also in the last Wednesday in May, 1741. Therefore, the Negroes celebrated their holiday during the Massachusetts General Election. According to authors such as Duane Hamilton, the General Election in Massachusetts was called "Nigger 'Lection Day" because African slaves and servants were authorized to celebrate with their white brethren. The celebration of the General Election Day in Massachusetts was open to everyone without regard to color. Negroes, Indians, and white counterparts celebrated the holiday together in the common. Negroes were allowed to enter in the common only the day of the General Election. The common was the property of the government where many celebrations were held in during the colonial era.

It appears that in Massachusetts, the Negro holiday was a privilege which every servant enjoyed in accordance with the law of the colony. Nathaniel B. Shurtleff notes that the Election Day which acquired the name of "Negro Election Day" was the General Election Day, in which the General Court of Massachusetts assembled and chose its officers, including in colonial times.[101] Charles Nutt, the author of *History of Worcester*, linked the Negro Election Day with the Massachusetts General Election. According to Nutt, the General Election Day was one of the great holidays of the year. It was the one day when persons of every degree, tongue, and color had a full right. Even the Negroes were allowed to buy gingerbread and drink beer. The occasion was called "Nigger 'Lection Day" to distinguish this event from "Artillery Election" on the first

---

99. Benjamin Lynde, *The Diary of Benjamin Lynde and of Benjamin Lynde, Jr.: with an Appendix*, Cambridge, Riverside Press, 1880, p. 109.
100. See Nathaniel B. Shurtleff, "Negro Election Day." *Proceeding of the Massachusetts Historical Society*, vol. 3, Massachusetts Historical Society, 1875, p. 45–46.
101. Ibid.

Monday of June.[102] If the records on the Negro Election Day noted by Shurtleff and Nutt are correct, the Negro Election Day in Massachusetts was not celebrated for the election of the Negro governor. It was just a holiday for them, as noted by Shurtleff. While Nutt and Shurtleff says that the "Negro Election Day" was named due to the participation of colored people in the celebration of the General Election in the Commons, Joseph Barlow Felt notes that "the slave election was used for the alleviation of their depressed condition, and the African slaves in Salem and other part of Massachusetts, had a vacation in the last Wednesday morning in May to the close of the week [and] in the imitation of their masters, they chose a governor for one year."[103] Felt did not list any names of an elected Negro governor in any city of Massachusetts. The omissions of those names make any statement elucidating that such an event happened in each colony difficult. Conversely, in Connecticut and Rhode Island, there are records of elected Negro governors, including the names of minor officers. Even though there is no record of the election of minor officers in Rhode Island, the black institutions in both colonies had many similarities. The election was celebrated with much pomp and enjoyment. Moreover, the parades were also executed in the same manners.

The celebrations of the Negroes for enjoyment were common during the colonial days. In Old New York, the Negroes also celebrated Pinkster Day with dancing and music. In Albany, in the areas inhabited by the Negroes, the celebration was enjoyed on Capitol Hill, which was known at that time as "Pinkster Hill." The Negro holiday was organized by King Charley, a Negro who was believed to be a prince in Africa. During this day, King Charley wore his military coat. Alice Morse Earle reports that "the Negroes were amused during this day. They played all kind of music with instruments such as drum or instruments constructed out of a box with sheepskin heads, upon which old Charley did most of the beating."[104] In Rhode Island and Connecticut colonies, in addition to the "Negro Election Day," African bondsmen were allowed to celebrate the day of Thanksgiving and the Annual Corn Husking

---

102. Charles Nutt, *History of Worcester and Its People*, vol. 1, Lewis Historical Publishing Company, 1919, p. 485.
103. Joseph B. Felt, *Annals of Salem*, vol. 2, W. & S.B. Ives, 1849.
104. Earle, 1896, pp. 195–97.

Day. Thomas Robinson Hazard and other Rhode Island and Connecticut authors have mentioned that Negroes enjoyed Corn Huskings as much as their masters. During Corn Husking celebration, the masters and their slaves celebrated the event together. The description of the Corn Husking was recorded by Thomas Robinson:

> The annual corn husking of Narragansett was in the olden time greatly enjoyed by the Negroes. Since my remembrance some of the large farmers had many hundred bushels husked of an evening. The refreshments provided consisted mostly of new cider, apple and mince pies, huge loaves of gingerbread, and never-to-be dispensed—with fiddle.[105]

Political Aspects of the Blacks' Election Day

African American governors were politically active in their respective towns as well as in surrounding towns under their jurisdictional power. Alice Morse Earle recorded that Cuddymonk, a black governor in the Narragansett, was a politician. His political qualification was based on his skills and strategies in dealing with his constituents and white inhabitants. In fact, he believed in himself that he was a politician. Earle writes that when Cuddymonk was asked about his real employment, he replied without hesitation that "I's er pollertishum [I am a politician]."[106] Cuddymonk was a politician because he played an important role in the Narragansett. He bridged a normal relationship between whites and blacks. According to Earle, "Cuddymonk arranged many matters in the relations of whites with the Negroes without the trouble of personal effort."[107] His diplomatic skills more than likely appeased many tensions between the two races. His efforts in creating good conditions between whites and black people possibly reduced the level of hate crime if there were any.

Cuddymonk was privileged to some respect due to his political status. He was always respected by people of his color and whites. He

---

105. Hazard, 1879, p. 119.
106. Earle, 1898, p. 80.
107. Ibid., p. 81.

resided in the same neighborhood with former rich slave-owners. Earle writes that "Cuddymonk had friendly intimacy with rich white people that was denied to a poor white man."[108] Cuddymonk was associated with rich white people due to his political status. Possibly, without such status, he would be treated like his fellow African Americans. In his case, he was above the poor whites.

Earle recorded an incident involving his arrest by Constable Cranston of North Kingston, Rhode Island. During the arrest, Cuddymonk was treated with civility compared to other blacks. According to Earle, he was accused for not paying the debts which he owed to the farmers. But when the constable went to arrest him, he denounced his arrest as being an act of injustice. But the constable did not take into consideration his complaints. During his communication with the constable, Cuddymonk was argumentative, but the constable did not overreact because he knew that the black governor was a political elite among the blacks.

In fact, due to his actions, Constable Cranston said to him that "it's most time for 'Lection Day [it's almost time for the Election Day], Cuddy, you'll never be elected again if you go to jail. They'll never want a rogue for gov'nor [governor]."[109] When the constable explained to Cuddy his concern, he replied to the constable as follows: "Cause de Governor am a rogue this year ain't no sign de next one won't be."[110] [Because I am a rogue governor this year, there is no sign that the next one will not be.] The constable did not expect such answer from Cuddy. He moved his head and said that "black politics were much like white." This assertion indicates that black governors indeed were politicians and practiced politics in their jurisdiction. During the same exchanges, Constable Cranston asked Cuddymonk, "I can't see why all you blacks are so dishonest and tricky?" Cuddymonk replied that "it was the fault of the Old George Washington. When he was dying, he rolled his eyes and said, 'forever keep all nigger down.'" Cuddymonk went on to note that "it can't take hundred years to work out a dying spell." The answers

---

108. Ibid., p. 79.
109. Ibid., p. 97.
110. Ibid.

of Cuddymonk were based on his political freedom. He was not afraid to reveal his political opinions to the constable.

On May 11, 1776, in Connecticut when John Anderson, the servant of Governor Philip Skene, was appointed governor of the blacks without holding the election, the event was politicized. The inhabitants of Hartford were alarmed to see that the servant of the enemy was appointed to the highest position among the blacks in the colony.[111] The appointment of Anderson happened in time when the Americans were at war against the British. Governor Skene was a loyalist and supporter of the British cause. Therefore, the appointment of his servant to high political position among the blacks was perceived as plot to the colonies. As a result, the governor and the councils convened in Hartford and appointed agents for the investigation regarding the appointment of John Anderson to the governorship in the black government.

Governor Philip Wharton Skene was sentenced to parole in West Hartford with his family. They resided in West Hartford for a year in the house Widow of Hooke but at their own expenses.[112] In West Hartford, Governor Skene and his family were always insulted by the inhabitants of the town. He was miserable, as he noted in his letter written in West Division in Hartford on May 5th, 1775. In his letter, Governor Skene wrote, "the insults I have been liable to here is worse than Death to me who never valued it above true liberty. I wish in my native country (even Newgate there) would be more preferable than the ills I have borne."[113] Even though Governor Skene complained about his treatment in Hartford, Governor Jonathan Trumbull of Connecticut believed that his treatment was not worse than his plan of plotting against the colony through the instrumental of his servants. Governor Trumbull agreed that a special committee was appointed for the investigation of the plot planned by Governor Skene.[114] The Connecticut governor also accused

---
111. Royal Ralph Hinman, *A Historical Collection from Official Records, Files, &c. of the Part Sustained by Connecticut, during the War of the Revolution*. E. Gleason, 1842, p. 31.
112. Ibid.
113. See *Collections of the Connecticut Historical Society*, vol. 2, published for the Society, 1870, pp. 300–301; Letter of Governor Skene, Tuesday morning, ye 5th of Sept. 1775 [Hartford] West Division.
114. Isaac W. Stuart, *Life of Jonathan Trumbull, Sen., Governor of Connecticut*, Cracker and Brewster, 1859, p. 218.

Governor Skene of having a design against the constitutional rights and liberties of the thirteen colonies.[115]

Governor Skene was prevented from communicating with any person whatsoever on any political subject during his term of parole. In 1776 when his servant was chosen governor of the blacks, Governor Jonathan Trumbull and the councils convened to see whether or not Governor Skene played any role in the appointment of his servant, John Anderson. For the investigation of the incident, a committee was appointed by the governor and the councils in Connecticut. It is possible that public opinion was in favor of an investigation for the matter in question. The inhabitants of Connecticut believed that the British were part of that plot. This reasoning can be supported by the account of the Connecticut Historical Society. According to the Journal, "the appointment of Governor Skene's Negro was the occasion of some uneasiness in the public mind lest there might be some plot on the part of the British officers."[116] Governor Skene was already on parole when his Negro servant was appointed governor of the Negroes.

The committee appointed by the governor and the council included Jeste Root, Esq. He was appointed chairman. A constable was also selected for the investigation.[117] When the committee went to the lodge of Governor Skene, they found that it was locked and the governor was absent. For precautions, one of the committee members remained at the lodge waiting for Governor Skene while others went to look for him. This was the first time in the history of Connecticut that that the election of the black governor took a different political dimension. The governor of the state and council members were involved. Additionally, inhabitants of Hartford were also troubled, fearing a plot orchestrated by Governor Skene and the African governor against the state.

On the way for his search, the committee found Governor Skene returning to his lodge. Without delay, he was brought before the committee. He was asked if he had any correspondence with the enemies of the United States, which he denied. The governor was very

---

115. Ibid., p. 217.

116. Major French's Journal, see *Collections of the Connecticut Historical Society*, vol. 1, published for the Society, 1860, p. 189.

117. Ibid.

cooperative. He gave his keys to the committee and his papers in his room were examined. After the examination of his papers, he was questioned about the appointment of his Negro servant to the position of governor of the Africans in Connecticut. He was also asked if he played any roles in the appointment of his Negro servant. The governor denied any roles for that appointment. Similarly, former Negro Governor Cuff and the current Governor John Anderson were questioned concerning Anderson's appointment. Governor Cuff was asked to reveal who told him to resign from his office. He noted to the committee that a certain group of Negroes advised him, but Governor Skene was not involved.

After the investigation, it was found that Governor Skene did not have any part in the resignation of Governor Cuff. In like manner, he was not involved in the process for the appointment of John Anderson as governor of the Negroes in Hartford, Connecticut. The official historical record on the appointment of Negro John Anderson and the resignation of Governor Cuff were collected from the Report of the Governor and Council relating to the affair of the appointment of Anderson. This report is recorded in the Connecticut State Archives, Revolutionary War, V.DOC., 392.[118] The same information was also related by Major Christopher French in his journal. He was a military officer of the 22d Regiment. Royal Ralph Hinman also mentioned the appointment of the slave of Governor Skene by Cuff, a Negro governor who resigned due to his health problem.[119]

From the violation of the election practices by Governor Cuff and John Anderson, it can be surmised that colonial officials and the inhabitants of Connecticut followed the process of the Negro Elections with much attention. Possibly, the all process was monitored consistently to see whether or not colored people worked against the security of the colony. Furthermore, the elected Negro governor was also monitored. If discovered that he [governor] was working against the interest of the state, sanctions might be imposed against him. The investigation

---

118. Ibid.
119. Royal R. Hinman, *A Historical Collection from Official Records, Files & of the Part Sustained by Connecticut*, printed by Gleason, 1842, p. 31.

conducted by the appointed committee on the appointment of the Negro servant of Governor Skene was an indication demonstrating that the Negro government was a government–by-proxy. The officials in the colonial government, as well as during the state, paid much attention to the affairs of the black government. The resignation letter of Governor Cuff and the appointment of Governor John Anderson read as follows:

Hartford, 11th May, 1776

I Governor Cuff of the Niegors in the province of Connecticut do Resine my Governmentship to John Anderson Niegor Man to Governor Skene.

And I hop that you will obeye him as you have Done me for this ten years past, when Colonel Willis Niegro Dayed I was the next But being weak and unfit for that office Do resine the Said Governorshipe to John Anderson.

I John Anderson having the Honour to be appointed Governor over you I will Do my utmost indevore to serve you in Every respect and I hop you will obey me accordingly.

John Anderson, Governor over the Niegors in Connecticut.

Witnesses present
The late Governor Cuff, Hartford
Quackow
Petter Wardsworth
Titous
Pomp Willis
John Jones
Fraday[120]

In Rhode Island, the elections of Negro governors were conducted to the same extent as in Connecticut. Black governors were elected in North and South Kingstown, Newport, and Narragansett. Prince Robinson, John, the slave of Elisha R. Potter, Guy Watson, and Cuddymonk

---

120. Ibid. See also the Journal of Major French.

were among the elected black governors in Rhode Island. In the same colony, Governor Cuddymonk was called a "black politician." Alice Morse Earle believed that the title of black governor was a political position in the state. Due to his status, he was respected by whites and the blacks alike. He was also integrated into the milieu of rich white people while poor whites were denied such access.[121] Thomas Robinson Hazard also believed that Cuddymonk was knowledgeable in the matter of political economy. The political ideas, legal decisions, and financial opinions of Cuddymonk were always quoted by the colonial governor while in session with his members.[122]

Cuddymonk was qualified like other politicians in the Narrangasset because he was devious in business affairs, according to his white and black neighbors. According to them, "he never paid for nothing if he could help it."[123] It seems that Cuddymonk did not honor his promises if he could get away with it. Unlike the citizens, Constable Cranston of Kingsport labeled Cuddymonk as being like white politicians due to his political maneuvering. In the Narragansett, Cuddymonk was a house and farm owner.

The involvement of blacks in politics was shown by Elisha R. Potter when he complained to his servant about the expenses of the elections. Thomas Robinson Hazard said to avoid financial difficulties for his election and that of his Negro servant, "Potter had a conference with the Negro governor, and stated to him that the one or the other must give up politics, or the expense would ruin them both. Governor John took the wisest course, abandoned politics and retired to the shades of private life."[124] The concern Potter expressed about the expense of blacks practicing in the political arena confirm that the process of the Negro Election Days and their government were not a farce, as more authors have claimed.

The elections of black governors sometimes were labeled as a mock election, or a farce. Were these elections significant? An examination of

---

121. Earle, 1898, p. 79.
122. Hazard, 1879, p. 25.
123. Earle, 1898, p. 87.
124. Bacon, 1904, p. 243.

the elections in the Connecticut and Rhode Island colonies will prove the validity of these elections.

The Significance of the Blacks' Election Day

In 1874, Frances Manwaring Caulkins said that African American performed a mock election of a Negro governor. Lorenzo Johnston Greene also notes that Negroes had a mock government. William Chauncey Fowler says King Caesar, a Negro, had a mock dignity. Much has been said about the process of the election of the Negroes, and for some, the dignity of the Negro governor seems to be a mockery. Some writers believed that the whole process of the Negro Election Day was a farce. The institution of the Negro government was portrayed as less significant by earlier writers of the history of Connecticut, and that perception has continued in our modern era. Was the election of a Negro governor and his dignity less important in the colonies? Was the election of the Negro governors and their administrations less significant to the colonial officials? These are pertinent questions which will address the magnitude of the power of the Negro governors as well as the weight of the Negro Election Day. It appears that some authors who had discussed the Negro governors and the Negro Election Day misunderstood the aim of the colonial officials in Connecticut and Rhode Island for allowing the establishment of black institutions. Therefore, the topic was examined lightly. The elections of the Negroes were considered to be an entertainment for them.

On the contrary, the Negro Election Day was given much consideration by the owners of slaves in Rhode Island and in Connecticut. In Rhode Island as well as in Connecticut, during the colonial era, slave owners spent much money for the preparation of the entire black election process. Clothes, military equipments, and horses were provided for the event. If the process were a mockery, would the slave owners spend so much money for the event? Would slave owners have missed their work days to enjoy with their slaves the celebration of the elected Negro governor? Would they let so many slaves miss their plantation duties? If the answers to these questions are "no," it is vital to note the reasons why slaves owners supported the political process of their slaves. The supports given to slaves shaped their working culture. Possibly, in return, slaves and servants were faithful to those of supported them.

In South Kingstown and North Kingstown, as well as Newport, slavery made up a segment of the economy. In Narragansett, the labor was performed by Negro slaves and Indians, as stated by Edgar Mayhew Bacon. In this colony, the elections of Negro governors were of much importance to the slave owners. As in Narragansett, in Newport, slave masters were interested in the elections of their servants and slaves. It is easy to refute the notion that the Negro election process was a farce or a mockery because there are many political concepts in the black government that were parallel to those of the colonial government. Some examples includes the counting of votes, the selections of qualified candidates, the scheduling of the election's date, celebrations, the power of the officers, and the composition of minor judiciary officers. The elections for the selection of colonial officers were conducted yearly in the same way as the election of officers of the black government. Prevention of election fraud was also observed by black officers in the same magnitude as white officers in the colonial government. In Rhode Island, voters were not allowed to move from their initial line to another avoiding the contamination of the election process.[125] These were very similar to the operation of the colonial government.

The entire process of the black government was very critical for the safety of the colony. Throughout the New England colonies, perhaps few insurrection attempts of the blacks were recorded. In general, African Americans in New England colonies were modest and docile. Possibly, due to the implementation of a proxy government, they felt included in the political process indirectly. Orville Platt believed that the policing of the blacks by people of their own color was healthy for the colony. Such strategies were more effectual than empowering white policemen to police the black.[126]

---

125. Earle, 1898, p. 82. Earle notes that "during the counting of vote, no person might change ranks or step from one end of the line to another, and thus fraudulently increase the number of voted."

126. Platt, 1900, p. 324. See *Negro Governors* in the Paper of the New Haven Historical Society, vol. 6.

Election Procedures

The election of a Negro governor was conducted like those of the white colonists although the process was not necessarily uniform throughout the territories. In New Hampshire, the election of the Negro governor was conducted in June. Likely, in the colony of Connecticut, the Election Day of the Negro was scheduled in June of each year on a Saturday following the Election Day of white officers. Negroes in the colony of Rhode Island held their annual Election Day on the third Saturday in June. It seems that in the town of Derby, the governor's election depended on the wish of the candidates. In Rhode Island, it appears that the election franchise was privileged to everyone, except in the city of Newport. In the town, only people who owned a pig and sty were allowed to vote.[127] This was the first franchise regulation discovered in the African American's government. In other towns, there were no elective rules. It does not appear that female slaves and maid servants were included in the voting process. They were there only to support the favorite candidates. In Massachusetts, the Negro Election Day was convened after the election of the colonial officers on the last Wednesday of May. According to Alonzo Lewis and James Robinson Newhall, both local authors in Lynn, Massachusetts, during slavery, slaves were allowed by their masters an annual vacation of four days when the General Court made their election for the selection of colonial officer.[128]

There were many similarities to the internal structure of the inaugurations of the governors. In each city where a government was elected, dancing, playing music, and sporting were the norms. There were also organizers for the inauguration for the parade. The slave owners, assisted by the older Negroes, were the organizers of the inauguration.[129] It was the responsibility of slave owner to provide food, drinks, the ta-

---

127. Federal Writer's Project, *Rhode Island, A Guide to the Smallest State*, Best Books On, 1937, p. 205.

128. Alonzo Lewis and James Robinson Newhall, *History of Lynn, Essex Counties, Massachusetts, Including Lynnfield, Saugus, Swampscat, and Nahant*, vol. 2, Shorey, 1897, p. 236. Also see, James Robinson Newhall, *Yet Great and General Courte in Collonie Times*, Nichols Press—T.P. Nichols, 1896, p. 100.

129. Platt, 1900, p. 324.

bles, chairs, and the attire for the governor-elect. In looking into the organizations of the dancing and music, in some towns, it is obvious that a music leader and a parade organizer were also assigned. To illustrate, in Windsor, Connecticut, General Ti, (a slave belonging to Col. Ellsworth), was the master of the ceremonies. This slave was well dressed in a military style when he trained regiment for the inauguration parade. Before the commencement of the training of the parade, General Ti gave the following order to the Negro that 'all you what got white stocca, rocker shoe, stain in the front.'"[130] His military men followed his order promptly. General Ti was the master of the ceremonies. He always wore his old uniform which he received from his master.[131] In Durham, Sawny Freeman was the official music leader of the inauguration. The musical contribution of Sawny Freeman is discussed in the following paragraphs.

The parade for the honor of the elected governor or king depended on the custom of the Negroes in each colony. The parade will be discussed later in this chapter. There were some differences with respect to the milieu of the celebrations. In New Hampshire, the inauguration party for the governor-elect was celebrated on the Portsmouth plains.[132] In Rhode Island, the inauguration of the newly elected governor depended on the town where the election occurred. In the Narragansett, the election of Cuddymonk was celebrated in the great Oak Grove on Rose Hill.[133] Sometimes, slaves in Rhode Island gathered under trees or an arbor for the inauguration of a black governor.[134] In Newport, the inauguration of the black governor was convened at the corner of Thames and Farewell Streets.[135] African slaves in Rhode Island to some extent selected an area the same way their father did. On the contrary, in Connecticut, the inaugurations of many Negro governors were held in the taverns. In the old town of Derby, the inau-

---

130. See Alfred E. Smith and Francis Walton, *New Outlook*, vol. 49, Outlook Publishing Company Incorporate, 1894, p. 744.
131. Ibid.
132. Brewster, 1859, p. 210.
133. Earle, 1898, pp. 81–82.
134. Hazard, 1899, p. 121.
135. Federal Writers Project, *Rhode Island: A Guide to the Smallest State*, Somerset Publishers, Inc., June 1938, p. 205.

guration of the Negro governor was celebrated sometimes in Warner's Tavern. In Hartford, the election of a black governor was inaugurated at Hinsdale's Tavern.[136] It appears that the tavern was a favorite place for the inaugurations of the Negro governor in Connecticut. It is possible that the tavern was a plausible location for the accommodation of a large number of participants.

In Rhode Island, there was a structured organization when the election commenced at one o'clock. Electors most of the time started arriving at 10 o'clock. Before the starting of the vote, electors were ordered to form two lines, one line for each candidate, and the chief marshal prohibited the changing of lines anticipating any manipulations. After the counting of the votes, Guy Watson, who was always the chief marshal, announced the result of the election attributed to each candidate. After the tabulations of the votes, the marshal proclaimed the name of the winner. The defeated candidate was introduced by him also following the norms of the election customs. After the presentation of the winner, the defeated candidate drank the first toast after the election ceremony. From this point, all animosities were forgotten.[137] When the celebration started, the governor-elect and the challenger with their wives sat at a long table. The day was celebrated with dancing and sporting. This was not the case in Connecticut, where the parade was grandiose.

African slaves and servants rode on saddle and pillions in chaise and farm wagons parading on the street. Sometimes, men and women rode in ox-carts during the parade. Children always accompanied their parents during this event.[138] Earle records that in the Narragansett, African slaves and servants wore their finest attire. Unlike the electors, the governor was also well-dressed. To illustrate, Cuddymonk, the black governor, wore a fine coat that was lent to him by his master, Colonel Gardiner. The gray horse which he rode on was also from Colonel Gardiner. While riding on the horse, Cuddymonk always wore his knee breeches given to him by his master.[139] He wore

---

136. Stuart, 1853, p. 39.
137. Updike, 1847, p. 178.
138. Earle, 1898, pp. 81–82.
139. Ibid.

knee breeches for his personal protection to avoid knee injury in case of an accident.

In the Connecticut records, there is no record indicating how the votes were tabulated. Orville Platt notes that it is difficult to ascertain whether or not the black votes were collected and put in a box and taken to Hartford.[140] But in the later years, sometimes the election was conducted through the measurement of physical strength through wrestling. Governor Eben Tobias, the strongest Negro governor won his governorship through wrestling.[141] It appears that method of selecting the black governor through sporting was introduced in 1800s. During the colonial era, there were no records for such a process. In the same colony, elections were sometimes conducted by proxy because some Africans did not attend.

The Parades during the Inauguration of Black Governors in Connecticut

The parade and the inauguration of the elected governor were an exciting moment for African bondsmen, slaves, and free people of color. Additionally, slave owners and their family shared the same joy. They sat with their slaves and celebrated the day together. The well-organized events were quite grandiose. African Americans from all levels of society attended the celebrations. All of them were well-dressed and ready for the inauguration of their governor or king. Unlike the ordinary black citizens, the elected king or the governor dressed elegantly. To illustrate, King Nero, of New Hampshire wore "a full dress in small cloths which required some filling in the back of the silk."[142] The attire of King Nero was majestic, and no one was dressed like him. His clothes were a sign of authority and power. Historically, in Portsmouth, Cyrus Bruce, a Negro servant of Governor Langdon, wore elegant attire. According to Charles W. Brewster, "for many years the waiter of Gov. Langdon was well dressed and exhibited a

---

140. Platt, 1900, p. 319.
141. Samuel Orcutt, *History of the Old Town of Derby, Connecticut, 1642–1880*, Springfield Print Co., 1880, p. 549.
142. Brewster, 1873, p. 210.

good appearance. His heavy gold chain and seal, his fine black or blue broadcloth coat and small cloths, his silk stockings, and silver-buckled shoe, his ruffles and carefully plaited linen were well remembered by many of the present generation."[143] Cyrus Bruce's attire was parallel to that of a king, and was probably one of the dignitaries among the blacks in Portsmouth. He was respected and considerate. With his employment connections, Cyrus Bruce was also respected by the white officials and others.

In Connecticut, after the proclamation of the winner of the position of governor, the Negroes organized a well-structured parade. Their masters provided horses, military trappings, money, and other materials for the party. Musical instruments of all kinds were played for the celebration as well as for the parade. Isaac William Stuart and W.M.B. Hartley, local Hartford historians, have recorded the Negro's parade during the inaugurations. The collection of Stuart on the Negro parade has remained authoritative. Most of the authors who have discussed the Negro parade in Connecticut during the colonial day rely heavily on the records of Stuart and Hartley.

The parade exhibited by people of African descent is worth recounting. It was a phenomenal event in Connecticut. People of European descent who witnessed the event observed the ceremony with curiosity. Orville Platt believed that the parade was incorporated into the inauguration of the newly elected governor by Negroes. According to him, the Negroes started using the parade before the colonial government earlier than 1830. He also went on to note that "the Negroes may claim that we copied that feature from them, for their parades were always as well as before as after 1830."[144]

On the contrary, during the inauguration of the black governor in Hartford, the elected governor rode throughout the street accompanied by a troop of black people in a military uniform. Stuart recorded the parade process exhibited by the Negroes in Hartford, Connecticut. He elaborated in detail that "a troop of blacks, sometimes on hundred in number, marching sometimes two and two on

---

143. Ibid.
144. Platt, 1900, p. 324.

foot, sometimes mounted in true military style and dress on horseback, escorted him through the street, with drums beating, colors flying, and fife, fiddles, clarionettes, and every 'sonorous metal' 'that could be found' 'uttering martial sound.'" After the troops marched, they would retire to some large room where they would engage deliberation and refreshments. Hinsdale's Tavern, on the site now occupied by H. Barnard, is well-remembered by an old gentleman now living, who informs us that Quaw, a Colonel George Wyllys' Negro, served as governor at this time to great satisfaction and was the stiffest and proudest "Darkie he never saw."[145]

The inauguration which Stuart recorded happened in 1760 when Governor Quaw was elected in Hartford. Possibly, the parade began with the election of Governor London, who was succeeded by Governor Quaw. The pomp of the parade commenced the sophisticated carriage and qualities of the Negro governor. In case of Governor Quaw, he was described as the stiffest and proudest "darkie." This statesman indicated that Governor Quaw was a proud and confident man. He believed in himself, and more likely he was an independent person. As a proud man, Governor Quaw valued his reputation. He was surely a responsible and respectable man in the community.

In Durham, Connecticut, it appears that the election of King Caesar was not celebrated with a troop of black soldiers as in Hartford, Connecticut. Fowler says that King Caesar after the election was escorted by a drummer and a fifer who played the music without interruption. During the celebration, Sawny Freeman, their musician, accompanied his violin with a sort of organ which he played with his foot. It was somewhat, in effect, like the Aeolian attached to the piano, said Fowler. This instrument increased the volume of the music. As the volume of the music increased, the Negroes jigged and reeled. They danced with much intensity and excitement.[146] In the later years, the parade was not conducted in the same magnitude as during the colonial era.

---

145. Stuart, 1853, pp. 38–39.
146. Fowler, 1866, p. 162.

In New England, African Americans were permitted to form social organizations among themselves. They were also allowed to establish a government for the management of their own affairs. The black government was formed of the governor, counselors, and various law enforcement officers. Officers of the black government also administered conflicts between masters and their slaves.

Chapter 9

Summary and Conclusion

African Descendants of Colonial America: Impact on the Preservation of Peace, Security, and Safety in New England, 1638–1783 reveals the omitted facts of the impact made by people of African descent in colonial New England. In addition, laws related to slavery and the militia were revealed and analyzed. Author Lievin Kambamba Mboma has examined each colony separately to make the work comprehensible and easy to read. Even though all the colonies of New England had similar laws, some religious and regional differences still existed. For example, the Massachusetts colony had a higher percentage of people of African descent than Rhode Island and New Hampshire. The flexibility in dealing with people of African descent in Massachusetts was not similar to the way New Hampshire and Rhode Island dealt with black people. As revealed in the text, fewer laws related to the status of people of color were established in New Hampshire and Rhode Island. In colonial Connecticut, no established laws for the bondage of people of African descent existed. Colonial officials enforced only laws relating to controlling the behavior of African Americans. Similar laws were also observed in the colony of Rhode Island.

The laws established in colonial New England had an impact on the relationship between slaves and their masters. From the documents consulted, records indicated people of color were treated humanely during the early years of the settlement. They were permitted to enjoy social activities such as the right of free movement, religion, property ownerships, marriage without restrictions, and the establishment of a Negro government. With the formation of their own government, Negroes freely elected their governors and other officers. The governor, on the other hand, had the executive power to appoint his minor officers.

Minor officers had judiciary power. They settled civil and criminal cases among their own race. Sometimes, these officers handled cases which involved Caucasians and people of color. Minor officers bore the same titles as those of the colonial government. Negro justices of the peace, sheriffs, constables, and judges were also established. These officers were sometimes selected throughout several cities in each colony in New England. Moreover, minor officers in the Negro government were sometimes the servants or slaves of colonial officers—such as governors and high-ranking military officials.

Like the authorization establishing a black government, facts collected from old documents revealed that the exclusion of people of African descent in the militia and the military was not permanent. The laws restricting their training or enlistment were sometimes overlooked by colonial officials. Laws sometimes were disregarded according to the circumstances of the time. Militia and military laws changed from time-to-time, especially during periods of war. Moreover, the same facts indicated that even though people of African descent were in slavery, they did not hesitate to fight side-by-side with their Caucasian counterparts in the pursuit of peace, security, and safety. Furthermore, voluntary enlistment was common among people of African descent during the French and Indian Wars and other battles.

In regard to the employment of a person of color in colonial government, Wentworth Cheswell was appointed justice of the peace, selectman, and other positions due to his skills and education. He was accepted and valued like a Caucasian. From several documents consulted, there was no indication that Caucasians opposed his appointment. This person of African descent was respected by many people of his era in the city of Newmarket, New Hampshire where he resided. He held several government positions in Newmarket even after the independence of the United States. This official also served during the Revolutionary War. The impact he made was tremendous. He was the first person to believe that city records were very important and should not be misplaced. He recorded historical facts of the city by hand for future use by others. Historian Jeremy Belknap was one of those who benefited from Wentworth Cheswell's records.

Furthermore, *African Descendants in Colonial America: Impact on the Preservation of Peace, Security, and Safety in New England, 1638–1783* reveals pertinent information on the inclusive militia policy observed for the liberation of North America. The end of the domination of the French in colonial America was accomplished by the military union of whites, the black militia, and loyal Indians. Similarly, the independence of the United States materialized from the same union. The policy observed in the military and militia domains was healthy for the colony and the United States. African Americans' services as military men caused the colonists to see black men differently. They were recognized as men who were reliable military companions.

People of color followed the example of their forefathers during the War of the Revolution in defending liberty and freedom. While some government officials disapproved of black enlistment, African Americans were eager to fight for justice, freedom, and the security of the United States. Crispus Attucks was the first person of color to die in the name of justice and freedom. Among those who fought, several were recognized for high honor after the war. Peter Salem helped with the killing of Major General Pitcairn of the British Marines and Prince with the capture of Major General Prescott. Salem Poor was honored for his fighting skills. While discussing the contributions of people of color in the Continental Army, the author revealed the change of policy for each state while dealing with the enlistment of people of African descent during the continuation of the war.

People of color were also employed as overseers and superintendents on the plantations and estates of their masters. In all the colonies of New England, private estates and farms were under the jurisdiction of an overseer. From the research, it was discovered that African Americans were overseers in cities such as Framingham, Massachusetts, and Hartford, Connecticut; some people of color also held the position of superintendent in private institutions.

In conclusion, this study is not the last work in this field. It is the intent of the author for *African Descendants in Colonial America: Impact on the Preservation of Peace, Security, and Safety in New England, 1638–1783* to be a motivation for those who would like to deepen the research on the impact made by people of color to the New England colonies. It is possible that there are more facts to be gleaned from forgotten documents, notes, reports, books, journals, and archives regarding the valuable contributions Africans and African Americans have made for peace, security, and safety of colonial America and the United States.

Appendix

In 1646, while on an African slave trade expedition, James Smith and his mate Keyser kidnapped two Africans after Africans had killed a hundred Londoners. According to John Winthrop, Smith and Keyser joined the Londoners who sought revenge against Africans who had injured the British in the past.[1] After kidnapping the two Africans, Captain Smith and Keyser brought them to New England. Upon reaching Boston, the Africans were sold to Francis Williams of Pascataqua, (now Portsmouth, New Hampshire). When the news of selling slaves reached members of the Massachusetts General Court, Williams, Smith, and Keyser were charged with kidnapping. After Smith and Keyser confessed to the kidnapping charge, magistrates ordered the return of the Africans to Guinea. As measure of deterrence to man-stealing, a law was passed on the subject in question. The law reads as follows:

> It was bound by the first opportunity to bear witness against the heinous and crying sin of man–stealing, as also to prescribe such timely, redress for what was past, and such a law for the future, as might sufficiently deter all others belonging to the colony to have to do in such vile and most odious courses, that the Negroes interpreter, with others unlawfully taken, be by the first opportunity, at the charge of the country for the present, sent to his native country, Guinea.[2]

The decision by the General Court of Massachusetts concerning the case of Smith and Keyser indicates that the slave trade was a

---

1. John Winthrop, *The History of New England from 1630–1649, with Notes* by S. Savage, vol.2, Boston: Printed by Thomas E. Wait and Son, 1826, p. 243.
2. Charles Sumner, *Defence of Massachusetts*. Buel & Blanchard, printers, 1854, p. xvi.

monopoly for government officials. Inhabitants of the colony were not allowed to engage in such commercial transactions. This assumption is supported by the Africans being returned to Guinea by one of the state ships. John Winthrop, the governor of Massachusetts, wrote, "One of our ships which went to [the] Canaries with pipestaves in the beginning of November last, returned now, and brought wine, and sugar, and salt, and some tobacco, which she had at Barbadoes, in exchange for Africoes (Africans), which she carried from the Isle of Maio."[3] Winthrop's account explicitly shows that the government was permitted to engage in the slave trade at any time without interference by any individual. Therefore, the decision of 1646 did not prohibit slave trade, but the decision deterred those who would compete with the government in this business. Conversely, the article of the Body of Liberties (1641) did not have the same aim as the law of 1646. The 1641 law authorized slavery in Massachusetts. It is a mistake that both laws have been interpreted by historians as having the same purpose or aim concerning slavery and the slave trade.

Abiel Holmes was pleased by the decision of the Massachusetts magistrates to order the return of the kidnapped Africans to their land. In his opinion, the judgment of the court was against buying and selling slaves.[4] It appears that Holmes was mistaken when he noted that the judgment was against slavery. Smith and Keyser were sanctioned due to misdemeanors they committed in a foreign land.

From the petition filed to the Massachusetts general court, Magistrate Richard Soltonstall, who sat in the court, detailed pertinently the reasons Smith and Keyser were summoned to the court. According to Soltonstall, his petition against Smith and Keyser was based upon religious convictions and the oath he took declaring he would serve the people faithfully by following the will of God. In his view, the acts committed by Smith and Keyser in Africa were contrary to the law of God and the law of the colony. He wrote that man-stealing was against the law of God and the colony. Similarly, chasing Africans during the

---

3. Winthrop, 1826, p. 219.

4. Abiel Holmes, *The Annals of America: from the Discovery by Columbus in the year 1492, to the year 1826*, vol.1, Hillard and Brown, 1829, p. 278.

Sabbath Day was also against the law of God and the colony. And finally, stealing Africans by force or theft was against the law of God and the colony. From his legal reasoning, it is a challenge to believe that the magistrate's aim was to stop the slave trade.[5]

---

5. For the petition of Magistrate Richard Soltonstal, see *A Discourse on the Life and Character of the Late Hon. Leverett Soltonstall: Delivered in the North Church, Salem, Mass., Sunday* 18, 1845, pp. 34–35. See also *Slavery Among the Puritans. A Letter to the Rev. Moses Stuart*. Boston: Charles C. Little and James Brown, 1850, pp. 13–14.

Selected Bibliography

Primary Sources

Manuscripts

Guide to Manuscripts at the Rhode Island Historical Society to People of Color. Compiled by Rice Stattler, June 24, 2004. See The Rhode Island Historical Society website. The number of manuscripts, MSS 673 Sg1, Military Papers Colonial Collection. Also MSS673, Roll of Captain Daniel Wall's Company. In these manuscripts, the names of African Americans who served in colonial wars are listed. More information can be collected by reading the entire document at the Rhode Island Historical Society website.

Connecticut Archives Index No. 61 War, Colonial 1765–1775. Ser. I V2 Hartford, Connecticut State Library, 1924. The document lists Jupiter, an African American, as a private in 1756. Likely, Mark, an African American, also a private in 1758 (pp. 74, 159), State Archives Record Group No. 003. New London Court, African Americans Collection, New London County African Americans and People of Color. Collection, 1701–1854, Judicial Department. In this manuscript, the account on Wait Wright, Jacklin, and Dowson are recorded. The Public Records of the Colony of Connecticut [1636–1776], Brown & Parsons, 1890.

African American Resources at the Connecticut Historical Society. Manuscript Resources. Important information on the election of black governors.

Public Documents of Colonial New Hampshire

Acts and Laws, Passed by the General Court or Assembly of His Majesty Province of New-Hampshire in New England. Printed by B. Gree [for] E. Russell, 1726. Accounts relating to the exclusion of African Americans from performing military duties.

Provincial Papers, Documents and Records Relating to the Province of New-Hampshire, vol. 20. Edited by Henry Harrison. Metcalf, 1851. The document relates the law enforcement position of Wentworth Cheswell (Chiswell). Also Provincial and State Papers, New Hampshire, vol. 14. Published by authority of the Legislature of New Hampshire, 1885. Names of colonial African American military men are listed. Provincial and State Papers, vol. 6, 1872. See the petition of John Gilman for his African American man who served in the 1757 expedition.

Report of . . . for the Year Ending June 1, 1866: Contains the Military History of New Hampshire from its Settlement, in 1623 to Year 1861. New Hampshire, Adjutant General's Office. G.E. Jenks, 1866. See information on the Law of 1718 excluding African Americans from military enlistment.

Public Documents of the Colonial Rhode Island

Acts and Orders made at the General Court of Election held at Warwick this 18th of May, anno, 1652. Proceedings of the Rhode Island General Assembly, Vol. 1, 1649–1669 (p. 25). The document is kept in the Rhode Island State Library in Providence. This act was the first of its kind abolishing slavery in Warwick and Providence Plantation.

Nine Muster Rolls of Rhode Island Troops Enlisted during the Old French Wars: To which is added the Journal of Captain William Rice in the Expedition of 1746. Providence, Printed for the Society by the Standard Print. Co., 1915.

Records of the Colony of Rhode Island and Providence Plantations, in New England: 1741–1756. A.C. Greene and Brothers, State Printers, 1860. See Letter to the government of Colonial Rhode Island intended for the expedition against Louisburg. Also the authorization for privateering against the enemies of His Majesty, the king of England. Additionally, see *Records of the Colony of Rhode Island and Providence Plantation in New England*, vol. 2, 1664 to 1677. Providence, RI: A. Crawford Greene and Brothers, State Printers, 1857. Important information on the census of 1676 during King Philip's War. Also see the authorization of African Americans to perform watch duties in the colony for public safety. African Americans were entitled to the same privileges as the English in communal law enforcement. *Records of the Colony of Rhode Island and Providence Plantations, in New England: 1707–1770*. Edited by John Russell Bartlett. A.C. Greene and Brothers, 1859. The record indicates how the war affected colonial military laws.

Public Documents of the Colony of Connecticut

Rolls of Connecticut Men in the French and Indian War, 1755–1762, vol. 2. Connecticut Historical Society. Albert Carlos Bates, 1905. Accounts of Connecticut colonial military men, including African Americans.

Public Records of the Colony of Connecticut, prior to the Union with New Haven, May 1665. Edited by James Hammond Trumbull. Brown & Parson, 1850. Important account concerning public defense. In the same records, the exclusion of African Americans and Indians from communal law enforcement is indicated. This is the first act prohibiting African Americans and Indians from performing watch and ward in the colony which was at the period equivalent to police duties.

Public Documents of the Colony of Massachusetts

Acts and Resolves, Public and Private of the Massachusetts Bay.

Charters and General Laws of the Colony and Province of Massachusetts Bay. Boston: T.B. Wait Co., 1814. Colonial Laws of Massachusetts.

Massachusetts Soldiers and Sailors in the War of the Revolution, 17 vols. Boston: Wright and Potter, 1896–1908.

Records and Files of the Quarterly Courts of Essex County, Massachusetts, 1636–1692, 8 vols. The record reveals the earlier African Americans subjected to punishment and the suing of an English by an African American family.

Records Relating to Early History of Boston, vol.1 Boston (Mass) Registry Dept. Boston Commissioners. Rockwell and Churchill, 1881. Account of African Americans employed as chimney sweepers.

Suffolk Deeds, vol. 2, by Frank Bradish (Elliot) S.n., 1883 Suffolk County. See Record of Bostian Ken for the bonding out of Angola from Anna Keayne.

The Earliest New England Code of Laws, 1641. Massachusetts, Nathaniel Ward. A. Lowell, 1896.

Vital Records of Andover, Massachusetts, to the End of the Year 1849 ... Andover (Mass) Topsfield Historical Society, 1912. Marriage of Salem Poor.

Vital Records of Andover, Massachusetts, to the End of the Year 1849 ... Andover (Mass) Topsfield Historical Society, 1912 (p. 573) Account on Abbot, Phillip, an African American killed during the battle of Bunker Hill.

Vital Records of Wakefield, Massachusetts, to the year 1850. Boston, MA, 1912. See Court Record of King Pompey, an African American in Lynn, Massachusetts. He was listed as married to Phebe, Negro Servant to Sweyn. Pompey was the servant to Daniel Mansfield of Lynn (p. 253).

Vital Records of Salem, Massachusetts to the End of the Year 1849, vol. 2. See Marriage of Read Joseph and Abigail Chiber, May 18, 1679.

Secondary Sources

Aldrich, Thomas B. *An Old Town by the Sea*. Boston: Houghton, Mifflin and Company, 1894.

Adams, Nathaniel. *Annals of Portsmouth*. Portsmouth: Published by the author, C. Norris, Printer, 1825.

Arnold, Samuel G. *History of the State of Rhode Island and Providence Plantations: 1701–1790*. New York: D. Appleton & Company, 1889.

Bacon, Edgar M. *Narragansett: Its Historic and Romantic Associations and Picturesque Setting*. New York: G.P. Putnam's Sons, 1904.

Bacon, Edwin M., *The Book of Boston, Fifty Year's Recollections of the New England Metropolis*. Boston: Book of Boston Company, 1916.

Bailey, Sarah L. *Historical Sketches of Andover: (Composing the Present Towns of North Andover and Andover)*. Boston: Houghton, Mifflin and Company, 1880.

Baldwin, Elijah C. *Branford Annals 1700. Read April 7, 1886*. Papers, Vol. 4. New Haven: New Haven Colony Historical Society, The Society, 1888.

Barry, William. *A History of Framingham, Massachusetts*. Boston: James Munroe and Company, 1847.

Belknap, Jerry. *History of New Hampshire*. G. Wodlleigh, 1862.

Bell, Charles H. *History of the Town of Exeter, New Hampshire*. Exeter: The Quarter-Millennial Year, 1888.

Bicknell, Thomas W. *The History of the State of Rhode Island and Province Plantations*, 3 vols. New York: American Historical Society, 1920.

Bodge, George Madison. *Soldiers in King Philip's War: Being a Critical Account of that War, with a Concise History of the Indian Wars of New England from 1620–1677*. Boston, Mass, 1906.

Brewster, Charles. *Rambles about Portsmouth, New Hampshire*, 2 vols. Portsmouth, 1859.

Caulkins, Francis M. *History of Norwich, Connecticut*. Norwich, 1845.

Channing, George A., *Early Recollection of Newport, Rhode Island from the Year 1793 to 1811*. Boston: A.J. Ward and Charles E. Hammett Jr., 1868.

Chapin, Howard. *Privateer Ships and Sailors: The First Century of American Privateers in King George's War, 1739–1748*. Providence, RI: Johnson, 1926.

———. *Rhode Island in the Colonial Wars: A List of Rhode Island Soldiers and Sailors in the Old French and Indian War, 1755–62*. Providence, RI: Rhode Island Historical Society, 1918.

Charlton, Edwin A. *New Hampshire as it is*. A. Kenney, 1857.

Clark, George L. *A History of Connecticut, Its People and Institutions*, 2nd ed. New York: G.P. Putnam's Sons, 1914.

Coburn, Silas R. *History of Dracut, Massachusetts*. Press of the Courier—Citizen Company, 1922.

Cole, J.R. *History of Washington and Kent County: Rhode Island*, vol. 1. W.W. Preston & Co., 1889.

Coolidge, Austin J. and Mansfield, John B. *History and Description of New England*. New Hampshire: A.J. Coolidge, 1860.

Corey, Deloraine P. *The History of Malden, Massachusetts*. Malden: Published by the author, 1898.

Daniels, George F. *History of the Town of Oxford, Massachusetts: with Genealogies and Notes on Persons and Estates*. Published by the author with the co-operation of the town, 1892.

Daniels, John. *In Freedoms Birthplace. A Study of the Boston Negroes*. The Southern House Association, 1914.

Davis, John, *An Oration Pronounced at Worcester (Mass) on the Fortieth Anniversary of American Independence*. Printed by William Manning, 1816.

Denison, Frederick. *Westerly (Rhode Island) and Its Witnesses, 1626–1875*. Providence, RI: J.A. & R.A. Reid, 1878.

Douglass, William. *A Summary, History and Political of the First Planting, Progressive Improvements, and Present State of the British Settlements in North America*. 1760.

Drake, Samuel G. *The History and Antiquities of Boston, the Capital of Massachusetts and Metropolis of New England from Its Settlement in 1630, to 1770. With Notes and Critical and Illustrative Material*, 2 vols. Boston: Luther Stevers, 1836.

Drake, Samuel A. *The Border Wars of New England: Commonly Called King Williams and Queen Anne's Wars*. C. Scribner's Sons, 1897.

———. *Old Landmarks and Historic Personages of Boston Profusely Illustrated*. Boston: James R. Osgood and Company, 1873.

Earle, Alice Morse. *Customs and Fashions in Old New England*. New York: Scribes, 1896.

Egleston, Thomas. *The Life of John Paterson: Major General in the Revolutionary Army*. G. Putnam's Sons, 1894.

———. *In Old Narragansett: Romances and Realities*. C. Scribner's Sons, 1898.

———. *Pinkster Day, New Outlook*, vol. 49. Outlook Publishing Company, Inc., 1894.

Estabrook, William. *Genealogy of the Estabrook Family: including the Esterbrokk and Easterbrook, in the United States*. Andrus & Church, 1891.

Fassett, James H. *Colonial Life in New Hampshire*. Ginn & Company, 1899.

Field, Edward. *State of Rhode Island and Providence Plantations*. Mason Publishing Company, 1902.

Felt, Joseph B. *The Annals of Salem: From its First Settlement*. W & S.B. Ives, 1827.

Fitts, James H. *History of Newfield, New Hampshire*. The Rumford Press, 1912.

Fowler, William C. *Historical Status of the Negro in Connecticut: A Paper Read before the New Haven Colony Historical Society*. Walker, Evans & Cogswell Company, 1901.

Frothingham, Richard. *The History of Charlestown, Massachusetts Part I*. C.C. Little and J. Brown, 1845.

———. *Life and Times of Joseph Warren*. Little, Brown & Company, 1865.

Garrison, William L. *The Loyalty and Devotion of Colored Americans in the Revolution and War of 1812*. R.F. Wallcut, 1861.

George, Nellie I. P. *Old Newmarket, New Hampshire: Historical Sketches*. News-Letter Press, 1932.

Goodrich, Charles A. *Lives of the Signers to the Declaration of Independence*. T. Mather, 1837.

Goodwin, Joseph O. *East Hartford: Its History and Traditions*. Case, 1879.

Greene, Lonrenzo J. *The Negro in Colonial New England 1620–1776*. Kennikat Press, 1966.

Hanson, John W. *History of the Town of Danvers, from Its Early Settlement to the Year 1848*. The author, 1848

Hazard, Caroline. *The Narragansett Friends Meeting in the XVIII Century with a Chapter on Quaker Beginning in Rhode Island*. Cambridge: Houghton Mifflin, 1900.

Hazard, Thomas R. *Collections of Olden Times*. J.P. Sanborne, 1879.

Hempstead, Joshua. *Diary of Joshua Hempstead of New London, Connecticut*. New London County Historical Society, 1901.

Hoyt, Epaphras. *Antiquarian Researches*. Ansel Phelps, 1824.

Hudson, Charles, and Lexington Massachusetts Historical Society. *History of the Town of Lexington, Middlesex County, Massachusetts: Genealogies*. Boston: Houghton Mifflin, 1913.

Hurd, Hamilton D. *History of Essex County, Massachusetts*. J.W. Lewis & Co., 1890.

Hutchinson, Thomas. *The History of... Massachusetts Bay*. M. Richardson, 1765.

Jesse, John H. *Memoirs of the Life and Reign of King George the Third*, vol. 2. Tinsley Brothers, 1867.

Johnson, Edward. *Wonder-Working Providence of Sions Savior in New England*. Andover: Warren Draper, 1867.

Johnston, William. *Slavery in Rhode Island, 1755–1776*. Providence, RI: Providence, Rhode Island Historical Society, 1894.

Josselyn, John. "An Account of Two Voyages to New England, Made during the Years 1638, 1663." *Massachusetts Historical Society Collection*, Third Series. Boston: Massachusetts Historical Society, 1833.

Kilbourne, Payne Kenyon. *A Biographical History of the County of Litchfield*. Clark, Austin & Company, 1851.

Kingman, Bradford. *History of North Bridgewater, Plymouth County, Massachusetts, from Its First Settlement to the Present Time*. North Bridgewater, Boston: Published by the author, 1866.

Lewis, Alonzo. *The History of Lynn*. Boston: Samuel N. Dickinson, 1844.

Lincoln, William. *History of Worcester, Massachusetts from Its Earliest Settlement to September 1836*. Worcester, MA: Charles Hersey, 1862.

Lincoln, Allen B. *A Modern History of Windham County, Connecticut: A Windham County Treasure Book*, vol. 2. Chicago: S.J. Clarke Publishing Company, 1920.

Lynde, Benjamin. *The Diaries of Benjamin Lynde and of Benjamin Lynde, Jr.: With an Appendix*. Boston: Privately printed, 1880.

Maverick, Samuel. *A Briefe Discription of New England and the Several Townes Therein*. Press of D. Clapp & Son, 1885.

McDuffee, Franklin. *History of the Town of Rochester, New Hampshire, from 1722 to 1890*. Manchester: J.B. Clarke Company, 1892.

Mirick, Benjamin, and John G. Whittier. *The History of Haverhill, Massachusetts*. Haverhill, MA: A.W. Thayer, 1832.

Moore, Frank. *Diary of the American Revolution from Newspapers and Original Documents*, vol. 1. C. Scribner, 1860.

Moore, George H. *Notes on Slavery in Massachusetts*. New York: D. Appleton & Co., 1866.

Mudge, Zachariah A. *Foot-Prints of Roger Williams, A Biography, with Sketches of Important Events in Early New England History, With which he was Connected*. New York: Carlton & Lanahan, 1871.

Nell, William C. *The Colored Patriots of the Revolution. With Sketches of Several Distinguished Colored Persons to which is Added a Brief Survey of the Conditions and Progress of Colored Americans*. Boston: Robert F. Wallcut, 1855.

Nutt, Charles. *History of Worcester and Its People*, vol. 1. New York: Lewis Historical Publishing Company, 1919.

Orcutt, Samuel, and Ambrose Beardsley. *History of the Old Derby, Connecticut, 1642–1880*. Springfield, MA: Press of Springfield Printing Company, 1880.

Paige, Lucuis R. *History of Cambridge, Massachusetts*. Boston: H.O. Houghton, 1877.

Palfrey, John. *History of New England*, 5 vols. D. Appleton and Co., 1918.

Perley, Sidney. *The Essex Antiquarian: An Illustrated Magazine Devoted to the Biography*. The Essex Antiquarian, 1897.

Perry, Arthur L. *Origins in Williamstown*. Charles Scribner's Sons, 1894.

Peterson, Edward. *History of Rhode Island and Newport in the Past*. New York: John S. Taylor, 1853.

Phinney, Elias. *History of the Battle of Lexington: Or the Morning of the 19th April, 1775*. Boston: Phelps and Farnham, 1825.

Piersen, William D. *Black Yankees: The Development of an Afro-American Sub Culture in Eighteenth Century New England*. Amherst: University of Massachusetts Press, 1988.

Platt, Orville H. "Negro Governor." *New Haven Historical Society Papers*, vol. vi. New Haven: The Society, 1900.

Quarles, Benjamin. *Black Mosaic: Essays in Afro-American History and Histography*. Amherst: University of Massachusetts Press, 1988.

———. *The Negro in the American Revolution*. Chapel Hill: The University of North Carolina Press, 1961.

Roads, Samuel. *The History and Traditions of Marblehead*. Boston: Houghton, Osgood and Company, 1880.

Robertson, William. *The History of America: Including the United States*, vol. 2. London: R. And A. Taylor, Shoe-Lane, 1821.

Sanborn, Edwin D., and Channing H. Cox. *History of New Hampshire, from Its First Discovery to the Year 1830*. Manchester: John B. Clark, 1875.

Sheldon, George A. *A History of Deerfield, Massachusetts. The Times When and the People by Whom it was Settled, Unsettled, and Resettled, with a Special Study of the Indian Wars in the Connecticut Valley with Genealogical Tables*. 2 vols. Deerfield, MA: Press of E.A. Hall & Co., 1895.

Staples, William R. *The Documentary History of the Destruction of the Gaspee*. Providence: Knowles, Vose and Anthony, 1845.

Sterling, Dorothy. *Speak Out in Thunder Tones: Letters and Other Writing of Black Northerners, 1787–1865*. Da Capo Press, 1973.

Stiles, Henry R. *The History and Genealogies of Ancient Windsor, Connecticut, including East Windsor, South Windsor, Bloomfield, Windsor Locks, and Ellington, 1635–1891*, 2 vols. Hartford: Case, Lockwood and Brainard, 1892.

Stuart, Isaac W. *Hartford in the Olden Time: Its First Thirty Years*. Hartford: F.A. Brown, 1853.

Thatcher, James. *A Military Journal during the American Revolutionary War from 1775 to 1783*. Boston: Cotton & Barnard, 1823.

Temple, Josiah H. *History of Framingham, Massachusetts Early Known as Donforth's Farms 1640–1880 with a Genealogical Register*. Framingham: Published by the Town of Framingham, 1877.

Trumbull, James H. *The Memorial History of Hartford County, Connecticut, 1633–1884*. 2 vols. Boston: Edward L. Osgood Publisher, 1886.

Updike, Wilkins. *History of the Episcopal Church in Narragansett, Rhode Island*. New York: Henry M. Onderdonk, 1847.

Washburn, Emory. *Slavery as It Once Prevailed in Massachusetts*. Boston: Press of John Wilson and Son, 1869.

———. *Historical Sketches of the Town of Leicester, Massachusetts: During the First Century from Its Settlement*. Boston: John Wilson and Son, 1860.

Wilkes, Laura E. *Missing Pages in American History: Revealing the Services of Negroes in the Early Wars in the United States of America*. R.L. Pendleton, 1919.

Wilson, Henry. *History of the Rise and Fall of the Slave Power in America*, vol. 1. Boston: James R. Osgood and Company, 1878.

Winsor, Justin. *Memorial History of Boston*, 4 vols. Boston: Ticknor and Company, 1881.

——— and Clarence F. Jewett. *The Memorial History of Boston: Including Suffolk County, Massachusetts, 1630–1880*. J. R. Osgood and Company, 1880

Winthrop, John. *History of New England, 1630–1649*. Edited by James Savage. Boston: Little, Brown and Company, 1853.

Woodson, Carter G. *The Negro in Our History*. Washington, DC: The Associated Publishers, 1922.

Index

Abbot, Nathan, 156, 166
Abbot, Philipp, 166
Abercrombie, James, 70, 173, 175
Abigail, 16
Adam, 198
Adams, Daniel, 184
Adams, Herbert Baxter, 62, 153
Adams, John Quincy, 51, 154, 161, 186
Adams, Josiah, 58
Adams, Nathaniel, 21
Affrica, Asa, 79
Aldrich, Thomas Bailey, 15, 193, 212
Allen, Samuel, 40
Amas, Negro, 98
Ambo, 77
Ames, Alexander, 164
Ames, Captain, 174
Amherst, Jeffrey, 72, 80, 145
Anderson, John, 195, 198, 221, 222, 223–24
Andrew, Mr., 148
Andros, Edmund, 39, 123–24, 125
Angola, 17, 107, 112
Anne, Queen, 40, 128, 129, 130
Archelus, 178
Arnold, Samuel Greene, 87, 88, 92, 175, 181
Asher, 79
Ashley, Parson/Reverend, 143
Ashley, Thomas, 144
Atkinson, Christopher Thomas, 114
Atkinson, Joseph, 49
Atkinson, Theodore, 48
Attucks, Crispus, xviii, 26, 159, 160–61, 237

Attucks, Peter, 140–41
Atwood, Thomas, 98
Austin, Cato, 187

Backos, 77
Bacon, Edgar Mayhew, 27, 201, 214, 227
Bacon, Edwin Monroe, 104
Bailey, Sarah Loring, 18, 153, 173, 174
Baldwin, Elijah C., 73
Bancroft, George, 114
Barjonah, Isaiah, 164
Barnard, H., 233
Barry, William, 6, 30, 135, 153, 167
Barton, Lieutenant-Colonel, 175
Bassett, Eben D., 200
Baylies, Francis, 121
Bean, Phoebe, 97, 100
Beex, John, 116
Belcher, Jonathan, 46, 138
Belknap, Jeremiah, 170, 172
Belknap, Jeremy, 6, 15, 25, 39, 47, 53, 54, 146, 237
Bell, Charles Henry, 42, 47, 50
Bellingham, Richard, 17
Bellomont, Earl of, 40, 46
Bennett, Samuel, 109
Benson, Abel, 162, 168
Benson, Henry, 111
Benson, Nero, 134, 135
Berbice, Louis, 14
Bernon, Emanuel, 20
Bernon, Gabriel, 20
Berry, Ephraim, 50
Bicknell, Thomas Williams, 18, 82–83

Bigelow, Captain, 168
Bigelow, Timothy, 163
Biglow, Jacob, 47, 50–51
Blake, General, 115
Bond, Lieutenant Colonel, 165
Boston (alias Burn, Boston), 51
Boston, Toby, 78
Bosworth, Nero, 100
Bow, Thomas Tracy, xiv, 6
Bowen, Clarence Winthrop, 60
Bowen, Ephraim, 184
Bowen, William, 45
Boyden, Captain, 140
Boylston, Joh'a, 164
Brackett, Captain, 126
Brewster, Charles Warren, xv, 23, 34–35, 37, 193, 203, 208, 214, 231
Brewster, Nero, 203–4
Brewster, William, 203–4
Brick, John, 188
Bridge, Ebenezer, 164
Bridges, Captain, 109
Brin, 167
Bristol, 77
Bristol, James, 51
Brooks, Charles, 9
Browen, Fortin, 100
Brown, Abiel, 196, 199
Brown, Barbara W., 197
Brown, John, 96, 182
Brown, Joseph, 182
Browne, George Waldo, 35, 179
Bruce, Cyrus, 30, 232
Buckminster, Dea Thomas, 30
Buckminster, Joseph, 30
Buckminster, Lawson, 167, 170, 172
Buel, Captain, 78
Bull, Jireh, 89
Bull, Jonathan, 214
Burk, John, 168
Burn, Boston, 51
Burn, Titus, 164
Burnee, Fortunatus, 144
Bus Bus, 20, 107, 112

Caesar, 20, 47, 108. *See also* Ceasar; Cesar
Caesar, King, 209, 226, 233
Cahoone, Sarah S., 174–75
Caldwell, James, 26, 161
Calis, Captain, 98
Campbell, Fox John, 70
Campbell, Susan, 197
Campbell, William, 169
Canada, Cuggo, 51
Carr, Patrick, 161
Case, Dudley, 199
Cato, 18, 77, 79, 143, 145, 164, 165, 191
Cato, Wood, 164, 166
Catto, Negro, 76
Caulkins, Frances Manwaring, 15, 32, 60, 61, 193, 197, 199, 226
Ceasar, 77, 98, 176–77. *See also* Caesar; Cesar
Ceasar, King, 193, 196–97
Ceasar, Negro, 76, 158
Cesar, 140–41. See also Caesar; Ceasar
Cesar, Negro, 141
Chace, Samuel, 98
Champlin, Christopher, 82, 98
Chapin, Howard, xiv, 3, 95, 96, 97
Charles, 80
Charles, King, 210
Charley, King, 218
Chase, Cesar, 98
Chauncey, Elihu, 76
Cheese, Peter, 100
Chester, Betty, 199
Chester, John, 158, 198, 204–5
Chester, London, 196, 198, 199, 204–5
Cheswell, Davis, 59
Cheswell, Hopestill March, xii, 54
Cheswell, Richard, 28
Cheswell, Thomas, 58, 59
Cheswell, Wentworth, xii, 28, 29, 52, 53, 54, 57, 58, 59, 236–37, 244
Child, Hamilton, 140
Childs, Samuel, 143

Index of Personal Names

Childs, Timothy, 142–43
Chiswell. *See* Cheswell
Church, Benjamin, 5, 6
Church, Major, 126–27
Clark, Anthony/Tony, 178
Clark, George Larking, 15
Clark, Isaac, 134
Clark, Stephen, 178
Clark, Thomas, 111
Clark, Tony/Anthony, 178
Clarkson, Willie, 204
Clement, 109
Clements, Job, 48
Cobb, Primus, 144
Coburn, Frank Warren, 163
Coburn, Silas Roger, 165, 189–90
Coffin, Newport, 98
Coggshall, John, 89
Cole, Jinny, 143
Collins, Primus, 202
Colton, John, 116
Compey, Captain, 100
Cooke, Captain, 97
Cookson, Mr., 149
Cooley, Timothy Mather, 157
Corey, Deloraine Pendre, xiv, 165
Cornish, Duddley Taylor, 1
Cornwallis, Charles, 178
Courant, Ben, 96
Cox, Channing Harris, 41, 42
Cranston, Constable, 220, 225
Cranston, John, 90
Cranston, Samuel, 84, 90
Creswell, Beatrix, 103–4
Cromwell, Oliver, 115
Cross, Peter, 111
Cross, Thomas, 111
Cross, Timothy, 111
Cuddymonk, Governor, 192, 202, 209–10, 212–13, 219–21, 225, 230, 231
Cudjo, 29–30
Cuff, Governor, 195, 198, 223, 224
Cuff, Negro, 79
Cuffee, 34

Cunningham, Valerie, 53, 203
Cutt, John, 39
Cutt, Richard, 38, 39
Cutt, Robert, 38–39

Darby, Roger, 111
Dartmouth, Lord, 22
Davenport, Addington, 127
Davenport, Lieutenant, 110
Davis, Jefferson, 31
Davis, Joe, 31
Davis, John, 173
Davis, Peter, 168
Dawson, Ben, 75
Dean, Charles, 25
Dean, John Ward, 29
Deane, Silas, 186
Dearborn, Arthur, 59
Dearing, Samuel, 60, 141
Denison, Frederick, 30
Denonville, Governor, 122
Devonshire, Duke of, 72
Dexter, Samuel, 15
d'Iberville, Pierre le Moyne, 122
Dick, King, 210
Dongan, Thomas, 122
Doolittle, Benjamin, 139
Dorcas, 109, 113
Douglass, William, 118, 137
Downing, Emanuel, 106–7
Drake, Samuel Adams, 4–5, 118, 124, 127, 129, 171
Drew, Richard, 148
Drury, Thomas, 167, 172
Duddingston, Thomas, 182
Dudley, Joseph, 129, 131
Dummer, William, 54
Durkee, John, 79
Durham, Caesar, 49
Dwight, Anthony, 145
Dwight, David, 145
Dwight, Mr., 21
Dwight, Theodore, 79
Dyer, Eliphalet, 76, 79

Earl, Richard, 40
Earle, Alice Morse, 22, 192, 202, 209–10, 212–13, 218, 219, 220, 225, 231
Easton, John, 90–91
Eaton, Benjamin, 109
Eaton, Theophilus, 67
Ebedmelecks, 109, 113
Edgell, Simon, 167, 170
Edmund, Welles, 78
Eliot, John, 15
Elizabeth, 107–8, 113
Elliott, Charles Wyllys, 53, 54, 57, 61
Ellsworth, Colonel, 229
Ellsworth, Jona, 64
Emery, Richard, 47, 50
Endicott, James, 144
Enos, Roger, 80
Equiano, Olaudah, 193
Estabrook, Prince, 163

Farman, Benjamin, 166
Felt, Joseph Barlow, 12, 102, 110, 115–16, 195, 215, 218
Field, David, 139
Field, Edward, 97, 100, 180
Field, Samuel, 139
Fish, Elihab, 144
Fiske, David, 109
Fitch, Adonijah, 78
Fitts, James Hill, 53, 54
Flanders, 144
Fletcher, Simon, 199
Follett, Robert, 178
Ford, John, 164
Foster, Benjamin, 183
Foster, Miles, 111
Fowle, Daniel, 20
Fowler, William Chauncey, 13, 14, 15, 17, 21, 61, 67, 175–76, 209, 226, 233–34
Fox, Henry, 70
Fraday, 224
Frank, 79
Frank, Andrew, 19, 100
Franklin, Benjamin, 154–55, 189

Freeman, Cuff, 187
Freeman, Nero, 187
Freeman, Roswell Quosh, 200–1
Freeman, Sawny, 229, 233
Freemen, Cato, 168
Freemen, Samuel, 51
French, Christopher, 195, 221–23
Frontenac, Count, 112, 125
Frumble, Ammy, 78
Fry, Cesar, 98
Frye, Colonel, 174
Frye, James, 166
Fuller, 77–78
Fuller, Eleazer, 144

Gardiner, Colonel, 231
Garrison, William Lloyd, 35
George, 190
George, Joshua, 101
George, King, 40, 68, 69, 80, 95, 131
George, Nellie Palmer, 53, 54, 57, 58, 59
Getchell, Sylvia Fitts, 53
Gift, 190
Gilman, Arthur, 171
Gilman, Captain, 178
Gilman, John, 43, 46–47, 50
Gilman, Samuel, 52–53
Gire, George, 144
Gleason, Captain, 170
Gloster, John, 48
Godfrey, Cuff, 98
Goodin, Prince, 68–69
Goodrich, Elizur, 70
Gookin, Captain, 109
Gooff, 78
Gordon, Thomas Francis, 114
Grant, Noah, 77
Gray, Samuel, 26, 161
Greene, Jeremiah, 101
Greene, Lorenzo Johnston, 4, 6, 19, 64, 94, 96, 99, 111, 127–28, 132–33, 198, 226
Greene, William, 94
Greenleaf, Major, 48
Gridley, Luke, 44

Index of Personal Names

Grusha, Blaney, 167
Gunnings, John, 147

Hagar, 14
Halifax, Lord, 70
Hall, Edward, 48
Hall, Judge, 179
Hall, Prince, 139
Hamilton, Duane, 217
Hanker, Cato, 168
Harcourt, Colonel, 175
Harris, Colonel, 101
Harris, Jack, 20
Harris, Katherine J., xv
Harrison, Benjamin, 155
Hart, Cato, 167
Hart, Richard, 23
Hartley, W. M. B., 232
Harvey, John, 167
Harvey, Joseph, 55
Hatch, N., 165
Hawkin, Captain, 101
Hawley, Elisha, 140
Hayden, Jabez Haskell, 18
Haynes, Lemuel, 157
Hazard, 82
Hazard family, 82
Hazard, Caroline, 16, 26, 201, 202
Hazard, Robert, 17, 89–90
Hazard, Rowland, 16
Hazard, Thomas Robinson, 201, 219, 225, 226
Heard, Richard, 145
Heath, Colonel, 164
Hemenway, Samuel, 172
Heminway, Adam, 168
Heminway, Jeffrey, 168
Hempstead, Joshua, 63, 198
Henchman, Captain, 109
Henchman, Nathaniel, 109
Hercules, Florio, 197
Hercules, Governor, 197
Hesilrigge, Arthur, 116
Hewes, Joseph, 186

Hierlihi, Captain, 80
Hill, 165
Hill, Henry, 164
Hill, Isaac, 17
Hills, Thomas, 165
Hilton, Colonel, 47
Hinman, Elisha, 188
Hinman, Royal Ralph, 223
Hinsdale, Colonel, 143
Hinsdale, Mr., 150
Hinsdale, Reverend, 30
Hitchcok, Aaron, 77
Hoady, Charles Jeremy, 71
Hobbes, Thomas, 115
Hobby, Captain, 76
Holmes, Abiel, 240
Hollowell, Benjamin, 138
Hope, 108
Hopkins, Edward, 67
Hopkins, Esek, 186–87
Hopkins, Pauline Elizabeth, 47, 50
Hopkins, Stephen, 186–87
How, Isaac, 167
Howe, Cato, 164
Hoyt, Jona, 143
Hubbard, David, Jr., 79
Hubbel, Samuel, 78
Hudson, Charles, 152
Hull, Joseph, 98
Humphrey, General, 206
Humphreys, Frank London, 61
Hun'ton, Sam, 32
Huntingdon, Lady, 22
Hurd, Duane Hamilton, 134, 145, 151, 170
Huntington, Sam, 199–200, 206
Huntington, Samuel, 32, 199, 206
Hutchinson, Edward, 113
Hutchinson, Thomas, 5, 103–4, 106, 144

Jack, 76
Jacklin, Robert, 62–63
Jackson, Hall, 178
Jackson, Joseph, 44

258   Index of Personal Names

Jackson, Prince, 214–15
Jacob, 100
James, 100
James II, King, 122, 123, 129
Jeffrey, 78
Jeffrey, John, 77
Jennings, James, 97
Jeremiah, 147–48
Jeremie/Jeremy, 148
Jethro, 120–21
Jewelt, Clarence F., 147
Jock, Lyn, 51
Joel, 78
John, 137, 202
John, Governor, 207–8, 224–25, 226
Johnar, Prince, 30
Johnson, Captain, 49, 51
Johnson, Edward, 104
Johnson, Samuel, 166
Johnston, William, xv, 15, 16, 17, 23, 27, 32, 99
Jones, John, 224
Jones, John Paul, 191
Jones, Thomas, 63
Joseph, 78
Joseph, John, 79
Joshua, 101
Josselyn, John, 12, 104
Joyliffe, John, 109
Judkins, Joseph, 55
Jupeter/Jupiter/Jupitur, 76, 77

Katharine, 113
Katz, William Loren, 139
Keayne, Anna, 107
Keayne, Robert, 107–8
Kemble, Thomas, 116
Ken, Bostian (Bus Bus), 20, 107, 112
Keniston, Catherine, 54
Keyser, Thomas, 14, 38, 239–41
Kidder, Frederick, 161
Kilbourne, Payne Kenyon, 77
King, Captain, 80
Knight, Charles, 114, 115, 136
Knoblock, Glen, 41–42

Lafayette, General, 177
Lambert, Edward Rodolphus, 61, 62
Lambert, John, 183
Langdon, Governor, 231–32
Langdon, John, 57, 186
Langston, Governor, 30
Lathrop, S. K., 153
Lawrence, William, 153
Lawson, King, 196–97
Ledyard, Colonel, 153
Lee, Captain, 103
Lee, Charles, 175-76
Lee, Richard Henry, 186
Lew, Barzillai, 140, 164–65
Lew, Priamus, 140
Lew, Primus, 165
Lewis, Alonzo, 209, 215–16, 228
Lewis, Joel, 101
Light, Prince, 51
Lillibridge, Prince, 98
Lincoln, Allen B., 65, 68
Lincoln, Waldo, 138
Lindal, Cato, 188–89
Lindsey, Jacob, 51
Lippit, Ann, 97
Livermore, George, 153
Locke, Benjamin, 164
Lomis, Captain, 76
London, 80
London, Governor, 196, 198, 204, 206, 233
Long, Peirse, 204
Loudoun, Earl of, 70, 71
Louis XIV, King, 122, 123–25
Lovewell, John, 45
Lowell, John, 109
Lyford, James Otis, 25, 26
Lyman, Phineas, 70, 71, 73, 75
Lynch, Thomas, 155
Lynde, Benjamin, 31, 195, 216–17
Lynde, Benjamin, Jr., 31, 216–17
Lynde, Jacob, 144
Lynde, Samuel, 132
Lyndon, Caesar, 20
Lyndon, Josiah, 20

Index of Personal Names

MacFarlane, Charles, 72
Maclay, Edgar Stanton, 96, 186
MacSparran, James, 18
Mansfield, Thomas, 215–16
Maricourt, Paul le Moyne de, 122
Mark, 18, 79
Martin, Jubil, 178
Martin, Scip, 49
Martin, Sidon, 178
Mary, 109
Mary II, Queen, 124, 125, 131
Mason, Captain, 65
Massasoit, 88
Mather, Cotton, 116
Matthew, 109
Maverick, Samuel, 12, 103, 104
Maxwell, Mungo, 191
Mayo, Lawrence Shaw, 71
McClintock, John Norris, 57
McCarty, John, 96
McManus, Edgar J., 194
McNeil, Hector, 187
Meade, Benjamin, 59
Mescheck, 20, 30, 150
Metacom/Metacomet, 88
Mew, George, 101
Middlesex, Salem, 170. *See also* Peter, Salem
Mighill, Samuel, 48
Mingo, the black servant, 108, 111, 144
Mirick, Benjamin L., 17
Molatto, Simon, 76
Molborne, Boston, 98
Moninah, 109
Monroe, George Lieutenant Colonel, 46, 78
Montcalm, Commander, 46, 47, 50
Montgomery, Hugh, 162
Montgomery, Benjamin T., 31
Moore, Captain, 183
Moore, George Henry, xvii, 4–5, 8, 112, 115, 117, 119, 124, 174
Morril, David Lawrence, 53
Mortimer, Thomas, 130, 124, 129, 130
Moulton, Ebenezer, 60, 141

Moyne, Charles le, 122
Mumford, King, 210
Mungaly, 109, 113

Nancy, 174
Negro, 80, 97
Negro, Ben, 98
Negro, Benjamin, 100
Negro, Benjamin Paul, 76
Negro, Caesar, 76, 77, 80, 139
Negro, Cicero, 178
Negro, Cuffe, 137
Negro, Dan, 145
Negro, Frank, 79, 80, 131
Negro, Fuller, 78
Negro, Hazard, 80
Negro, Jupeter/Jupiter/Jupitur, 77, 79
Negro, Newport, 77
Negro, Prince, 76
Negro, Sipio, 77
Negro, Syphax, 137
Negro, William, 178
Nell, William Cooper, 34
Nep/Neptune, Squire, 213, 214
Nero, Caesar, 43, 47, 50, 51
Nero, King, 203–4, 209, 214–15, 232
Newcastle, Duke of, 94, 95
Newhall, James Robinson, 215–16, 229
Newport, 77, 79
Nichols, Moses, 179
Nichols, Mr., 199
Niles, Grace Greylock, 140
Nixon, Captain, 145
Nixon, General, 172
Nixon, John, 170
Nixon, Thomas, 172
Norton, Benjamin, 97
Norton, Frederick Calvin, 208, 211
Nott, Peleg, 205–6, 207
Noyes, John, 145
Nutt, Charles, 163, 168, 217–18

O'Brien, Jeremiah, 182, 183
O'Brien, John, 182, 183

O'Brien, William, 183
Odell, Ned, 78
Odiorne, Jock, 204, 214–15
Oliver, Aaron, 165
Opdyck, Gysbert, 14
Orcutt, Samuel, 19, 200, 201
O'Suluvan, Dennis Ambrose, 134

Paige, William, 144
Palfrey, John Gorham, 114
Parker, Captain, 163
Parkman, Francis, 112–22
Paterson, John, 75
Patterson, John Prentice, 74
Patterson, Major, 77
Paul, Caesar Nero, 50
Paul, John, 191
Payes, Joseph, 148
Pearce, Captain, 80
Pearse, Abraham, 114
Peck, Captain, 76
Pembleton, Cato, 188–89
Pepperell, William, 69, 146
Perkins, John, 67
Perkins, Mary Elizabeth, 201
Perry, Arthur Latham, xv, 141
Peter, xiv, 48, 80, 190
Peterson, Edward, 83
Petro, 78
Philip (Metacom/Pometacom/
    Metacomet; King), 41, 86–87, 88, 119,
    120, 121
Phillips, Negro Hanley, 101
Phillips, Samuel, 18
Phinney, Elias, 6, 152
Phipps, Spencer, 137
Phipps, William, 125–26
Pierce, Samuel, 100–1, 112
Pierce, William, 12, 101–2
Piersen, William Dillon, 4, 6, 61, 209, 210
Pitcairn, Major, 29, 170–71, 175, 237
Pitkin, John, 70
Pitt, Robert, 72
Pitt, William, 69, 72, 78

Platt, Orville, 192, 193, 228, 231, 232–33
Pometacom, 88
Pomp, 52, 53, 55–56
Pompey, 99, 108
Pompey, King, 193, 194–95, 209, 215–16
Pompy, 163–64
Poor, John, 174
Poor, Rebecca, 174
Poor, Salem, xviii, 173, 174, 175
Potamea, Job, 164
Potter, Aaron, 202, 207–8
Potter, Elisha Reynolds, 83, 202, 207, 208,
    224–25, 226
Potter, Simeon, 182
Prentice, John, 74
Prescott, Colonel, 175
Prescott, General, 29–30
Preston, Captain, 162
Priamus, 140
Primas, 79
Primus, 20, 29, 76, 131
Primus, Doctor, 22, 79
Prince, 29, 174–75
Prince, Abijah, 139
Prince, Charles, 199
Prince, Hills, 165
Putnam, Israel, 77

Quackow, 224
Quam, 165
Quam, Prince, 189
Quarles, Benjamin, 4
Quartus, 144
Quaw, Governor, 196, 198, 206, 233
Quimons, Simpson, 98
Quosh, 31
Quosh, Governor, 206–7

Rantoul, Robert, 8
Read, John, 20
Read, Joseph, 73
Reed, Christopher, 109
Reed, John, 189
Rice, William, 99

Rich, Robert, 116
Richard, 75, 109
Richman, Irving Berdine, 201, 204
Richmond, Mr., 182
Riggs, Jim, 167, 168
Ring, King, 209
Roads, Samuel, 103
Roberts, George Simon, xv, 208
Roberts, Reuben, 178
Robertson, William, 60
Robin, 177–78
Robins, Samuel, 96
Robinson, Caroline Elizabeth, 90
Robinson, Hazard, 16, 208
Robinson, Prince, 14, 202, 208, 224–25
Robinson, Rowland, 16
Robinson, Thomas, 16
Robinson, William, 80, 82
Rogers, Adam, 63
Root, Jeste, 222
Rose, David, 156–57
Rose, James M., 197
Rouville, Hertel de, 133
Rowe, John, 145
Rowley, Mr., 107
Royal, Silas, 189–90
Royall, Hector, 144
Rumbale, Daniel, 113
Russell, John Henderson, 34

Saffin, John, 121
Saint Helene, Jacques le Moyne de, 122
Salem, Peter, xviii, 5, 29, 153, 165–66, 168–72, 173, 237
Salter, Samuel, 149
Sambo, 100
Sammons, Mark J., 53
Samuel, Chace, 98
Sanborn, Edwin David, 41, 42
Sanford, John, 89
Savage, Edward Hartwell, 25
Scipio, 49, 99, 108, 138, 191
Scippio, 142
Seymour, Captain, 198

Seymour, Major, 200
Sheldon, George, xv, 8, 20, 30, 139, 142, 143, 150
Shelton, Jane De Forest, 19, 31, 65, 206
Sherman, Andrew M., 183
Shirley, William, 41, 48, 69, 94, 95, 137
Shores, Pharaoh, 204, 215
Shurtleff, Nathaniel B., 217, 218
Silvy Antoine, a Jusiut, 122
Simeon, Colonel, 209
Simon, Lieutenant, 199
Sipio, 77
Sippio, 178
Sippo, 49
Skene, Philip Wharton, 195–96, 221–24
Smith, Isaac, 200
Smith, James, 14, 38, 239–41
Smith, William, 98
Smith, William J., 142
Soltonstall, Richard, 240–41
Southack, Cyptian, 138
Sprague, Governor, 155
Staples, William Read, 84
Stark, James Henry, 161
Stattler, Rick, 97, 98, 99
Steven, Cezar, 98
Stiles, Henry Reed, xv, 63, 64, 79
Stoddart, Colonel, 140
Stone, Micah, 167
Stoughton, Mr., 113
Stride, John, 148
Stuart, Isaac William, 66, 147, 198, 205, 206, 208, 211–12, 213, 232, 233
Swett, Samuel, 153, 170, 171
Swift, Rev. Mr., 135
Sylhax, 137
Sylvester, Herbert Millon, 45
Syphax, 138

Tash, Thomas, 47, 49
Taylor, George, 98
Taylor, James P., 46
Temple, Josiah Howard, 135, 151, 161, 167, 168, 172

Index of Personal Names

Thatcher, James, 153, 174–75
Theophelus, 80
Thomas, General, 154
Thompson, David, 39
Thomson, C. L., 122
Thomson, Thomas, 72
Thornton, Mr., 22
Ti, General, 64, 229
Timon, 157
Titous, 224
Titus, 143
Tobey, 78
Tobias, Eben, 200, 231
Tobie, 149
Tomlinson, Agar, 31, 206–7
Toogood, Edward, 44
Torrey, John, 184
Tossett, Ira, 201
Towne, Ezra, 165
Trowtrow, Boston, 193, 199, 205
Troyes, Chevalier de, 122
Trumbull, Benjamin, 71
Trumbull, James Hammond, 65, 66, 67, 70, 71, 158
Trumbull, Jonathan, 14, 221–22
Tucker, Judge, 15, 25
Tucker, Samuel, 187
Tuveson, Erick R., 37
Tyng, Colonel, 126
Tyng, Edward, 137, 138

Underwood, Cato, 165
Updike, Daniel, 82
Updike, Wilkins, xv, 32, 90, 196, 202
Usher, John, 40

Van Tromp, Admiral, 115
Varnum, James B., 189–90
Vaudreuil, Governor, 126, 131
Vincent, John Martin, 153

Wadsworth, Jeremiah, 205–6
Wadsworth, Peleg, 165
Walker, Augustine, 116

Walker, Daniel, 97
Walkup, William, Sr., 172
Wallace, James, 182
Wallace, Lucy Sessions, 60
Wallis, David, 60
Walls, Daniel, 100
Walpole, 78
Walpole, Premier, 72
Ward, Andrew, Jr., 77
Ward, Constance Brickwell, 42
Ward, Edward, 144
Ward, Governor, 29, 97
Ward, Hezekiah, 140
Ward, Nathaniel, 13, 23
Wardsworth, Petter, 224
Warner, Seth, 190
Warwick, Hannah, 34
Washburn, Emory, 6, 105, 153, 170
Washington, George, 6, 13, 35, 153–55, 167, 178, 183, 185, 220
Waterhouse, Benjamin, 210
Waters, Wilson, 165
Watson, Guy, 202, 224–25, 230
Webb, General, 46
Weeden, William Babcock, 21, 93, 97, 103, 113–15, 118
Weeks, Doctor, 182
Welcome, Jack, 108
Wells, Thomas, 20
Wentworth, Benning, 40, 48, 49
Wentworth, Cheswell, 52, 53, 54, 55–59
Weston, Juba, 206
Wheatley, John, 22
Wheatley, Phyllis, 22
Wheelwright, John, 38–39
Whipple, Abraham, 180, 181–82
Whipple, John, 142
Whipple, Prince, 34–35
Whipple, William, 35–36
White, John, 140
White, Sunday, 187
White, Thomas, 164
Whiting, Nathan, 70, 73, 78
Whiting, Samuel, 80

Whiting, William, 76
Whitmore, William Henry, 9
Whitney, David, 71
Whitney, Tarball, 79
Whittaker, 17
Whittemore, Cuff, 164
Whittemore, Nathaniel, 51
Whittier, John Greenleaf, 17
Whitting, John, 101
Whittlesey, Chauncey, 71
Whittlesy, Eliphalet, 77
Wiggin, Mark, 58
Wiggin, Simon, 54
Wilkes, Laura Eliza, 4, 44
Will, 24, 109, 147 168, 202
Will, Black, 113
Will, Cesar, 200
Willcox, Caesar, 199
Willcox, Joseph, 199
Willett, Hezekiah, 120–21
Willett, Thomas, 120
William, 78, 79
William, Abraham, 145
William, Elijah, 20
William, John Foster, 189
William, Jonathan, 188
William, Mr., 132
William, Plato, 189
Williams, Mr., 14, 38
Williams, Ephraim, Jr., xv, 141
Williams, Francis, 239
Williams, George Washington, 6, 12, 102, 104

Williams, John, 133
Williams, Roger, 15, 84
William III, King, 125, 126, 128, 129, 131
Willis, Pomp, 224
Wilson, Joseph Thomas, 1
Winslow, Captain, 137
Winsor, Justin, 137
Winthrop, James, 15
Winthrop, John, 13, 14, 17, 102, 103, 106, 107, 113, 239–40
Wodsworth, Tim, 149
Wolcott, Doctor, 22
Wolcott, Roger, 69
Wolcott, Captain, xxx, 80
Wood, Cato, 164
Wood, Scippio, 141–42
Wooster, Captain, 200
Wootonekanuse, 121
Worcester, Daniel Thomas, 56
Wormwell, Benjamin, 184
Wright, Hagar, 74
Wright, Theodore, 73
Wright, Wait, 74
Wright, Will, 198
Wyatt, Thomas, 96
Wyllys, George, 198, 206, 207, 233
Wyllys, Governor, 207

York, Jeffrey, 137
Young, Joseph, 58
Youngey, Prince, 30

Zekera, 78

www.ingramcontent.com/pod-product-compliance
Lightning Source LLC
Chambersburg PA
CBHW020418010526
44118CB00010B/306